The

EVERYTHING Music Theory Book

Dear Reader,

As someone who has been an academic music student, a composer, and a professional musician in all areas of music, I see clearly the divide that has made theory such a hard topic to teach. I love music theory because it fascinates me. But at the same time, I understand that it serves a purpose and that purpose is different for each reader.

To try to tackle this, I opted for a few unique things. First, the examples in the book range from classical music to pop and jazz in an effort to reach as many readers as possible. Also, the notation is presented for single-line instruments, mainly piano and guitar. This is also meant to motivate you to play the examples because theory does not live on paper. Music is not a theory; it is a real thing that I want all of you to experience in full. I hope no matter who you are, you leave this book with a deeper understanding of something that you and I love so much: music.

Best,

The EVERYTHING® Series

Editorial

Publishing Director	Gary M. Krebs
Director of Product Development	Paula Munier
Associate Managing Editor	Laura M. Daly
Associate Copy Chief	Brett Palana-Shanahan
Acquisitions Editor	Lisa Laing
Development Editor	Jessica LaPointe
Associate Production Editor	Casey Ebert

Production

Director of Manufacturing	Susan Beale
Associate Director of Production	Michelle Roy Kelly
Cover Design	Paul Beatrice Erick DaCosta Matt LeBlanc
Design and Layout	Heather Barrett Brewster Brownville Colleen Cunningham Jennifer Oliveira
Series Cover Artist	Barry Littmann

THE EVERYTHING® MUSIC THEORY BOOK

A complete guide to taking your understanding of music to the next level

Marc Schonbrun

Adams Media
Avon, Massachusetts

This book is dedicated to Joshua Barry Schonbrun, my nephew.

An Everything® Series Book.
Everything® and everything.com® are registered trademarks of F+W Publications, Inc.

Published by Adams Media, an F+W Publications Company
57 Littlefield Street, Avon, MA 02322 U.S.A.
www.adamsmedia.com

ISBN 10: 1-59337-652-9
ISBN 13: 978-1-59337-652-9

Printed in the United States of America.

J I H G F E D C B

Library of Congress Cataloging-in-Publication Data.
Schonbrun, Marc.
The everything music theory book : a complete guide to taking your understanding of music to the next level / Marc Schonbrun.
p. cm. — (Everything series)
Includes bibliographical references and index.
ISBN-13: 978-1-59337-652-9
ISBN-10: 1-59337-652-9
1. Music theory. I. Title.

MT6.S325 2007
781–dc22
2006032602

Contents

Introduction / xi

1

Review of the Basics / 1

Ins and Outs 2 • Notes 2 • Clefs 3 • Time 7 • Basic Rhythms 8 • Rests 12 • Meter 12

2

Intervals / 16

Go the Distance 17 • Intervals from Scales 21 • The Simple Intervals 26 • Advanced Intervals 30 • Inverted and Extended Intervals 33

3

The Major Scale / 36

Scales Defined 37 • Spelling Scales 38 • Scale Tones 44 • How Scales Are Used in Music 45

4

The Minor Scale / 47

Minor Colors 48 • The Definitive Approach 48 • The Derivative Approach 52 • Degrees in Minor Scales 53 • Multiple Scales—Scale Clarity 54 • Variant Variables 57

5 **Musical Keys and Key Signatures / 64**
Musical Organization 65 • The System of Key Signatures 68 • Relative Minor Keys 71 • Minor Keys on Paper 74 • Keys Change 76

6 **Modes and Other Scales / 79**
Modes—The Other Side of Scales 80 • Seven Modal Scales 81 • Looking at Modes on Their Own 86 • Other Important Scales 90 • Time for Etudes 95

7 **Etude One: Scales and Keys / 96**

8 **Chords / 108**
What Is a Chord? 109 • Building Chords 110 • Minor Triads/Chords 112 • Diminished Triads 114 • Augmented Triads 115 • Chords in Scales 118 • Diatonic Chords 119 • Minor Scale Harmony 122

9 **Seventh Chords and Chord Inversions / 123**
Seventh Chords 124 • Seventh Chord Construction 125 • Seventh Chord Recap 131 • Inverted Chords 132 • Quick Study: Bach Prelude in C 137

10 **Movements: Chord Progressions / 141**
What Is a Chord Progression? 142 • Progressions in Time 143 • Diatonic Progressions and Solar Harmony 144 • Solar Harmony and the Chord Ladder 148

11 **More Chord Progressions / 153**
Tonic and Dominant Relationships 154 • Using Dominant Chords in Minor Keys 158 • Harmonic Rhythm 161 • Voice Leading 162

12 **Melodic Harmonization / 165**
What Is Melody? 166 • Chord Tones and Passing Tones 169 • True Melodic Harmonization 172 • Single Line Harmony 175 • Dealing with Accidentals 177

13 **Etude Two: Chords and Harmony / 178**

14 **Advanced Harmony / 189**
Beyond Diatonic 190 • Modal Mixture 198 • Modulation 201

15 **Jazz Harmony / 207**
What Is Jazz? 208 • Jazz Harmony 208 • Jazz Progressions 212 • Blues Forms 219

16 **Transposition and Instrumentation / 223**
What Is Transposing? 224 • Transposing Chant 227 • B♭ Instruments 228 • E♭ Instruments 229 • F Instruments 230 • Octave Transposes 230 • Analyzing Scores 231 • Instrument Ranges 237

17 **Etude Three: Advanced Harmony, Jazz Harmony, and Transposition / 242**

Appendix A: Glossary / 253
Appendix B: Additional Resources / 263
Index / 265

Acknowledgments

Thanks to my family: Mom, Dad, Bill, Trish, Joshua, and David. Many thanks again to Joe Mooney for his time, also to Dr. Paul Siskind for his guidance. Thanks to Ernie Jackson for the formative ideas. To the Crane School of Music for my education, and Dr. Doug Rubio for my start!

To Karla, life is a journey and it's better with you as a partner on the road.

Introduction

▶ MUSICIANS OFTEN START at an early age with study in school that typically includes learning how to read music notation. Many of you who play traditional instruments got your start in public schools. Traditional instruments include band and orchestral instruments like flute, clarinet, violin, and cello. If you were able to study in school, you probably got a good foundation of practical work on your own instrument, including reading music and performance. Many schools only offer instruction in band and orchestral instruments, although that is starting to change. If you studied a nontraditional instrument, such as guitar, bass, or piano, chances are that you didn't do so in school. You probably did it totally on your own, either teaching yourself or through private instruction. Depending on the instrument you chose, you may or may not have a strong background in reading music. Pianists typically are grounded in reading, while many guitarists' learning rarely includes reading.

When you study a musical instrument, you typically work in stages. The first stage is learning the basics of your instrument. You can devote years to learning about the techniques and practices that make your instrument work. After you have attained some mastery of your individual instrument, things start to change, and the instrument becomes simply a vehicle for musical expression. As a musician, you begin to look at the larger picture of what makes music work and hold together.

The word *theory* is almost always thrown around as an elusive second step toward understanding music. Many musicians view the study of music theory as a chore, akin to "I have to paint the house" or any other tedious task. But music theory is not a task. It is an educated look back at what happened throughout music history. Music has undergone a slow evolution, and theory looks back at what's happened and tries to make sense of it. Theory will put words to concepts that you hear and have understood all of your life. Studying music theory won't necessarily make you a better player, but it could. In a sense, achieving an understanding of music theory is very much like buying a new instrument: In the hands of a skilled player, it can be a powerful tool for self-improvement.

This book is a follow-up to *The Everything® Reading Music Book*. The purpose of that book was to give a logical way for all players to learn to read musical notation. Understanding musical notation is a critical step in the process of reading music, and if you are not comfortable with it, you should check out that book as well. This book will review basic concepts of reading musical notation in the first chapter, but music reading will not be covered in depth and you will need knowledge of notation. You can learn theory without strong music-reading skills, but strong reading skills will make everything, at every step, easier.

This book is different from many other theory books. Many theory books simply start off too hard for many people. They presuppose too much information and typically put the reader off to the idea of music theory. They often cater to college-level music-theory topics. Rarely are they suitable for self-study. The other problem of many theory books is their failure to speak to a large cross section of readers, including a range of instruments played, abilities, and styles of music. Many texts focus solely on classical music, using examples from the canon of classical music only—totally ignoring popular music. This book will remedy that so you can get the most out of your experience. If your goal is to be on an advanced track to music theory, this book will give you the foundation you will need to go further, and you will be able to tackle a much harder book with ease.

Chapter 1

Review of the Basics

Everyone needs a good review! You might not know everything you need, or even have read any other music-theory books in your life, so the purpose of this chapter is to give you a very brief overview of some of the visual concepts of music, such as notes, clefs, and rhythms, so that you can look at the forthcoming examples in the book and decipher them with ease.

Ins and Outs

Since you will see the language of written music throughout this book, you must make sure that you will be able to read it. Many of the concepts will reinforce themselves through the use of the accompanying audio CD, but there is no way around an inability to read notation. You might be sitting there saying, "I can read just fine," but the real question is, "How well do you read in other clefs?"

IN TIME

In Europe, musical tradition began with the simple monophonic (one voice) chants of the early Christian era. This was the most common type of music during the Early Middle Ages (from about A.D. 350 to 1050). Polyphonic liturgical music, composed of more complex composition with multiple melodies, developed in the High Middle Ages (from about A.D. 1050 to 1300).

Music theory is all about looking at what's been done, and through the study of other music, you can come to a greater understanding of what's up. You will need to know how to read in multiple clefs, since standard notation uses treble and bass clef at a minimum, and often throws in alto clef, too. In order to see what's going on, you need to be able to read those clefs as well! Here is some basic review so that you can make sense of what you are reading. There is also a review of rhythms in some detail as rhythm can be a concept that is very difficult to understand, and even if you know how to decipher the notes on a staff, you still may be uneasy with the counting aspect. If this chapter is already scaring the heck out of you, try picking up *The Everything® Reading Music Book* and keeping that around, as it will help you greatly in understanding this material!

Notes

What better place to start than notes? Here's a short sample of music; try to dissect what's going on and see if you have all you need to know.

FIGURE 1.1 Musical Elements

As you can see from **FIGURE 1.1**, this is a short excerpt from a piece of solo piano music. Here is what you are seeing:

1. There are notes placed on two musical staffs: one treble staff and one bass staff.
2. The staffs are further defined by their clefs.
3. The notes are identified only by use of a clef; otherwise, they are simply dots sitting on lines and spaces.

If you want to talk about the notes, you have to talk about clefs because clefs actually define the name of the notes in a staff.

Clefs

A clef is a symbol that sits at the beginning of every staff of music that you look at. A staff contains five lines and four spaces. How do you know where the note A or the note C is? The missing element needed is the clef. The clef defines what notes go where, functioning a lot like a map. Placing a treble clef at the start of the staff defines the lines and spaces with note names. **FIGURE 1.2** shows the notes of a treble staff.

FIGURE 1.2 Treble Clef Staff

The treble clef circles around the note G. This is why it's commonly called the G clef. As for the notes, there is an important pattern. Look at the lowest line, which is designated E. Follow the musical alphabet to find where the next note is. The F is in the space just above the E. The staff ascends in this fashion—line, then space, then line—as it cycles through the musical alphabet (A–B–C–D–E–F–G).

Extra Credit

Even though you may understand the notes on both clefs, the only way to get proficient is to read other clefs as often as you can. Set aside a few minutes a day to look at other clefs so you can easily identify their notes. Since clefs define notes, you can almost think of being able to read in many clefs as a kind of musical literacy.

The bass clef is a different clef than the treble and identifies not only different note names, but also notes in different ranges. The bass clef is used for instruments that have a lower pitch, like a bass guitar. Even though the bass clef sits on the same five-line staff, it defines very different note names. Many musicians read treble clef because it is the most common clef. Because of this, too many musicians have a greater difficulty reading bass clef than reading treble clef. In order to progress your understanding of theory, you will need to be adept at reading all clefs. **FIGURE 1.3** shows the notes of a bass clef staff.

FIGURE 1.3 Bass Clef Staff

Grand Staff and Middle C

When the bass clef and the treble clef are grouped together, it creates something called the grand staff. The grand staff is used in piano writing. To make a grand staff, all you have to do is connect a treble and a bass staff, or clef, with a brace, which is shown in **FIGURE 1.4**.

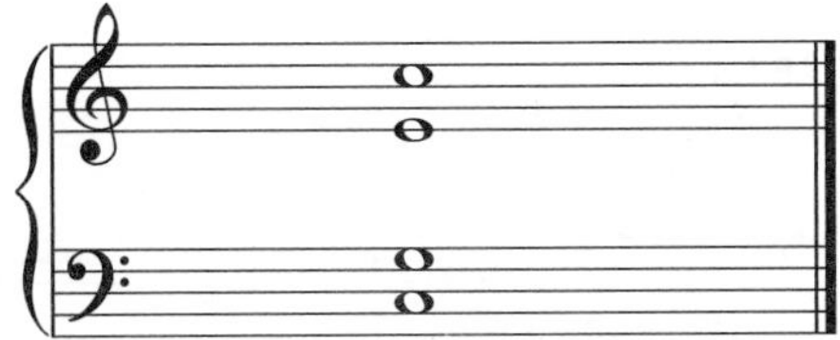

FIGURE 1.4 A Brace

What a grand staff shows is a very important note: middle C. **FIGURE 1.5** shows a middle C.

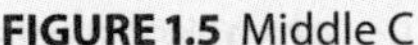

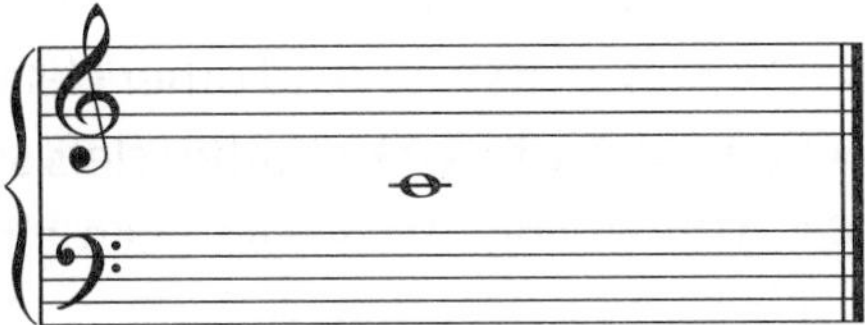

FIGURE 1.5 Middle C

When you look at **FIGURE 1.5**, can you tell whether the note belongs to the bass clef, or the treble clef? Actually, it belongs equally to both. If you trace down from the treble clef, one ledger line below the staff is a C. If you look at the bass clef notes, one ledger line above the staff is also a C. They are, in fact, the same pitch on the piano. This is called middle C because it's right in the middle of everything. Middle C will come up throughout this book, so keep track of it!

Moveable "C" Clefs

The last type of clef is called the C clef. Typically, you see this clef associated with the viola because it's the most common instrument that reads in that clef; however, more instruments than just the viola read it. When the C clef is used with the viola, it is called the alto clef. Thankfully, this clef is very easy to read because the symbol for the C clef has two semicircles that curve into the middle of the staff and basically "point" toward the middle line, which is a C. It's not just any C, it's middle C. **FIGURE 1.6** shows the notes for alto clef.

FIGURE 1.6 Alto Clef

Since this is a movable clef, you can place the clef anywhere you want, and whatever lines its two semicircles point to become middle C. Some very old choral music uses a different movable C clef for each part (tenor clef, alto clef, and soprano clef). Just as long as you know that the clef always points toward middle C, you will be able to decipher the notes in this clef.

As a little exercise, here are a few lines of music, each in a different clef. Below the music, there is space for you to write the note names in. Go ahead and do so right in the book.

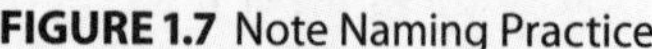

FIGURE 1.7 Note Naming Practice

Notice anything about your answers from the four examples? If you did it correctly, you should have come up with the exact same answer for each line. This was intentional! Look at how different each line looks. At first glance, you never would have thought that they were the same! This is the power of clefs and why it's so important to be able to read well in all clefs—sometimes it looks much more difficult than it really is!

Point to Consider

When notes use ledger lines that are extremely high or extremely low, they can be difficult to read; it's much easier to read notes that sit in the staff you are reading. Using different clefs allows you to move the location of middle C in such a way that the majority of your notes are in and around the staff.

Time

Even though this is in the "review" section of this book, time is a fundamental aspect of music theory that is often left out of formal music-theory study. Time has more to it than just counting beats and bars. Time can dictate the feel and flow of a piece, and even harmony has a rhythm to it, aptly called "harmonic rhythm." You'll start with time signatures, as they are the first time-related aspect you want to understand in detail.

Time Signatures

Music is divided into bars, also called measures, for reading convenience and for musical purposes. Most music adheres to a meter, and that affects the phrasing of the melody. If you don't have a lot of experience with reading, rhythm can be a very difficult concept to grasp.

The most standard time signature is $\frac{4}{4}$ time, which is also called "common time" and is abbreviated by this symbol c. Common time looks like a fraction and it signifies two things. First, the top number 4 means that every measure will have four beats in it. The bottom number 4 indicates what note value will receive the beat; in this case, 4 stands for a quarter note (♩). So common time breaks up each measure into four beats, as a quarter note receives one beat. You can, of course, further divide the measure into as many small parts as you feel like, but in the end, it must add up to four beats.

Rhythm

Music is composed of pitch and rhythm. While there are finer elements that come into play later on, such as dynamics and expression, music can be made by knowing simply this: which note and how long to hold it. Without rhythm, people couldn't fully read music.

Rhythm is music's way of setting the duration of a note. Music accomplishes this task by varying the appearance of the notes that sit on the staff. Different rhythms indicate different note lengths. To get rolling, you need to hear about an essential concept: beat. Have you ever been to a concert and clapped along with 30,000 other fans? Have you ever noticed how everyone claps together in a steady pattern? Did you ever wonder how 30,000 people could possibly agree on anything? If you have been to a dance club, you may have noticed that there is always a steady drumbeat or bass line, usually up-tempo, to drive the music along. Those are examples of pulse and beat in music. Rhythm is a primal element and pulse and beat are universal concepts.

Basic Rhythms

In music, changing the appearance of the notes indicates the rhythm. As you will remember, the location of the notes is fixed on the staff, which will never change. The appearance of the note varies, indicating how long that note should be held. Now, you'll go through all the basic musical symbols for rhythm.

Quarter Notes

A quarter note (♩), which is signified with a filled-in black circle (also called a notehead) and a stem, is the simplest rhythm to talk about. Quarter notes receive one count; their duration is one beat (see **FIGURE 1.8**).

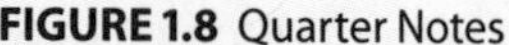

FIGURE 1.8 Quarter Notes

Half Notes

The next in our series of simple rhythms is the half note: (𝅗𝅥). As you can see, the half note looks similar to the quarter note, except the circle is open and not filled in. Like a quarter note, it also has a single stem that points either up or down. The half note receives two counts; its duration is two beats. In relation to the quarter note, the half note is twice as long because it receives two counts (see **FIGURE 1.9**).

FIGURE 1.9 Half Notes

Whole Notes

A whole note is a rhythm that receives four beats. It's twice as long as a half note and four times as long as a quarter note—count to yourself: one, two, three, four. It is represented as an open circle without a stem. The whole note is probably the single longest rhythmic value that you will come across. Whole notes are easy to spot because they are the only notes that lack a stem (see **FIGURE 1.10**).

FIGURE 1.10 Whole Notes

Eighth Notes

The smallest rhythm you have encountered thus far is the quarter note, which lasts for one beat. Chopping up this beat into smaller divisions allows musicians to explore faster rhythms and faster passages. Chopping the quarter note in half gives us the eighth note, which receives half of one beat (see **FIGURE 1.11**).

FIGURE 1.11 Eighth Notes

Sixteenth Notes

The beat can be broken down even smaller for the faster note values. The next rhythm is called the sixteenth note. A sixteenth note breaks the quarter note into four equal parts and the eighth note into two equal parts (**FIGURE 1.12**).

FIGURE 1.12 Sixteenth Notes

Faster Note Values

It's possible to keep chopping the beat up into smaller and smaller parts. The next step beyond sixteenth notes is the thirty-second note. A thirty-second note breaks one beat into eight equal parts. Just like the transition from eighth to sixteenth notes, going from sixteenth to thirty-second notes will add another flag or beam to the notes. You can keep adding another flag and it will simply make the note value half the length of the previous note. **FIGURE 1.13** shows faster note values.

FIGURE 1.13 Faster Note Values

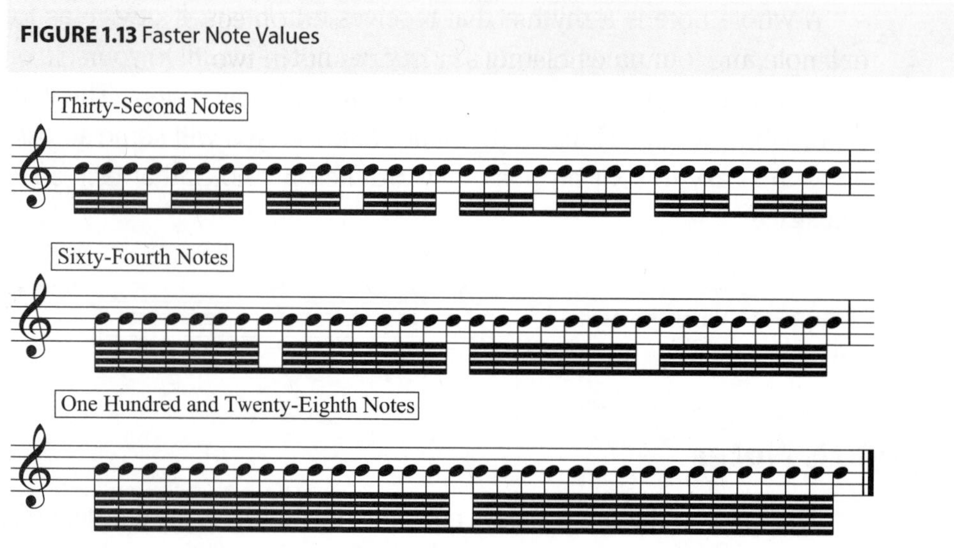

Augmentation Dots

FIGURE 1.14 Dotted Rhythms

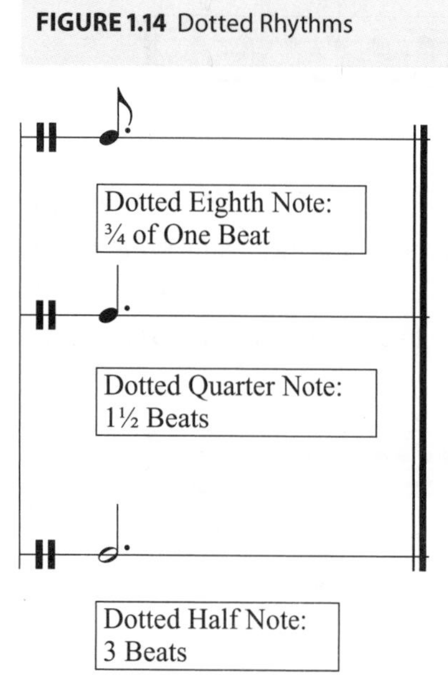

You have focused on making note values smaller and smaller, but you can make them larger by using what's called an augmentation dot. Placing a small dot directly to the right of any note increases the duration of that note by one half. For example, placing a dot after a half note makes the dotted half last for three beats. The original half note receives two beats and the dot adds half the value of the original note (a half note): The dot adds one extra beat (a quarter note), bringing the total up to three beats. Any note can be dotted. **FIGURE 1.14** is a chart of dotted rhythms and their duration.

Point to Consider

A dot extends the value of a note. A tie also extends notes. Both do the same thing but they do it differently visually. A dot added to a note requires that you figure out what half of the note value is and count it. A tie is sometimes easier to read as the notes are visually "glued" together.

Tuplets

Up to this point, rhythms have been based on equal divisions of two. For example, breaking a whole note in half results in two half notes. In the same way, dividing a half note in two parts results in two quarter notes. As the divisions get smaller, going through eighth and sixteenth notes, the notes are continuously broken in half equally. However, beats can also be broken into other groupings, most importantly groupings based on odd numbers such as three. Such odd groupings are commonly referred to as tuplets.

When you break a beat into three parts, you give birth to a "triplet." The most basic triplet to look at is the eighth-note triplet. An eighth-note triplet is simply three eighth notes that equally divide one beat into three parts (see **FIGURE 1.15**). You could also look at it like a ratio: three notes equally divided in the same space as one beat. Since there are three notes in each beat, eighth-note triplets are faster than two eighth notes taking up the same beat. The more notes per beat, the faster they progress.

FIGURE 1.15 Eighth Note Triplets

Tuplets don't have to be in threes, although that is the most common tuplet in music. You can have tuplets that divide a beat into any number of parts: five, seven, even eleven. The number above the grouping of notes indicates how it's supposed to be divided.

Rests

FIGURE 1.16 Rests

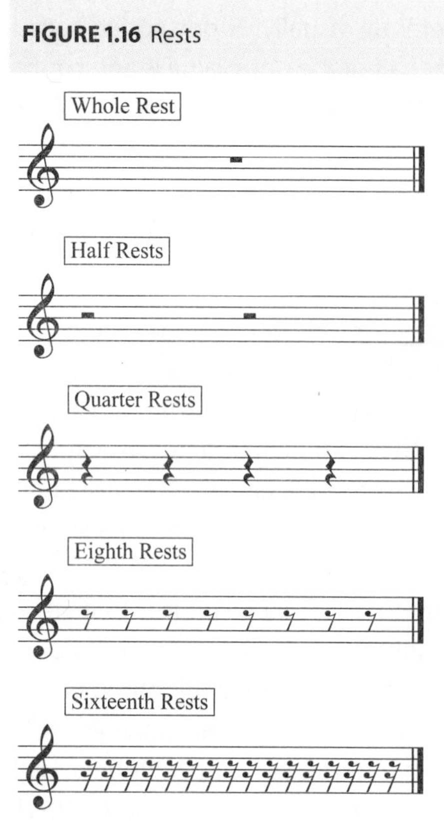

All this talk about notes and rhythms wouldn't be complete without some discussion about rests. The best news of the day is that everything you've learned about rhythms also applies to rests. The only difference is that a rest tells you not to do anything! At last, you get a break.

Every pitch needs duration. Rhythm defines how long notes should be sustained. Music isn't always about sound—rests are as common as pitches. Rests indicate a spot in the music where you don't play a sound. Since a rest does not have a pitch associated with it, it requires a different symbol. Here's a chart of the rests (**FIGURE 1.16**) and their associated notes.

Meter

The last thing to briefly explain is meter. You encountered one meter at the beginning of this chapter: common time, or $\frac{4}{4}$, meter. Now take a little bit of time and look at the different meters.

Simple Meter

A simple meter is any meter that breaks the beat up into even divisions. This means that whatever the beat is, whether it's $\frac{4}{4}$, $\frac{3}{4}$, or $\frac{2}{4}$, each beat (which is a quarter note) is equally divided. The beat is broken into even divisions of two (eighth notes), four (sixteenth notes), or eight (thirty-second) notes.

FIGURE 1.17 Common Simple Meters

What sets simple meter apart from other meters is how the beats are grouped together. The clearest way to see how beats are grouped is the use of eighth and sixteenth notes. Since the flags join and are visually grouped together, you can clearly see how the notes and the beats break down. In a simple meter, you place slight natural accents on the strong beats, which are always on the first note of any rhythmic grouping. Whenever you see notes grouped together in twos or fours, you know that you are in simple time. Since $\frac{4}{4}$, $\frac{3}{4}$, and $\frac{2}{4}$ are the most common meters and all are in simple time, you will become a pro at simple meters in short order!

Compound Meter

Simple meters have one important feature: groupings of two or four notes. The next meters are compound meters. A compound meter breaks itself into groups of three. This is what makes compound time different from simple time. Common compound meters are $\frac{3}{8}$, $\frac{6}{8}$, $\frac{9}{8}$, and $\frac{12}{8}$. Compound meters usually have an 8 in the lower part of the meter because the meter is based on eighth notes receiving the beat.

Compound time relies on groupings of three notes; you need to adjust how you view beat durations. A click on the metronome does not always signify a quarter note. What it does signify is the "pulse" of the music. In common time, that click could be a dotted quarter note, so keep your concept of time elastic.

FIGURE 1.18 Common Compound Meters

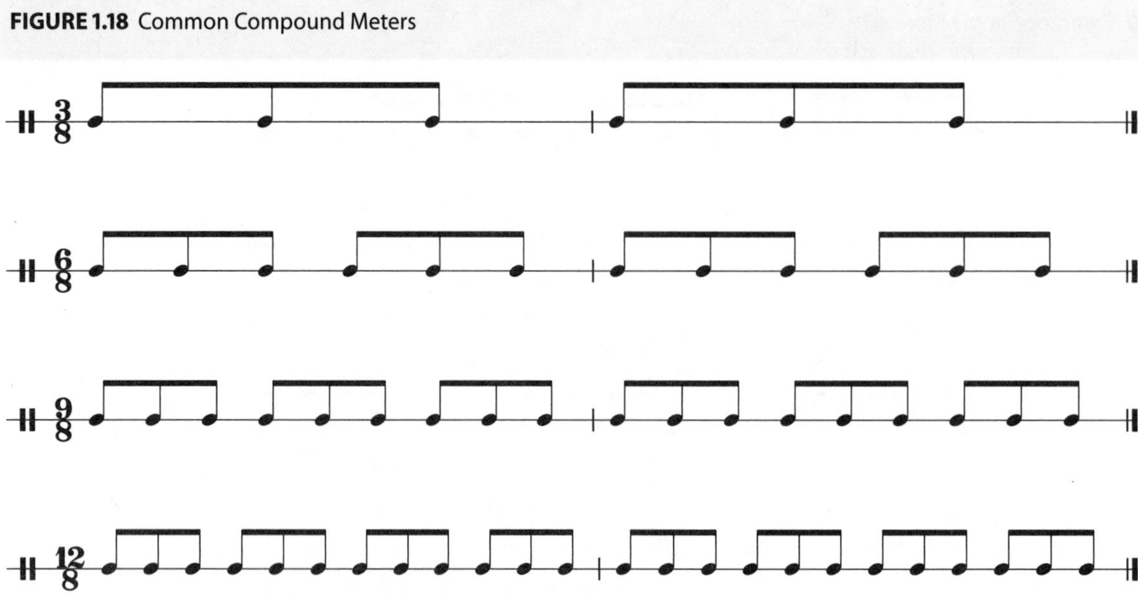

As you can see in **FIGURE 1.18**, compound meters visually group sets of three notes. That is, $\frac{3}{8}$ simply contains one grouping of three, $\frac{6}{8}$ two groupings of three, and so on. Counting in $\frac{4}{4}$ and other simple meters hasn't been such a big deal. You simply set your metronome or tap your foot along with the quarter notes. In compound time, your beat becomes a grouping of three notes—more specifically, a grouping of three eighth notes (although if you were in $\frac{3}{16}$, three sixteenth notes would get the beat, but since time is all relative, it all works out the same).

Other Meters

In music, the combination of simple and compound time signatures will get you through the majority of the music you'll encounter. Even so, composers and musicians love to stretch the boundaries. All of the meters you've learned about so far have been divided into easy groupings. Other music exists in unusual groupings, called odd time.

Odd time and odd meter is simply a meter that is asymmetric, or a meter that has uneven groupings. Odd time can be expressed anytime that 5, 7, 10, 11, 13, and 15 are the top value in a time signature. The bottom of the signature can be any rhythmic value; it's the top number that determines if it's symmetric (simple) or asymmetric (odd) time. Take a look at a basic odd meter like $\frac{5}{4}$ (see **FIGURE 1.19**).

FIGURE 1.19 Odd Time

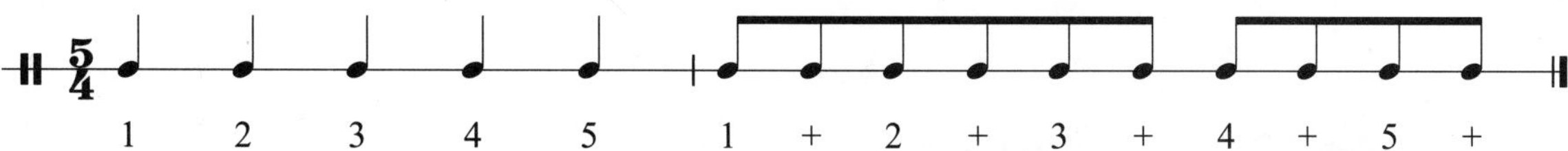

Chapter 2

Intervals

The most elemental part of music theory is understanding the relationships between single notes. The distance between those notes is an interval, which will serve as the foundation for practically every single concept that you will explore throughout this book. Understanding intervals is extremely important.

Go the Distance

An interval is defined as the distance from one note to another. Intervals are going to provide the basic framework for everything else in music. Not only is knowledge of intervals as a subject itself important, but intervals are used everywhere. Small intervals combine to form scales. Larger intervals combine to form chords. Intervals will aid you in voice leading, composition, and transposition. There are virtually no musical situations where intervals aren't used (barring snare drum solos), and even in some of the extremely dissonant music of the twentieth century, intervals are still the basis for most composition and analysis.

There are five different types of intervals:

- Major intervals
- Minor intervals
- Perfect intervals
- Augmented intervals
- Diminished intervals

You will learn all about the five types of intervals in this chapter, but before you go any further, you must have a visual helper, kind of a musical slide rule: the piano keyboard. Intervals can seem like an abstract concept, but when you have some visual relationships to reference, the abstract concept becomes something more concrete and easier to grasp. **FIGURE 2.1** shows the piano.

FIGURE 2.1 The Piano Keyboard

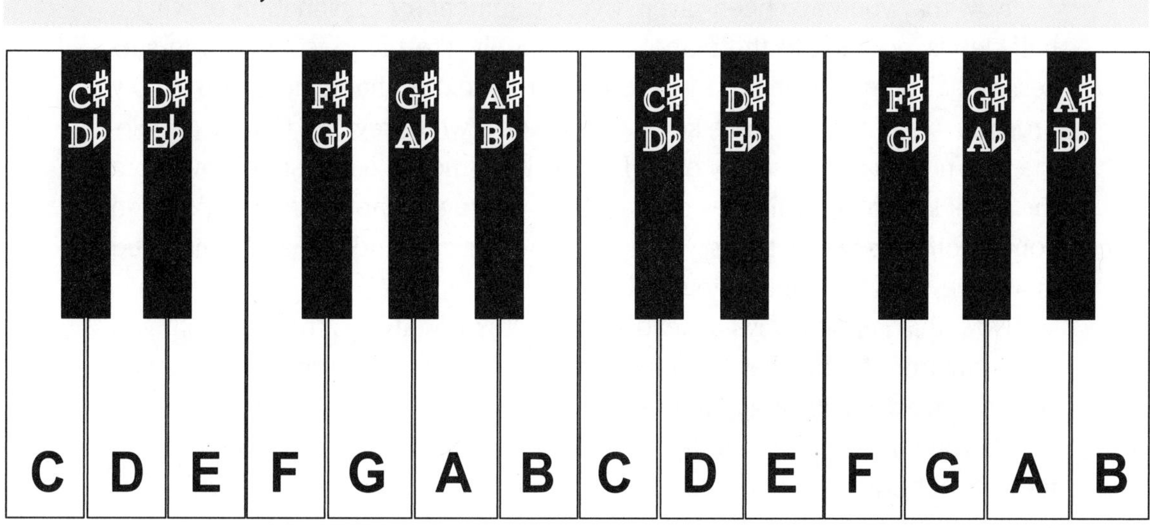

This image will repeat at different times throughout this book, but you can earmark this page for reference as you're going to need it.

The keyboard shows you where all the notes are within one full octave on a piano. It also shows you all the sharps and flats on the black keys.

Point to Consider

Notice how C♯ and D♭ occupy the same key. This situation, where one key can have more than one name, is called an enharmonic. This happens on all of the black keys on the keyboard. The white keys have only one name whereas the black keys always have a second possibility. This will be explained further along in this book.

Half Steps

The first interval to look at is the half step; it is the smallest interval that Western music uses (Eastern music uses quarter tones, which are smaller than a half step), and it's the smallest interval you can play on the majority of musical instruments. How far is a half step? Well, if you look at a piece of music, a great example of a half step is the distance from C to C♯ or D♭—remember that C♯ and D♭ are the same thing. **FIGURE 2.2** shows the half step in a treble staff.

FIGURE 2.2 Half Step

Now that you have been given a very rudimentary explanation of what a half step is, go back to the piano. Stated simply, the piano is laid out in successive half steps starting from C. To get to the next available note, you simply progress to the next available key. If you are on a white key, like C, for example, the next note is the black key of C♯/D♭. You have moved a half step. Move from the black key to the white key of D and you've moved another half step. When you've done this twelve times, you have come back around to C and completed an octave, which is another interval.

Now, this is not always a steadfast rule. It is not always the case that you will move from a white key to a black key, or vice-versa, in order to move a half step. **FIGURE 2.3** will illustrate an example of this.

As you can see from the figure, the movement between E and F and the movement between B and C are both carried out from white key to white key, with no black key between them. This means that B and C, and E and F, are a half step apart. This is called a "natural" half step, and it is the only exception to our half-step logic. The good news is that if you keep this in the front of your mind, all intervals will be much easier to define, not just half steps.

FIGURE 2.3 Hidden Half Steps

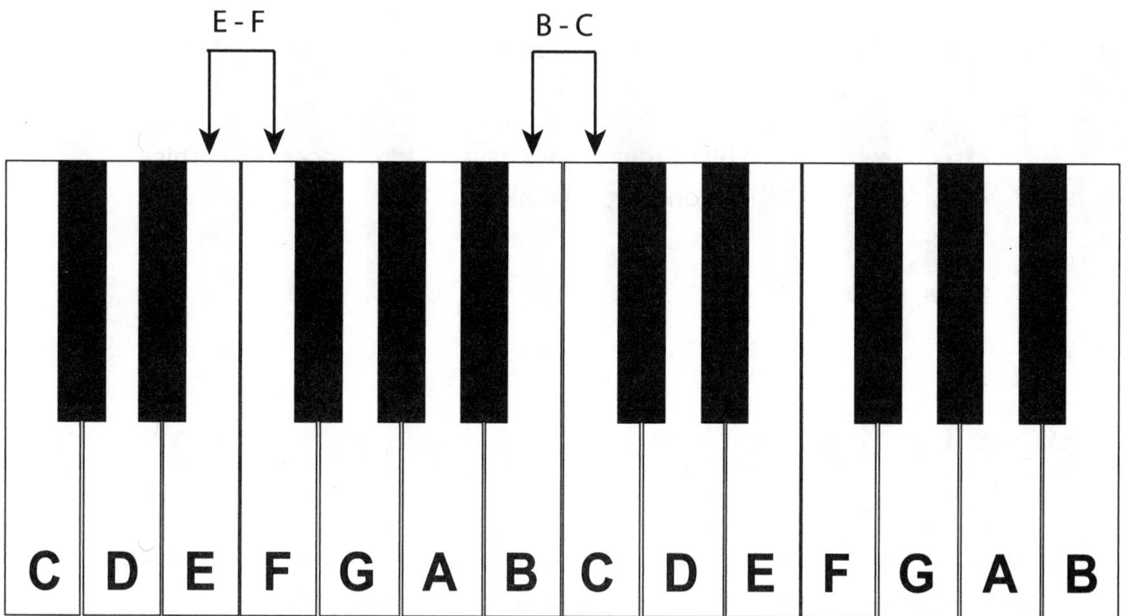

Why is there a half step between B and C and E and F when everywhere else it takes a whole step to get to the next letter name? The answer is simpler than you think. The sound of the C major scale (C–D–E–F–G–A–B–C) came first. The scale happened to have a half step between E and F and B and C. When the system of music was broken down and actually defined, that scale was laid out in white keys and had to fit the other half steps between the other notes. It really is an arbitrary thing more than anything else. It's another argument for the fact that sounds come first and then you figure out a way to name/explain them.

Whole Steps

A whole step is simply the distance of two half steps combined. Movements from C to D or F♯ to G♯ are examples of whole steps. If you are getting the hang of both whole and half steps, you can actually take this information quite a bit further. You could skip to scales, which would, in turn, lead you to chords.

The intervals between E and F and B and C are still natural half steps. Look at **FIGURE 2.4** to see an example.

FIGURE 2.4 Unusual Whole Steps

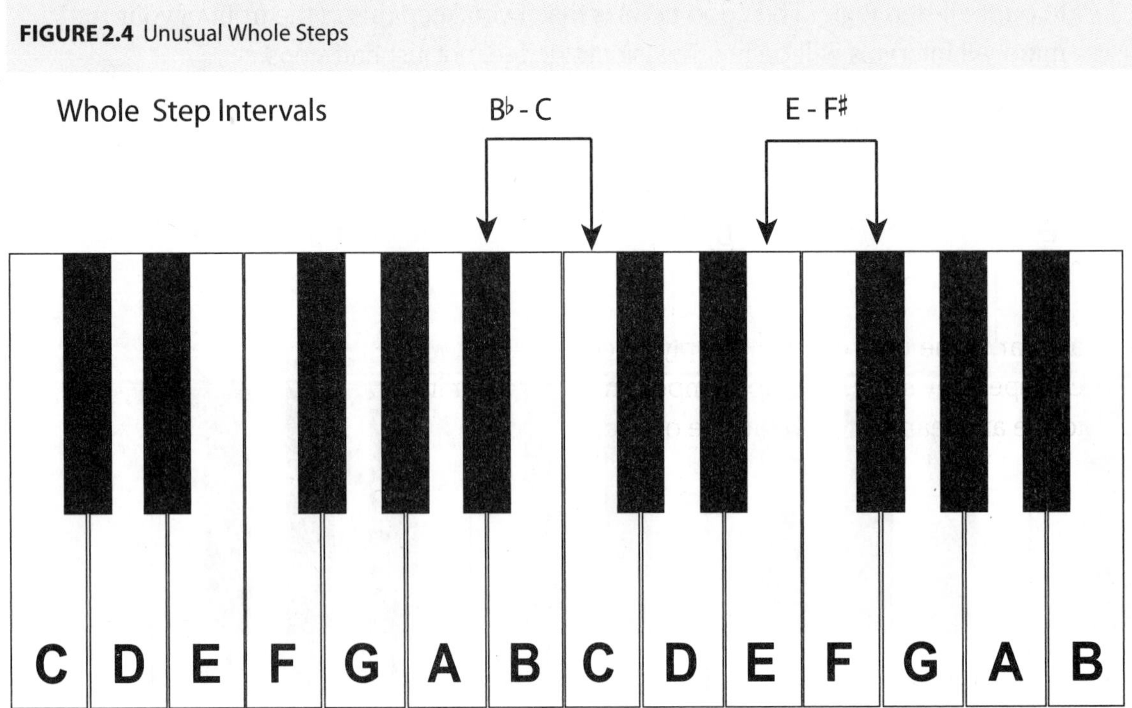

A whole step from E ends up on F♯ because you have to go two half steps to get to F♯, passing right by F natural. The same holds true for B♭ to C.

Now it's time for you to put this information to work. **FIGURE 2.5** is a worksheet for half and whole steps. You'll be asked to name some intervals by looking at them and also write an interval from a single note. There are a few different clefs, to make this exercise fun and challenging. Feel free to write in your book, but use a pencil!

FIGURE 2.5 Half and Whole Step Practice

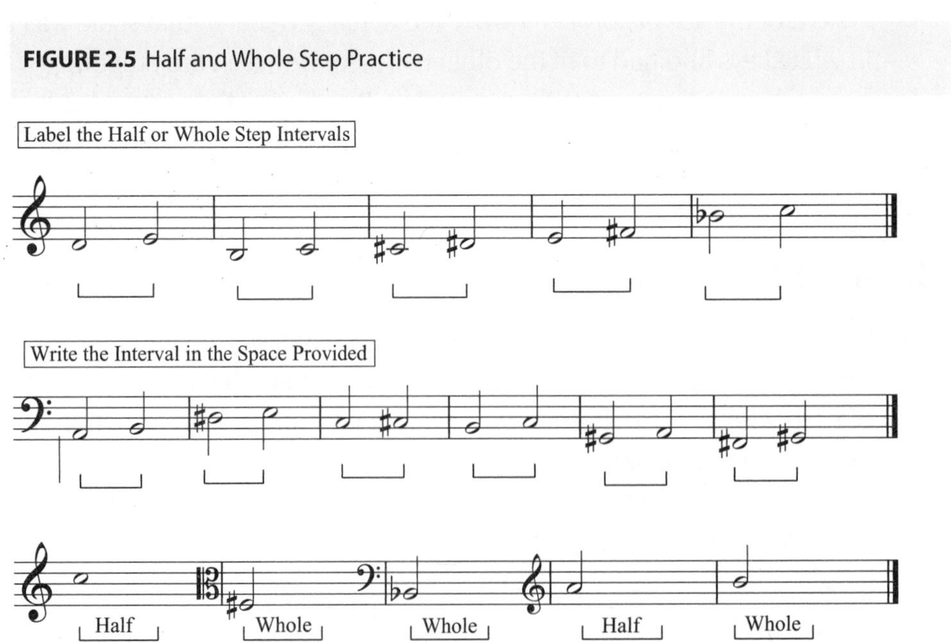

Now that you have gone through half and whole steps, the next step is a look at the C major scale, to get to some of the other types of intervals out there.

Intervals from Scales

Now, you may be wondering why a discussion of the C major scale appears here in the interval chapter, when, according to the plan of the book, scales appear in the next chapter. Simply, once you know whole and half steps, you can spell any scale, but more importantly, the other intervals are much easier to see and learn through the use of a scale.

Point to Consider

When many musicians name a large interval they usually don't count the numbers of half steps that they need to figure out the answer. Typically, most musicians are so familiar with scales that they use that information to solve their puzzle. Scales are such useful bits of information, and they are, of course, made up of simple intervals!

This will become clearer as the book progresses, so consider this a sneak peek at scales; you will get the full scoop in the next chapter.

Intervals in the C Major Scale

Forming a C major scale is pretty simple: You start and end on C, use every note in the musical alphabet, and use no sharps or flats. Because the C major scale contains no sharps or flats, it's very easy to spell and understand. It's the scale you get if you play from C to C on just the white keys of a piano. So, here is the scale spelled out.

FIGURE 2.6 The C Major Scale

If you look at the distance between any two adjacent notes in the scale, you will see that this is simply a collection of half and whole steps. Now try skipping around the scale and see what intervals you come up with. Start with C as a basis for your work for now. Every interval will be the distance from C to some other note in the C scale.

To start simply, measure the distance where there is no distance at all. An interval of no distance is called unison.

TRACK 1

FIGURE 2.7 Unison Interval, C to C

Unison is more important than you think. While you won't see it in a solo piano score—you couldn't play the same key twice at the same time—when you learn to analyze a full score of music, it's really handy to be able to tell when instruments are playing exactly the same notes and not other intervals, like octaves and such.

The movement from C to D is a whole step, but the interval is more formally called a major second. Every major second comprises two half steps' distance.

TRACK 2

FIGURE 2.8 Major Second, C to D

The next interval would be from C to E, which is four half steps' distance and more formally called a major third.

TRACK 3

FIGURE 2.9 Major Third, C to E

Next up is the distance from C to F, which is five half steps, and is formally called a perfect fourth.

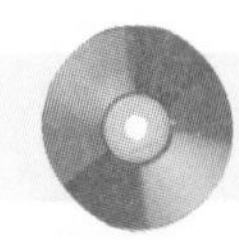

TRACK 4

FIGURE 2.10 Perfect Fourth, C to F

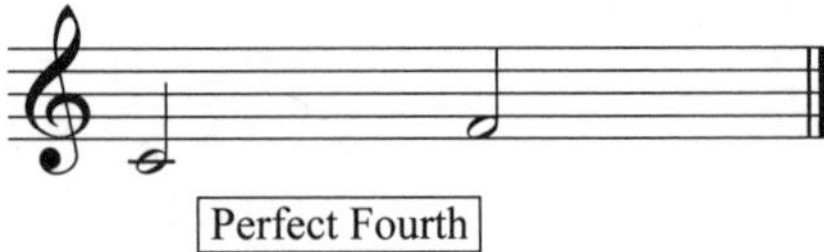

Perfect fourth? Are you confused yet with the naming of these intervals? Hang in there! Before you get to the why and the logic behind this, finish the scale. You have only begun to chip away at intervals.

The next interval is the distance from C to G, which is seven half steps and is formally called a perfect fifth.

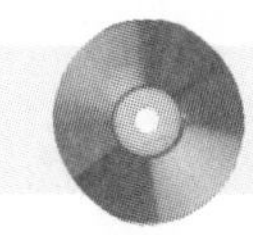

TRACK 5

FIGURE 2.11 Perfect Fifth, C to G

The interval from C to A, which is nine half steps, is formally called a major sixth.

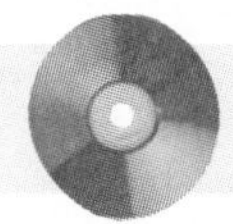

TRACK 6

FIGURE 2.12 Major Sixth, C to A

The next interval, from C to B, is eleven half steps and is formally called a major seventh.

TRACK 7

FIGURE 2.13 Major Seventh, C to B

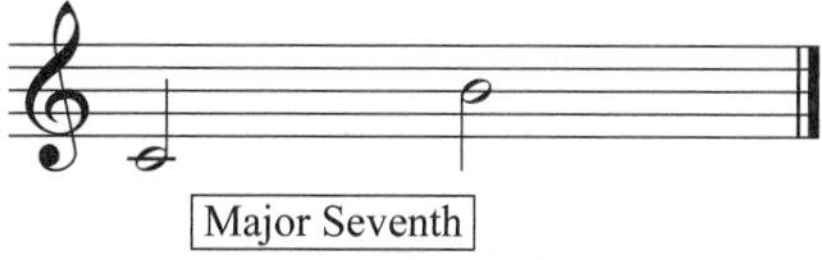

To complete this scale, the last interval will be C to C, a distance of twelve half steps, or an octave.

TRACK 8

FIGURE 2.14 Octave, C to C

Intervals in the C Minor Scale

Now that you've seen the intervals in the C major scale, here is the whole C minor scale and all of its intervals.

FIGURE 2.15 Minor Scale Intervals

Perfect Unison

Major Second

Minor Third

What do you see here? For starters the third, sixth, and seventh intervals are now minor. That makes sense because those are the three notes that are different if you directly compare a C major and a C minor scale side by side, as in **FIGURE 2.16**.

FIGURE 2.16 Major and Minor Scale Comparison

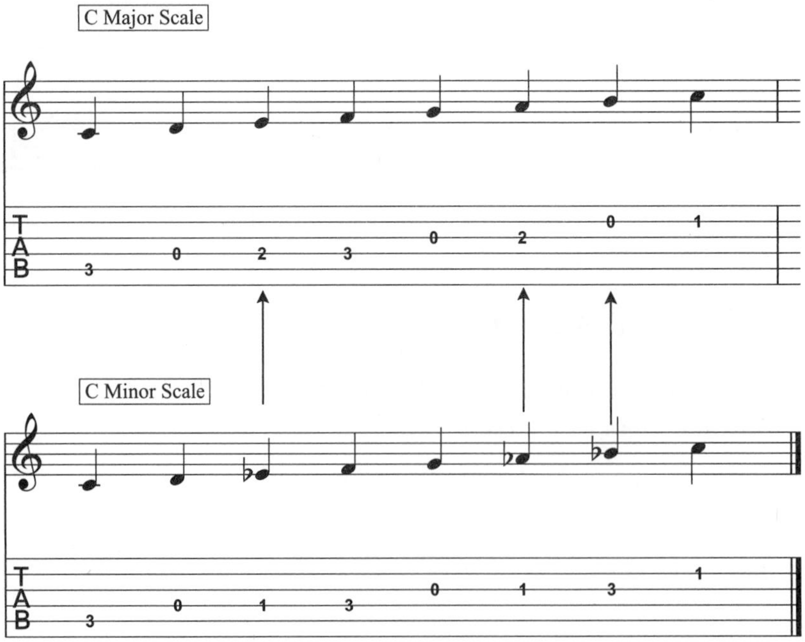

C Major Scale

T
A
B
3 0 2 3 0 2 0 1

C Minor Scale

T
A
B
3 0 1 3 0 1 3 1

Only the 3rd, 6th and 7th change.

The intervals that were "perfect" in the major scale remain the same between both scales. However, the second note of the scale (C to D) remains the same in both scales, yet that interval is called a "major second."

Why are scales so important when dealing with intervals? Aren't intervals something that you can measure on their own, separately from a scale? Yes, of course, that's right, but most musicians get very comfortable with scales and they use them to figure intervals out because scales are a point of reference. If you ask a musician what the interval is between A and F, it's likely that he or she will think of an A major scale first and try to see if F♯ is in the A scale. Since F♯ is, he or she will quickly lower the F♯ from a major sixth down to a minor sixth and that's the answer. Otherwise, half steps would have to be counted, which is tedious, or every possible interval combination in music would have to be memorized, and that has it's own obvious disadvantages. (It might happen naturally over time, but it certainly wouldn't happen overnight.) Certain intervals are easy to memorize, and you do learn to memorize some of them, but scales still remain in most musicians' heads since they know them so well.

What you don't see in either the major or minor scale is diminished or augmented intervals. That's not to say they aren't there; it all depends on how you look at it. Suffice it to say that major, minor, and perfect intervals are the most basic intervals, and they are the easiest to spell and understand as they naturally occur in the major and minor scales that you play so much. Augmented and diminished intervals are less common but are equally important to know and understand.

Point to Consider

When measuring musical intervals, always count the first note as one step. For example, C to G is a fifth because you have to count C as one. This is the most common mistake that students make when they are working with musical intervals, they often come up one short of the real answer because they simply forget to count the starting spot as one!

Quality and Distance

Intervals have two distinct parts: quality and distance. Quality refers to the first part of an interval, either being "major" or "perfect," as you saw from the C major scale intervals. Now, these are not the only intervals in music, these are just the intervals in the C scale; you will see the rest of the intervals shortly. Distance is the simplest part—designations such as second, third, fourth, and so on refer to the absolute distance of the letters. For example, C to E will always be a "third" apart, because there are three letters (C, D, and E) from C to E.

The numerical distance is the easiest part of intervals: You simply count the letters! Determining the quality of an interval is a different story. In the C major scale, there are two different qualities of intervals: major and perfect. Why were some of them major and what's so perfect about the fourth and the fifth? At first, learning all of these rules can be a challenge, but when you understand the basics, you can do so much. As for interval quality, it's only when you understand all of the different qualities that you can name any interval.

Enharmonics

An interval has to determine the distance from any note to another note. As you can see above in the C major scale, every interval has a distance and a quality to it. Where the real confusion comes in is that notes can have more than one name. You might recall enharmonics, mentioned earlier, where C♯ and D♭ sound the same yet are different notes on paper.

When you analyze written music, you have to deal with what you are given. When you listen to any interval, you don't listen to the spelling, you hear the sound, so the distance from C to D♯ will sound just like C to E♭. What you hear is the sound of those notes ringing together, but if you had to analyze it on paper, you'd be looking at two different intervals (one is a minor third and the other is an augmented second), with two different names. This is exactly why the system of intervals has evolved somewhat strangely and with a certain amount of ambiguity, because written music has the enharmonic issue built in.

IN TIME

Many modern theorists and composers don't use the traditional intervallic system. Instead, they base their intervallic measurements on pure distance-based relationships in half steps. This solves the ambiguity with enharmonic intervals completely. So, instead of a major third, it would be a "five." This more numerically based system of organization for music is called "set" or "set theory."

The Simple Intervals

As previously mentioned, there are five distinct types of interval qualities to deal with: major, minor, perfect, diminished, and augmented. The "distance" of an interval will always consist of the quality first, followed by the numerical measure of how many notes you are traveling, for example, "major sixth." Go through the "simple" intervals—major, minor, and perfect—first, and you'll deal with diminished and augmented intervals in the next section.

Major Intervals

Major intervals can apply only to distances of seconds, thirds, sixths, and sevenths. A quick trick to spell any major interval would be to look to the major scale you are working with. For example, if you wanted to find out what a major third was from the note E, you could spell the scale and simply name the third note of the E major scale and that would be your answer. Many musicians use this method to spell intervals and scales.

The other way to look at these intervals is to look at the distance in half steps (or whole steps). This is another way to figure out an interval, and it precludes knowing the scale (which this book doesn't officially get to until next chapter). Here is a table of all the major intervals and their intervallic distance.

Table of Major Intervals

Type	Distance in half steps	Distance in whole steps
Major Second	two	one
Major Third	four	two
Major Sixth	nine	four and one half
Major Seventh	eleven	five and one half

That's all there is to major intervals! **FIGURE 2.17** is a short quiz that asks you to name a bunch of major intervals. Use whatever method you are familiar and comfortable with to name these, either using scales if you know them already or simply counting the steps. Just remember, there are no trick questions here—all of these intervals are major intervals: seconds, thirds, sixths, or sevenths. Write your answers below the intervals.

FIGURE 2.17 Major Interval Practice

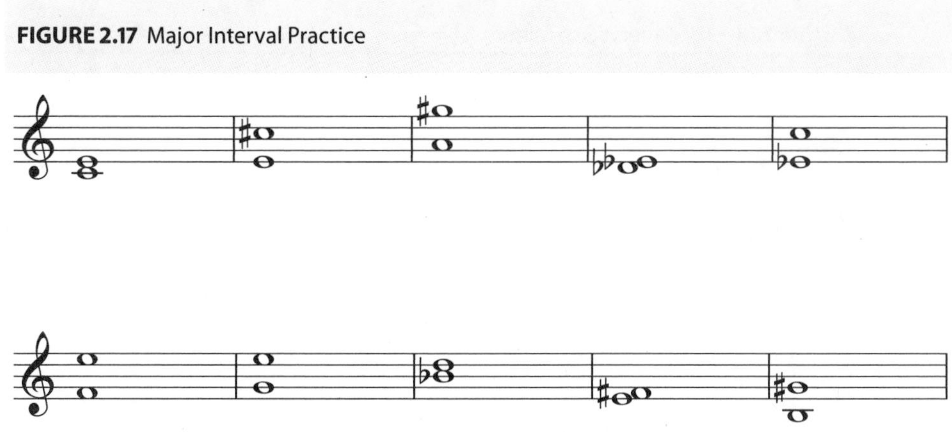

Minor Intervals

Minor intervals are next up, and they are closely related to major intervals, as they both only exist as seconds, thirds, sixths, and sevenths. So, what's the difference between a major and a minor interval? Simply, a minor interval is exactly one half step smaller than a major interval. Take a look at the table below and compare it to the table presented above for the major intervals.

Table of Minor Intervals

Type	Distance in half steps	Distance in whole steps
Minor Second	one	one half
Minor Third	three	one and a half
Minor Sixth	eight	four
Minor Seventh	ten	five

With the major intervals, you are lucky enough to be able to name any major interval simply by looking at a major scale and counting. This sort of works for the minor scale, but it's not perfect. If you spell out the minor scale, you do, in fact, get the minor third, minor sixth, and minor seventh, but beware of the second. A minor scale's second note is a major second from the root. If you need to measure a minor second, just remember that a minor second is the smallest interval in music, the half step.

What you realize about the minor intervals is that they are always exactly one half step lower than their major counterparts. So, if you have to name a minor interval and you're super fast at the major intervals, simply lower any major interval exactly one half step and you will be there. **FIGURE 2.18** shows how this works.

FIGURE 2.18 Major Intervals to Minor

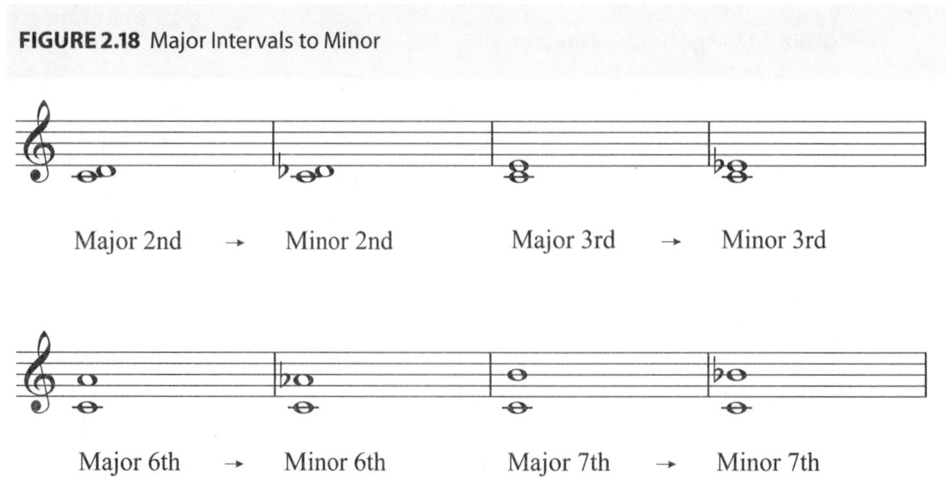

See, that isn't so bad! Just remember that major intervals are the larger of the two intervals when you compare major and minor intervals.

Extra Credit

Strengthen your vocabulary! Instead of talking about half and whole steps, call them by their proper names. A half step is a minor second and a whole step is a major second.

Perfect Intervals

So far, the logic to naming interval quality has made sense: Major intervals come from major scales, and minor intervals (all except one) come from the minor scale. Now you come to perfect intervals, and you may be wondering what is so "perfect" about them. Here is a very brief history lesson. As music was evolving, most music was monophonic, meaning that you sung or played only one line at a time. Once they got daring enough to add a second line of music, only certain intervals were considered "consonant" and could be used. In the early days of polyphony, fourths and fifths were commonly used, so *perfect* seemed to fit their name as they almost never sounded bad. To modern ears, fourths and fifths don't always sound as nice as thirds or sixths do, but that's just a matter of taste. Back to the intervals! Perfect intervals encompass the following distances: unison (no distance at all), fourth, fifth, and octave.

Perfect intervals are fairly easy to spell because all the perfect intervals appear in both the major and the minor scales, so no matter what you are more comfortable spelling in, you'll find all your perfect intervals there. If you're up for counting in steps, here is another table!

Table of Perfect Intervals

Type	Distance in half steps	Distance in whole steps
Unison	n/a	n/a
Perfect Fourth	five	two and a half
Perfect Fifth	seven	three and a half
Perfect Octave	twelve	six

In contrast to major intervals that can be made into minor intervals by simply lowering them a half step, the perfect intervals are stuck. If you do anything to a perfect interval (flat or sharp one of the notes), you are changing interval type away from being perfect. It always becomes something else. What it actually becomes is something discussed in the next section. Before you move on to the more advanced intervals, practice spelling some perfect intervals. **FIGURE 2.19** will help you practice identifying perfect intervals.

FIGURE 2.19 Perfect Interval Practice

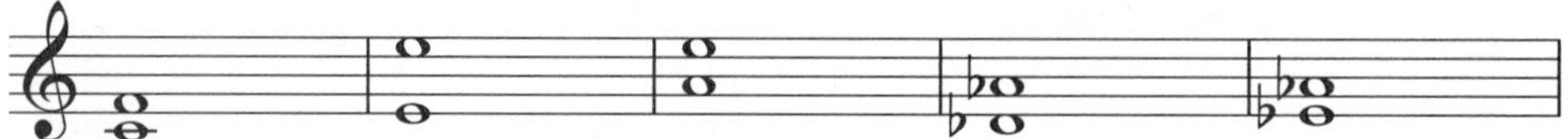

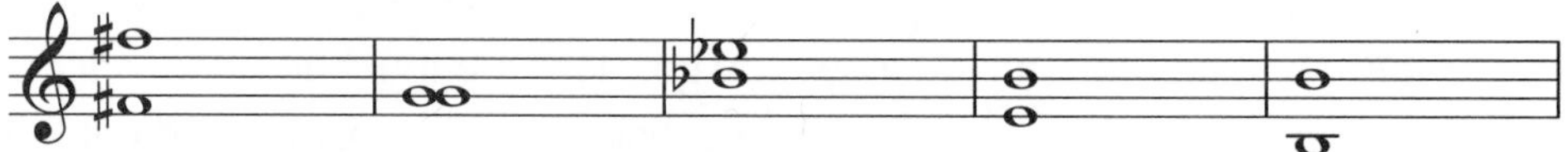

See, this isn't that bad. Intervals are a fairly concrete thing that have an absolute distance and you can name them based on those parameters. But as stated before, naming an interval comprises two parts: quality and distance. You have two more qualities to explore: augmented and diminished.

IN TIME

The term *octave* has the root *oct* like *octagon* does. *Oct,* of course, is the prefix indicating eight, and an octave is the distance spanning eight notes. More importantly, an octave is the same letter name repeated at a higher part of the musical spectrum.

Advanced Intervals

The basic intervals of music are major, minor, and perfect. If you stopped there, you would have more than just a cursory understanding of intervals; you could do more than just get by. However, there are two more types of intervals, which deal with the issue of enharmonic spellings of notes and other such anomalies: augmented and diminished intervals.

As you know, the interval of C to E♭ and that of C to D♯ sound exactly the same. The only thing that's different is the spelling of the D♯ and the E♭. If you remember, that's called an enharmonic.

Now, the spelling of those intervals will change as the note changes its name—this is regardless of whether or not those intervals "sound" exactly the same. For example, if the interval is spelled C to E♭, the interval is called a minor third. If the interval is spelled C to D♯, you can't call it a minor third anymore. Third intervals are reserved for intervals of three notes (C to E). Since this interval is from C to D, it must be called a second of some sort. In this case, the correct name is an augmented second. Enharmonic spellings give birth to the need for terms like *augmented* and *diminished intervals*.

Augmented Intervals

An augmented interval is any interval that is larger than a major or perfect interval. **FIGURE 2.20** shows a few examples of augmented intervals.

FIGURE 2.20 Augmented Intervals

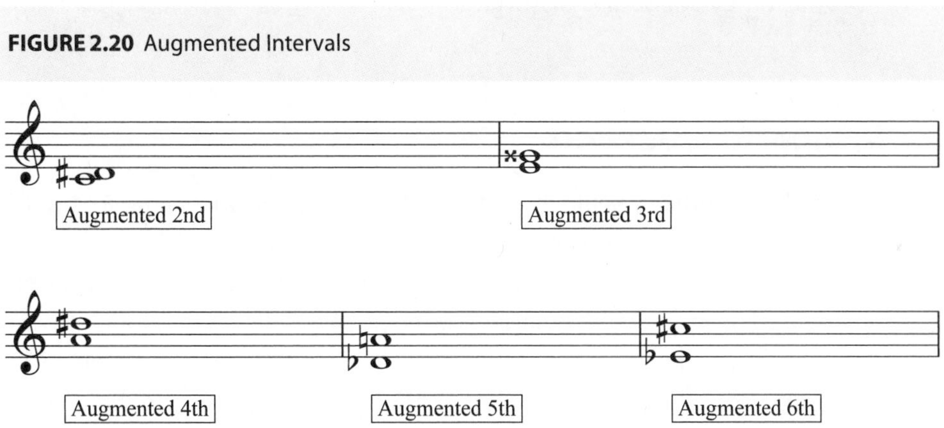

Traditionally, you can only augment second, third, fourth, fifth, or sixth intervals. Use augmented intervals when the notes are spelled in an unusual way and you have to adhere to the rule of "it's three notes apart, so I must call it some sort of third, but it's larger than a major third." The deciding factor in all of this is how the interval is spelled on paper. Look for the distance between the notes and use that as your guide. Again, augmented intervals are used when an interval is too large to be called major or perfect.

Diminished Intervals

Diminished intervals are more specialized. A diminished interval names an interval that has been made smaller. Typically, diminished intervals are used only to make the perfect intervals smaller. In reality, this is just another spelling convention more than anything else. You can make a fourth or a fifth diminished by lowering any of the perfect intervals one half step. You can also make a minor interval diminished by simply lowering a minor interval one half step down. The interval of C to E♭♭ would be a diminished third. The interval of a diminished fifth is commonly called a tritone because, at six half steps, it splits the octave evenly in half (twelve half steps in an octave).

IN TIME

Both the diminished fifth and the augmented fourth are considered tritones—the spelling is not important, only the distance. The tritone is such a dissonant interval it was called diablo en music ("the devil in music") during the Middle Ages, and was something to avoid at all costs. Things have changed, and you do hear tritone intervals in modern music, but they still sound dissonant.

Chromatic Intervals

The chromatic scale includes all twelve tones (including all the half tones) in the octave. Thus, chromatic intervals are a semitone apart.

FIGURE 2.21 provides a full chart of every possible interval and enharmonic spelling in one octave to show you how all this lays out. Notice how the number of half steps an interval has is not always the deciding factor in its name. Because of enharmonic spellings, there are pluralities to deal with. Always remember to look at the distance between the written notes and then look for the quality.

Here is another way to understand intervals. If the top note of the interval exists in the major scale of the bottom note, the interval is major or perfect. If not, it's minor, diminished, or augmented. Here is a little chart to help you. An arrow in either direction indicates movement of a half step.

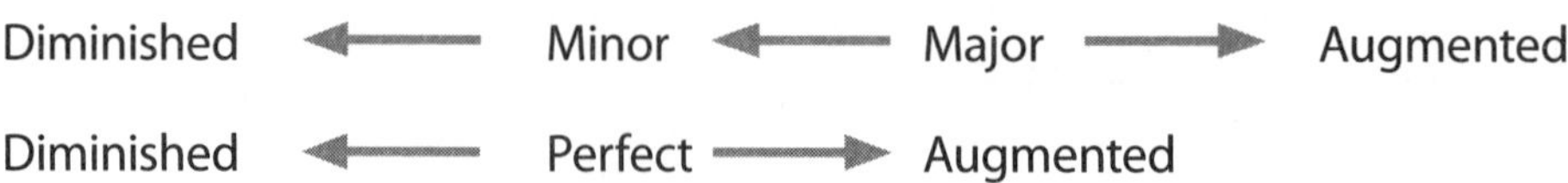

FIGURE 2.21 Chromatic Intervals

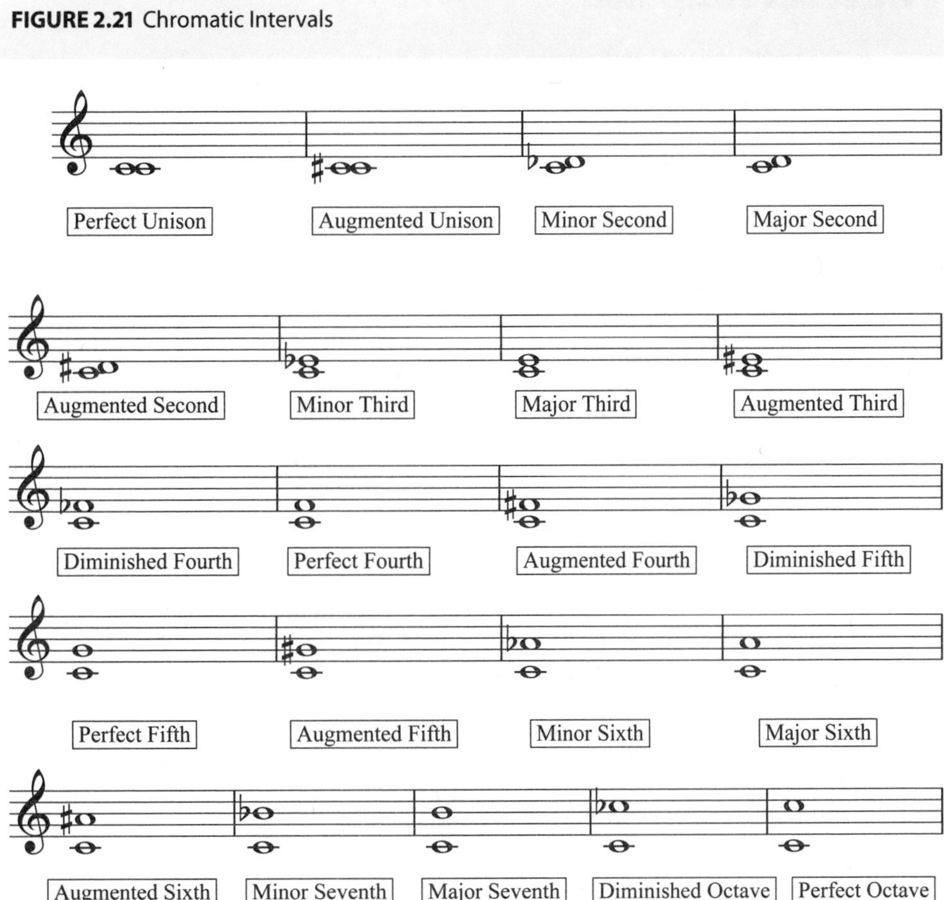

Inverted and Extended Intervals

How far is it from C to G? You might say a perfect fifth. You might be right. However, what if the interval went down? What if the C were written higher on the staff than the G? Would it still be a perfect fifth? In this case, it would actually be a perfect fourth.

So far, this text has dealt with ascending intervals. But what happens when you read an interval down? When you name any interval, such as C to G, you must specify if it's an ascending interval or if it's descending. If the interval ascends, no worries, you've been trained to handle that without a problem. On the other hand, if the interval descends, it's not spelled the same way. A fifth interval, when flipped around, is not a fifth anymore. This is because the musical scale is not symmetric.

Interval Inversion

Any interval that ascends can be inverted (flipped upside down). **FIGURE 2.22** looks at the example of C to G from the last section. When you flip the perfect fifth, it becomes a perfect fourth. Wouldn't it be great if there were a system to help you invert any interval? Thankfully, there is. You are going to learn to use the rule of nine to invert any interval with ease.

FIGURE 2.22 Inverted Intervals

The Rule of Nine

The rule of nine is defined as such: When any interval is inverted, the sum of the ascending and descending intervals must add up to nine. Using the first example, the interval from C to G is a perfect fifth. The interval from G to C is a perfect fourth. When you add up 5 and 4, you get 9. Test this out in a few notation examples in **FIGURE 2.23**. What's the inversion of a third? It's a sixth, because 3 and 6 add up to 9. This works on any interval.

FIGURE 2.23 Inverted Intervals and the Rule of Nine

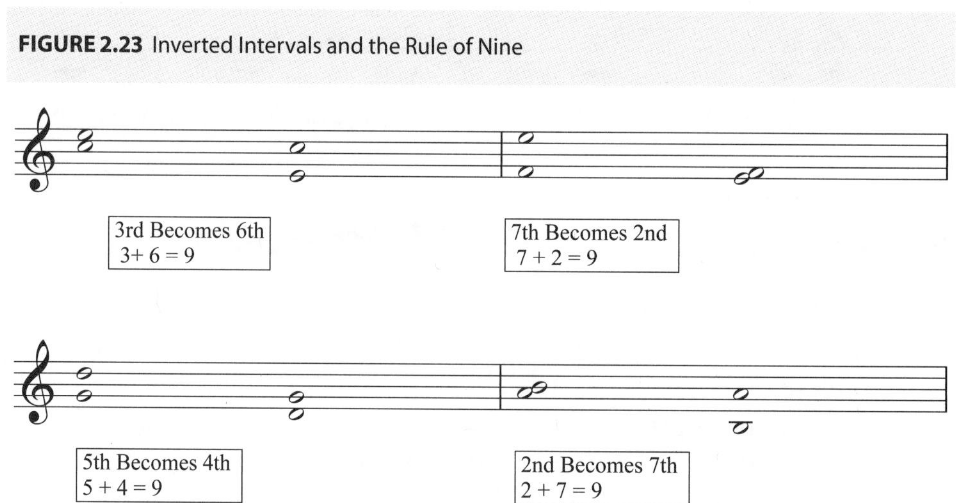

Inverted Qualities

When using the rule of nine, it's easy to flip the intervals over and get the correct inversion. But the type of interval, or quality of the interval, also changes as you invert it. The rule of nine tells you the name of the interval numerically, but the type of interval that it becomes (major, minor, perfect) will change as intervals are flipped over. The answer to this problem has a simple solution. Here is what happens to interval qualities when the intervals invert.

- If the interval was major, it becomes minor when inverted.
- If the interval was minor, it becomes major when inverted.
- If the interval was perfect, it remains perfect when inverted.

This is easy to remember. Major becomes minor, minor becomes major, and perfect stays perfect. As you can see, by using the rule of nine and changing the type of interval accordingly, you can invert intervals like a pro!

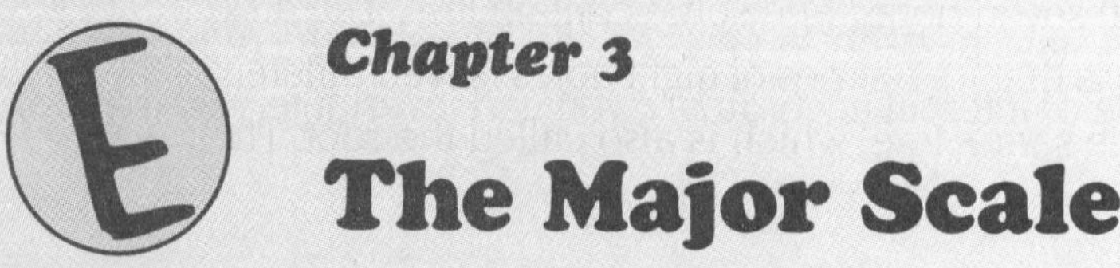

Chapter 3
The Major Scale

The major scale is one of the first structural elements that you should look at in music. A simple formation of notes can bring you into the mind of the composer, allowing you to see what elements are used in composition. Major scales are multifaceted and are used for melodies and harmonies. Anyone interested in learning about music theory should know as much as possible about the major scale.

Scales Defined

You've heard the term major scale many times before. Many of you play scales in some shape or form and don't even know it. Scales have been mentioned already in this book. Now it's time to look more closely at what makes them tick. For starters, here's a basic definition of what a scale is: A scale is a grouping of notes together that makes a key. Most of the scales that you will encounter have seven different pitches (but a total of eight notes, including the repeated octave) in them. Some scales that you'll learn about later in the book contain more than seven notes, and some contain less. The bread-and-butter definition of a scale is that it's a series of eight notes (seven different pitches) that start and end on the same note, which is also called the root. The root names the scale. If a scale starts and ends on C, the root is C and the scale's name is the C something (major, minor, etc.) scale. What that something is depends on its intervallic formula. Thankfully, you know a thing or two about intervals. Since this chapter focuses on major scales, look at a very basic C major scale in **FIGURE 3.1**.

FIGURE 3.1 The C Major Scale

TRACK 9

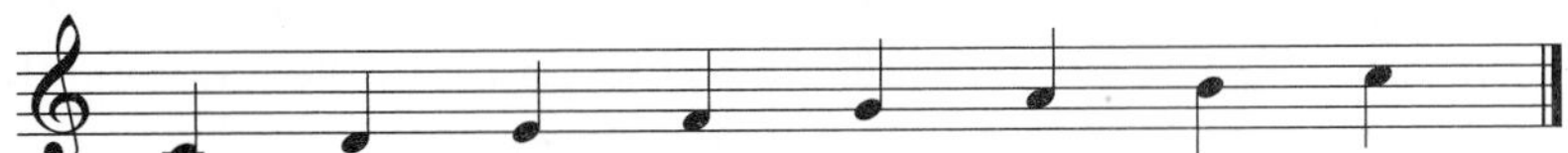

As you can see, the scale starts and ends on C and progresses up every note in order. Since C major contains no sharps and no flats, it's an easy scale to understand and remember. On the piano, it's simply all the white notes. The C scale contains seven different notes: C, D, E, F, G, A, and B. The last C isn't counted, as it's just a repeated note. The major scale has eight notes in total, though.

What makes this a major scale is not the fact that it uses the notes C–D–E–F–G–A–B–C. That only tells you that it's one particular key. Music theory looks for larger scale ideas and tries to tie them together. What makes that scale a major scale are the intervals between the notes. If you simply look at the distance from each note in the scale to the next, you see a pattern of half or whole steps in a series. This series, which you can also call a formula, is exactly what you are going to learn about now. **FIGURE 3.2** shows the C major scale with the intervals defined.

FIGURE 3.2 Intervals of the C Major Scale

Whole Whole Half Whole Whole Whole Half

What you come up with is the interval series of Whole, Whole, Half, Whole, Whole, Whole, Half, or WWHWWWH for short. This is the only thing that makes any scale different from any other scale: the formula of the intervals. As long as that interval formula is present, you have a major scale. It's an absolutely perfect system, because you can start on any note you feel like (any of the twelve chromatic notes, that is) and follow these simple rules:

1. Pick a root note.
2. Progress up seven notes until you reach the octave.
3. Use the formula of WWHWWWH between your notes to ensure that you have the correct spelling.
4. Make sure that you use any letter only once before the octave.

If you can follow those rules, you can spell any scale. Here's how.

Spelling Scales

FIGURE 3.7 will be an exercise where you will be given four different notes to start on, and you will be asked to fill in the correct notes to spell the major scales. To see how it's going to work, try one now. Start out with a root note, which in this example will be A♭, as seen in **FIGURE 3.3**.

FIGURE 3.3 Building a Scale: *Step One*

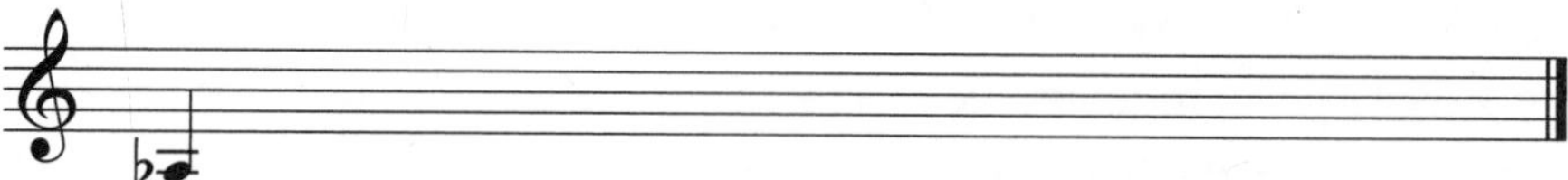

Next, place the rest of the notes on the staff. Now, don't be too concerned about whether you have the correct intervals or even the right spellings, you just need to have one of each letter name, in order, up to the octave. So simply add a B–C–D–E–F–G and A to **FIGURE 3.4**.

FIGURE 3.4 Building a Scale: *Step Two*

Now that you have the raw notes in, you need to add the intervals. The formula is WWHWWWH, so you add the intervals between the notes of the scale, as seen in **FIGURE 3.5**.

FIGURE 3.5 Building a Scale: *Step Three*

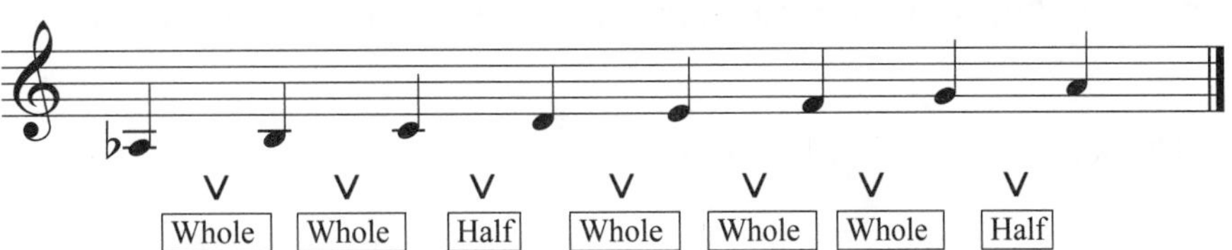

You're nearly done. All you have to do is actually "engage" the intervals and make sure your scale is spelled correctly. Follow this process:

- You need a whole step from A♭. A whole step away would be B♭. Add a B♭ to the scale.
- You need a whole step from B♭. A whole step away would be C, which you already have written down, so you don't have to change anything.
- You need a half step from C. A half step away would be D♭, so you put a flat in front of the D to make it D♭.
- You need a whole step from D♭. A whole step away is E♭, so make the E an E♭.
- You need a whole step from E♭. A whole step away is F, which you already have, so no change is needed.
- You need a whole step from F. A whole step away is G, which you also already have, so no change is needed.
- You need a half step from G. A half step away is A♭. Change the A to A♭. (Coincidentally, since this is a ♭ scale, every A in this scale is flat, so you could have just made it flat.)

Now, look at **FIGURE 3.6**.

FIGURE 3.6 Building a Scale: *Step Four*

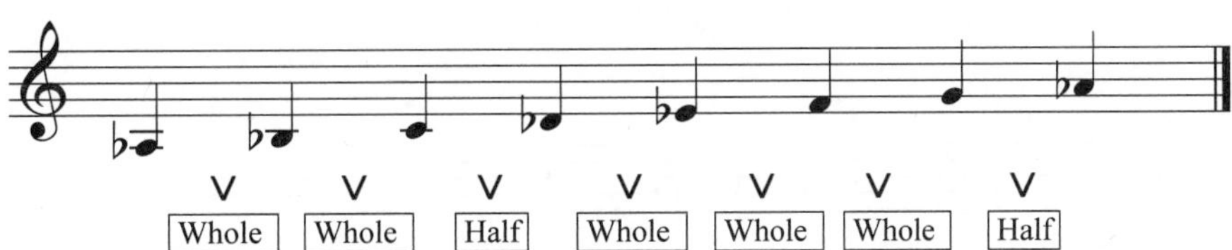

That's it! You have a scale that ascends up using every letter of the musical alphabet once. The scale follows the pattern of WWHWWWH, which all major scales follow. Play it on your instrument just to be sure, and that familiar sound will tell you that you're correct.

FIGURE 3.7 is practice time. Start on each note and spell your major scales. You can use the method above or go your own way. Just remember that you have to use the WWHWWWH interval pattern, otherwise they won't be major scales.

FIGURE 3.7 Major Scale Spelling Practice

Using the space provided, spell the D, G, B♭, and E Major scales. Use the WWHWWWH interval pattern to spell the scale tones.

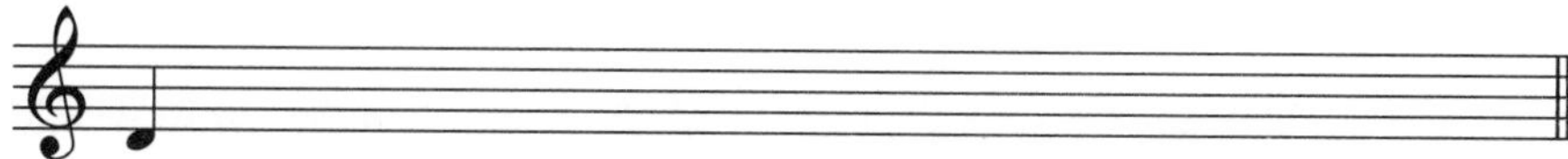

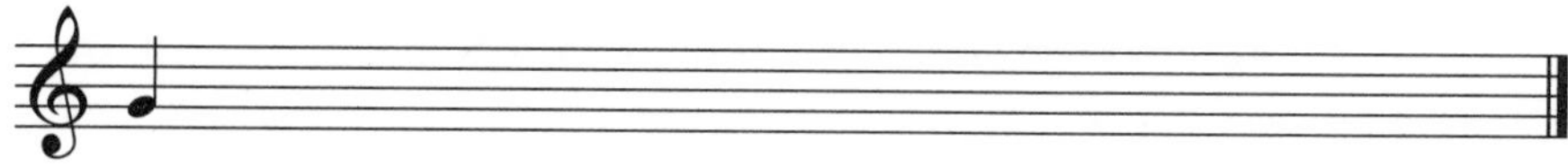

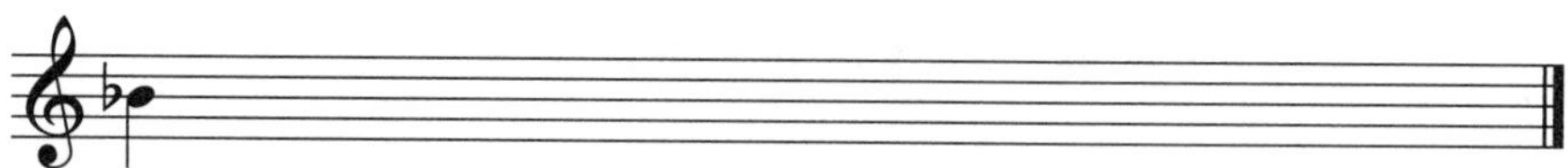

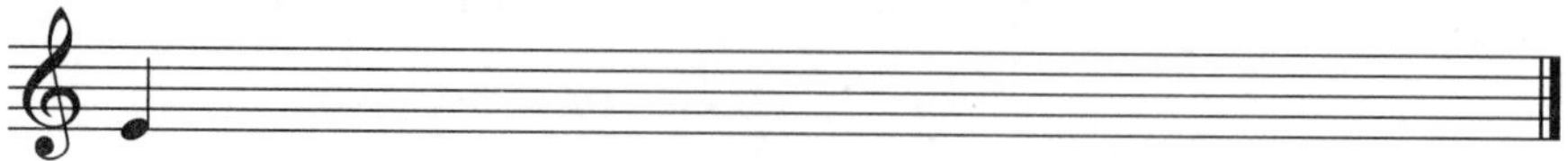

Some Thoughts

We have now seen a total of six major scales: the two you have been shown in full (C and A♭) and the four you have just done. This is a good time to pause and point out some very interesting things that you should notice.

First, each of the scales is totally unique. What does that mean? Well, each of them has different pitches. No two scales look the same on the surface. While it's true that each of the scales uses the exact same interval pattern, that fact is not clear until you analyze the scale. The fact that each scale uses a unique set of pitches is what makes each one unique, and that is something that you can clearly see.

IN TIME

Ludwig van Beethoven (1770–1827) composed in almost every genre of music during his lifetime, including piano sonatas, chamber music, nine symphonies, and an opera. Although born in Bonn, Germany, he moved to Vienna, Austria, as a young man, and it was there that he wrote his most celebrated works, including the famous "Ode to Joy."

Scales are a bit like DNA in that each one is unique. This fact makes them pretty easy to spot if you know what you're looking for.

Second, did you notice that the scales that contain sharps use only sharps and never throw in a flat or two? Also, the scales that contain flats use only flats and never sharps? That's right, when you spell scales or analyze in music, you will notice that scales have either flats or sharps; you rarely see both sharps and flats in the same scale (see Chapter 4 for the rare exceptions to this rule, posed by the harmonic and melodic minor scales). These two points will help you understand scales so much better and make your life in music theory so much easier.

At this point, you might want to see all the scales, just for reference. Here are all of the chromatic major scales, starting on every possible chromatic note, including the enharmonics (**FIGURE 3.8**).

Notice that based on which chromatic note you start your scale on, you may get a scale that spells pretty easily. On the other hand, certain scales contain double flats or double sharps in order to keep the WWHWWWH pattern going and utilize one of each note in the alphabet. Some spell easily and others are a pain. Because of that, you don't see all the chromatic major scales often; you typically see about scales, which are the ones that spell without constant use of double sharps and double flats.

Because of enharmonic notes, you're going to have scales that have the exact same sound but are spelled differently. A good example is A♭ and G♯.

The key of A♭ has four flats and isn't too hard to spell and/or read in. The key of G♯ has six sharps and a double sharp. Which would you rather read in if both scales actually sounded the same? Even though there are twenty-four possible scales, there are only twelve chromatic notes in the scale, and you will find yourself reading in the easiest twelve keys. Remember, music isn't just for the composer; it also has to suit the player as well.

FIGURE 3.8 All Your Major Scales

FIGURE 3.8A All Your Major Scales

Point to Consider

Now that you know that flats and sharps are mutually exclusive items in scales, this should help you spell your scales more accurately. If you're working on spelling a scale and you're seeing a mixture of flats and sharps, you did something wrong. If you see mostly flats and one sharp, you did something wrong. Scales will simply always look cohesive this way, and that will make your job a bit easier.

Scale Tones

Each scale has seven tones (eight if you include the octave). There are two ways to talk about notes in the scales: by number and by degree.

Scale Tones by Number

In a C major scale, the note C would be considered "one" because naturally, it's the first note of the scale. A different note can then be assigned to each of the scale tones, one through seven. This is useful for a few reasons. First of all, regarding intervals, the distance of an interval is measured with a number, which is often taken from a scale. Second, since all major scales are made of the same pattern, theory once again looks to a "universal" system for naming these scales. If a piece is said to start on the third note of a scale, you can later take that idea and use it in any key. If you simply say, "It starts on E," you lose the context of what scale/key you are in and need extra information in order to work with the idea. Using numbers is a handy way to think about scales and scale tones. It's also going to come in handy as chords and chord progressions are discussed, as chord progressions are labeled with Roman numerals exclusively in music theory.

IN TIME

Originating in the thirteenth century, the motet (derived from the French *mot,* meaning "word") is an early example of polyphonic (multivoice) music. Motets were generally liturgical choral compositions written for multiple voices. Johann Sebastian Bach wrote many motets, seven of which still exist today.

Scale Tones by Degree

The other way that you can describe the tones of the major scale is by giving a distinct name to each degree, instead of a number. This is traditionally used in classical/academic music theory contexts, but some of the terms have become universal and you should at least be aware of them. You might have seen the term *tonic* used to refer to the root of any scale, and that is an example of the names given to each note in the major scale. The chart below will show you how to name each note in the major scale.

Names of Notes in the Major Scale

Scale Degree	Name
First	Tonic
Second	Supertonic
Third	Mediant
Fourth	Subdominant
Fifth	Dominant
Sixth	Submediant or Superdominant
Seventh	Leading Tone
Eighth (the Octave)	Tonic

These names are also used when talking about chords and chord progressions, so knowing them will aid you in understanding progressions. While these terms aren't thrown around nearly as much as the numerical names for the tones, certain names such as the tonic, dominant, and leading tone are used in the everyday vernacular of musicians despite the fact that numerical naming is more widespread and easier to use. If you find yourself in a formal theory situation, you will find these names of scale degrees used, and luckily, now you'll know what they mean!

How Scales Are Used in Music

Scales are everything. That's a huge statement, but as you're going to see, scales are going to spin off into all sorts of directions. By itself, a scale is an organization of pitches, which are called sounds. This organization makes scales more than just a set of random pitches; it makes them into a set of sounds that musicians and theorists call a key. A key is a concept you will see in much more detail throughout this book.

To understand the concept, consider that a key is like a family: Everyone's related in some way. When you use a scale to compose a melody, those notes sound like they belong together. When you stay exclusively in a scale, or a key, you get a very regular and expected sound. Composers use scales to construct melodies. Because keys already have the built-in feeling of "belonging together" or, better yet, "sounding together," it isn't hard to take a scale and make it into a memorable melody. Literally hundreds of melodies that everyone knows and can hum at the drop of a hat come from a scale of some sort. So think of a scale as a vocabulary for musical phrases, much like letters form words that, in turn, form sentences—see the parallels?

When you play a scale one note at a time, you get a melody. When you takes notes from scales and combine them by playing them together, you get harmony. This is something that you will look at in more depth later in this book. For now, just accept that you can break the vast majority of music down into melody and harmony. Now that you know that scales can give us melodies and harmonies, you start to understand the importance of scales.

Major scales are not the only scales in the musical universe. The major scale is very important, but a true understanding of music would be incomplete without a look at the minor scale, the other basic scale of music. Now it's time for some minor exploration.

Chapter 4

The Minor Scale

The next stop on your journey into musical understanding is a closer look at the minor scale. Minor scales have their own distinct pattern and, more importantly, their own sound. In contrast with major scales, minor scales have a darker and heavier sound. They, too, have their own construction and order. Major and minor make up the two fundamental elements of musical scales that are commonly used and practiced in musical theory and writing and performance.

Minor Colors

By this point, you have learned a lot about the major scale. The major scale is an essential, commonly used musical scale. It represents a certain "color" or type of sound. The minor scale is a different color, a darker sound. It's also the other main musical scale. As a musician, you'll encounter the minor scale often.

The minor scale is an alternative to the major scale, yielding a different musical color than the major scale. Certain pieces can convey moods and feelings based on the key and type of scale they're written in. Major scales definitely have a bright and cheery sound to them. Since music is all about contrast, the minor scale and its darker sound are needed to juxtapose with the major scale. Think of it as another flavor in your spice rack.

There are a few ways to look at the minor scale. One is a definitive approach and the other is the derivative approach. You will explore the derivative approach later. For now, treat the minor scale as a very separate entity that has its own formula, intervals, and usage. Later on, you can take a look at the bigger picture and make some fun connections.

The Definitive Approach

In Chapter 2, in the explanation of intervals, the example of the C minor scale illustrated some minor intervals and also showed a contrast against C major. **FIGURE 4.1** shows the C minor scale.

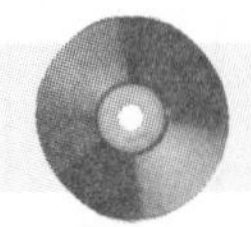

FIGURE 4.1 The C Minor Scale

TRACK 10

By now, you should have in your head that C major has no sharps or flats—that's what makes it such an easy key to work with. Now, if you take a peek at **FIGURE 4.1** again, you will notice that it's different. Sure, it's a different scale, even though it has the same root of C. You learned about the differences in the intervals present in this scale in Chapter 2, but you need to learn the underpinnings of the intervals between the notes so you can come to a formula that enables you to spell any minor scale you need to. Remember that theory is an attempt to find universal parts of music, elements that apply over the entire range of music. Simply knowing that a C minor scale is spelled C–D–E♭–F–G–A♭–B♭ gives you the ability to recognize, spell, and work with only one key. However, if you look at the scale for its intervallic content, you can take that information and apply it anywhere. Time to break the scale into pieces. **FIGURE 4.2** shows the pattern of half and whole steps that are present in the C minor scale.

FIGURE 4.2 The Intervallic Pattern of the Minor Scale

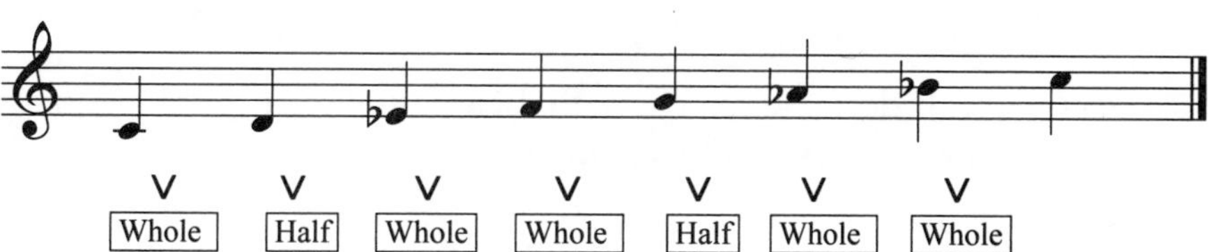

Not surprisingly, there is a different interval pattern than in the major scale. It is WHWWHWW. You can use that interval pattern as a construction blueprint and spell any scale you need to. Now take a step-by-step look at how to create any minor scale.

First start out with a root note, such as C, as seen in **FIGURE 4.3**.

FIGURE 4.3 Building a Minor Scale: *Step One*

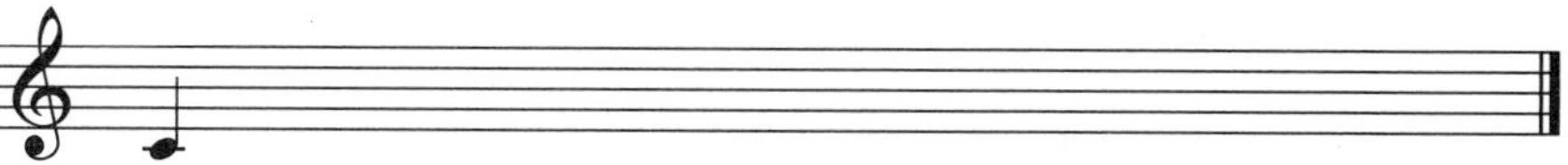

The next thing you want to do is place the rest of the notes on the staff. Now, don't be concerned with whether you have the correct intervals or even the right spellings. You just need to have one of each letter name, in order, up to the octave. So simply add a D–E–F–G–A and B to **FIGURE 4.4**.

FIGURE 4.4 Building a Minor Scale: *Step Two*

Now that you have the raw notes in, you need to add the intervals. The formula is WHWWHWW, so add the intervals between the notes of the scale, as seen in **FIGURE 4.5**.

FIGURE 4.5 Building a Minor Scale: *Step Three*

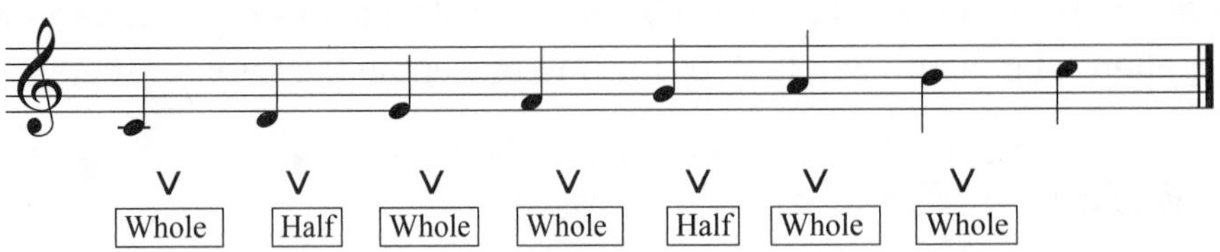

You're nearly done. All you have to do is actually "engage" the intervals and make sure your scale is spelled correctly. Here's the process:

- You need a whole step from C. A whole step away would be D, which you already have.
- You need a half step from D. A half step away would be E♭, so you add a flat before the E.
- You need a whole step from E♭. A whole step away would be F, which you already have.
- You need a whole step from F. A whole step away is G, which you also already have.
- You need a half step from G. A half step away is A♭, so you add a flat before the A.
- You need a whole step from A♭. A whole step away is B♭, so you place a flat before B.
- You need a whole step from B♭. A whole step away is C.

Now to see your full scale, look at **FIGURE 4.6**.

FIGURE 4.6 Building a Minor Scale: *Step Four*

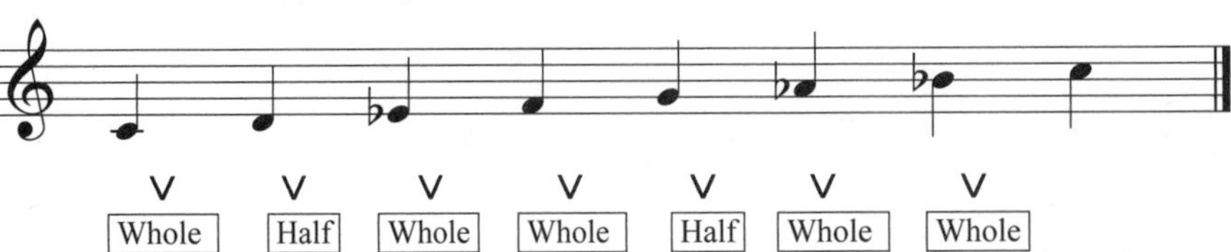

That's it! You now have a scale that ascends up using every letter of the musical alphabet once. Your scale follows the pattern of WHWWHWW, which all minor scales follow.

Now try another one: **FIGURE 4.7** is your practice time. Start on each note and spell your minor scales. You can use the method above or go your own way. Just remember that you have to use the WHWWHWW interval pattern, otherwise they won't be minor scales.

FIGURE 4.7 Minor Scale Spelling Practice

Using the space provided, spell the F, D, A and G♯ Minor scales. Use the WHWWHWW interval pattern to spell the scale tones.

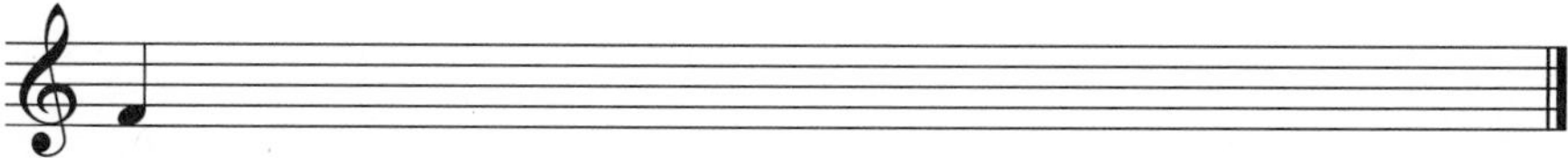

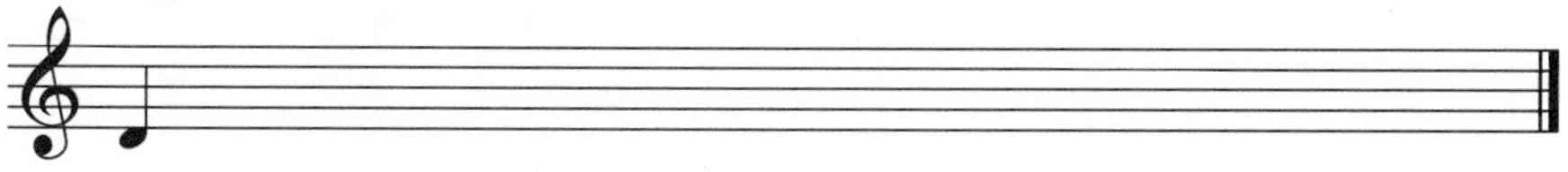

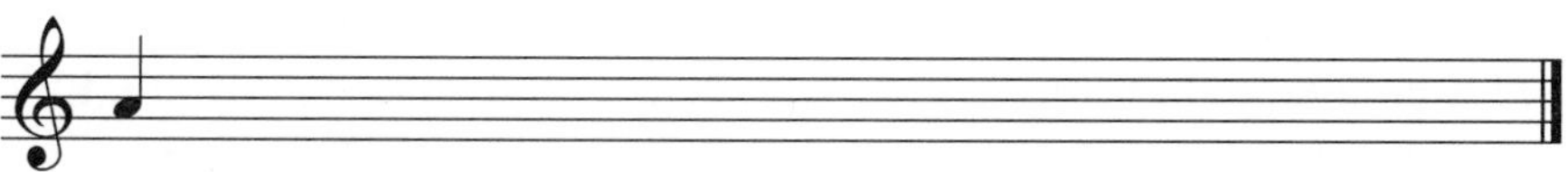

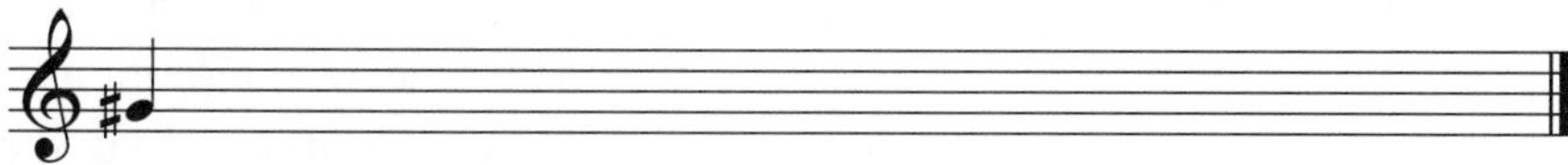

The Derivative Approach

Being able to form scales from pure intervals is a common and useful way to spell scales. Another convenient way to spell minor scales is to derive them from major scales. Many students become comfortable with spelling major scales and find it easy to recall those scales. If you look at the difference between a major scale and a minor scale with the same root, you can form another way to spell minor scales: deriving them from modifications to the major scales. **FIGURE 4.8** shows a C major scale on the top line and a C minor scale on the bottom line.

FIGURE 4.8 Major and Minor Scale Differences

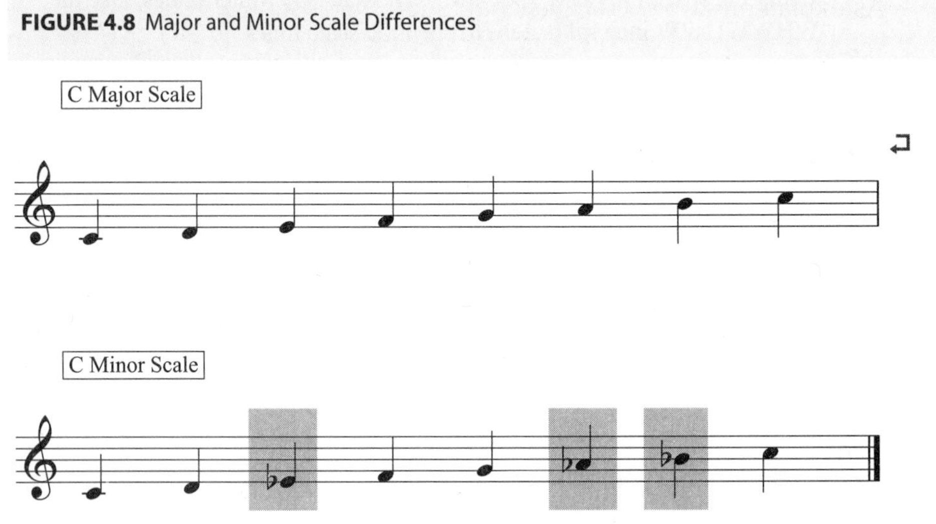

The Highlighted Notes Are The Only Changes Between C Major and C Minor

What you see is that the scales are very similar. The notes C, D, F, and G stay the same. What is changing is that the third, sixth, and seventh note are changing from the major scale to the minor scale. More specifically, the third, sixth, and seventh scale degrees are lowered exactly one half step down from their spelling in the major scale to make the minor scale.

Since you have dealt with intervals in detail, take a closer look at what happened when you went from the major scale to the minor scale. Simply, the intervals of the major third, major sixth, and major seventh (when measured from the root of C) are all changed from major intervals to minor intervals by simply lowering each of the intervals one half step. If you remember from our discussion of intervals, the only difference between a major interval and a minor interval is that the minor interval is one half step smaller than the major interval, or vice versa.

So, what this means is that you can take any major scale and make it into a minor scale by simply lowering the third, sixth, and seventh scale degrees one half step. Doing this, you are deriving the minor scale from the spelling of the major scale—using the derivative approach. This is one more way to look at spelling the minor scale, and you should be comfortable with all the different ways to spell scales as you never know which one will work the best for you!

Degrees in Minor Scales

As explained in the previous chapter on major scales, minor scales can have scale degrees. Also, as with major scales, you can refer to the tones in the minor scale numerically, just like you did when looking at the derivative approach for spelling minor scales (talking about the third, sixth, and seventh scale degrees). In case you skipped the major scale chapter, here is an explanation of scale degrees.

The other way to describe the tones of the minor scale is to give a distinct name instead of a number to each degree. This is traditionally used in classical/academic music theory contexts, but some of the terms have become universal, and you should at least be aware of them. The term *tonic*, used to refer to the root of any scale, is an example of the names given to each note in the minor scale. The table below will show you how to name each note in the minor scale.

Names of Notes in the Minor Scale

Scale Degree	Name
First	Tonic
Second	Supertonic
Third	Mediant
Fourth	Subdominant
Fifth	Dominant
Sixth	Submediant or Superdominant
Seventh	Leading Tone
Eighth (the Octave)	Tonic

These names are also used when talking about chords and chord progressions, so knowing them will aid you in understanding progressions. While these terms aren't thrown around nearly as much as the numerical names for the tones, certain names such as the tonic, dominant, and leading tone are used in the everyday vernacular of musicians despite the numerical naming being more widespread and easier to use. If you find yourself in a formal theory situation, you will find these names of scale degrees used, and luckily, now you'll know what they mean!

Multiple Scales—Scale Clarity

In contrast to the major scale, which comes in only one variety, the minor scale comes in a few different forms. What you have begun to explore is the natural minor scale. When people talk about minor scales, they are typically talking about the natural minor scale, which has the formula of WHWWHWW. However, there are two other minor scales that you need to know about, which have different interval patterns than the natural minor scale: harmonic and melodic minor.

Point to Consider

The natural minor scale is called natural because it's a naturally occurring extension of the major scale, also called a related or relative minor. Relative minors will be discussed in Chapter 5. The other minor scales are derivatives of the natural minor scales and are made by modifying the original natural minor scale.

Harmonic and melodic minor scales have a slightly controversial stance in traditional music theory. Some theorists argue that they are not "true" scales because they are not naturally occurring patterns. But music theory is about identifying what you see and hear in music and whether or not you believe that the scales should have their own names, they are found in music often enough that you need to know about them. In any case, harmonic and melodic minor scales are part of the basic level of theory knowledge, and you simply have to know what they are.

Harmonic Minor

Harmonic minor is the first variation of the minor scale you should know. It's a simple change of the natural minor scale. To form the harmonic minor scale, simply take a minor scale and raise the seventh note up one half step. What you are doing is creating what is called a leading tone to the scale. It simply gives a very strong pull from the last note of the scale back to the tonic. All major scales already have the leading tone built in, but natural minor scales do not; they have a whole step between the sixth and seventh tones. Interestingly, this is not why composers use the harmonic minor scale. If you look at the name of the scale, you gain some insight into why the scale exists. Simply, the raising of the seventh tone gives composers a slightly better harmonic palette to work with—it gives us better chords. The harmonic minor scale provides a major chord on the dominant degree and a diminished chord on the leading tone degree. Both of these chords are extremely important to composers and musicians and are used so frequently that the harmonic minor scale actually became a "scale."

Here is the D harmonic minor scale.

TRACK 11

FIGURE 4.9 The D Harmonic Minor Scale

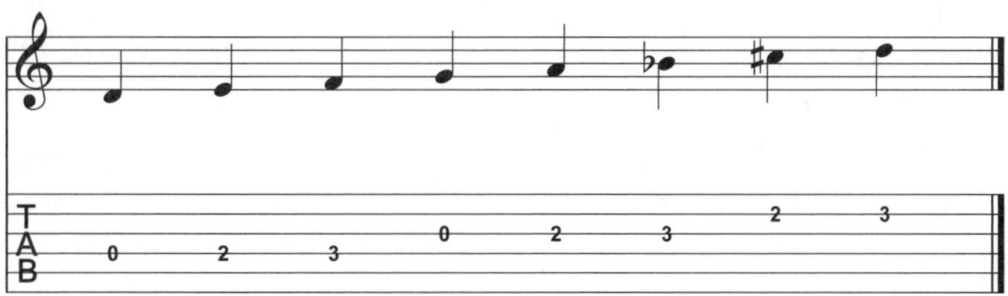

The formula of the scale is interesting in that you no longer strictly keep to whole and half steps. In fact, between the sixth and seventh tone, you have a step and a half (an augmented second to be more exact). That large leap between the sixth and seventh tone is awkward melodically.

If you play the scale by itself, you may conjure up images of the Middle East and the traditional melodies of the Jewish religion, which uses the harmonic minor scale as material for melodies. It's hard to use the scale by itself and not have it sound "ethnic."

Melodically, you are left with an awkward scale to work with. To work around this, composers created yet another scale to solve this dilemma: the melodic minor scale.

Melodic Minor

To fix the strange sound that the harmonic minor scale makes, the melodic minor scale was born. The melodic minor scale is made by raising the sixth and seventh tones of a natural minor scale one half step each.

The whole point of the melodic minor scale is to smooth out the skip between the sixth and the seventh tones in the harmonic minor scale. The raised seventh tone in harmonic minor is crucial to minor scale harmony, but the scale when played alone sounds strange. By raising the sixth as well, the melodic minor scale works better for melodies and harmonies. You lose that augmented second interval between the sixth and seventh tone and you get back to using whole and half steps.

Because the change in the scale makes it melodically smoother, it's called the melodic minor scale. Both the harmonic and melodic minor scales fall under the umbrella of basic music theory, which is important to understand to make sense of reading music.

Here is the melodic minor scale in the key of D minor.

FIGURE 4.10 D Melodic Minor

TRACK 12

Classical Melodic Minor Versus Jazz Melodic Minor

Here is a bit of very specific information for you. The melodic minor scale when used and practiced in a classical setting has some odd usage rules. The rule is that when you play the scale and ascend with it, you sharp the sixth and seventh tones, just like in the construction of the melodic minor scale. The odd part is, when you go to descend with the same scale, you return the sixth and seventh tones back to their natural minor spellings. This is something that is taught in classical music traditions, and if you study an instrument with a classical teacher, you may practice your scales that way: ascending one way and descending another way. **FIGURE 4.11** is what that scale would look like:

FIGURE 4.11 Classical Melodic Minor

Nowadays, and especially in jazz circles, the melodic minor scale is not altered depending on its direction; it is the exact same scale no matter which direction it's played in (the sixth and seventh remain raised the whole time).

Rather than do all your practice in this book, consider keeping a separate notebook of staff paper in which to practice spelling scales and other concepts and to jot down notes. Do as much as you can to reinforce the material presented here, to accelerate your learning and mastery of music theory.

Variant Variables

One of the points made about scales earlier in this book is that they are composed of half and whole step intervals. Harmonic minor has proved that scales don't always have to have that interval pattern. The addition of the augmented second (a step and a half) breaks that pattern. Also worth mentioning is that although it was earlier stated that all scales use either flats or sharps but not both, in the case of the harmonic and the melodic minor scales, that rule is thrown out the window (not for all the scales, but for some of them). On a positive note, anomalies like this make the scales easier to spot when you analyze music, as mixtures of sharps and flats can be the calling cards of these scales.

Take the time on your own instrument to play through all of these scales on a regular basis. Being able to play these scales and recognize them visually and aurally will help you understand them on a deeper level. For your reference, all of the chromatic minor scales are on the following pages.

FIGURE 4.12 All Natural Minor Scales

FIGURE 4.12A All Natural Minor Scales

FIGURE 4.13 All Harmonic Minor Scales

FIGURE 4.13A All Harmonic Minor Scales

FIGURE 4.14 All Melodic Minor Scales

FIGURE 4.14A All Melodic Minor Scales

Chapter 5

Musical Keys and Key Signatures

As you learned earlier in this book, intervals are the smallest element of music. Intervals combine to form scales. Scales, in turn, make up melody and harmony, the lifeblood of music. The key is the next major level of organization in music and one of the major elements of musical analysis. In this chapter, you will learn what makes a key, how to identify a key, and why you should care about the musical key.

Musical Organization

Now that you have explored the principal scales that make up music, it's time to explore the idea of what a key actually is. A key is the first level of organization in tonal music. An oversimplified definition of tonal music is music that is composed of keys, chords, and scales. Of course, there are forms of music that do not rely on keys, such as modern and atonal music. For the purpose of this book, tonal music makes up the majority of music from the "common practice" period (circa 1685–1900) and is still very much in use today. When you study theory, you start in the common practice period and move forward. If you want to study tonal music, keys are going to be very important to you!

The concept of musical keys is very closely tied to scales, both major and minor. The simplest definition of a musical key is: A key defines the basic pitches for a piece of music. A key does not have to use those notes exclusively, but the majority of the notes will come from the scale of that key. You know from studying the major and minor scales that no two scales are ever spelled alike. Because each scale/key is unique, it is fairly easy to spot them in music and understand some of the musical structure involved. More than anything else, keys are the DNA of music.

Point to Consider

Key signatures correspond with major and minor scales. Since a great deal of written music adheres to major and minor scales, key signatures are a convenient way to indicate keys and scales that are frequently used. Key signatures can also visually tell you what key a piece may be in, simply from looking at it.

A key is a slightly abstract concept, which can be a challenge to describe. A key defines what notes can be used to create an "expected" sound, such as consonant and not dissonant. As you progress as a musician, keys and key signatures will become more important than just defining what notes to play. Keys can give you a glimpse into the mind of the composer and help you unravel how music is composed. In any event, you need to know a lot about keys and their key signatures if you want to be a competent music theorist.

What Is a Key Signature?

You know all about sharps and flats now. You can comfortably spell scales in any key. That knowledge is one step removed from real music and how it functions. Observe the spelling of the A major scale in **FIGURE 5.1** versus **FIGURE 5.2**. Instead of having each sharp and flat spelled out, you can use a key signature to simply make all the Fs, Cs, and Gs sharp. Most musicians would rather read **FIGURE 5.2** any day of the week.

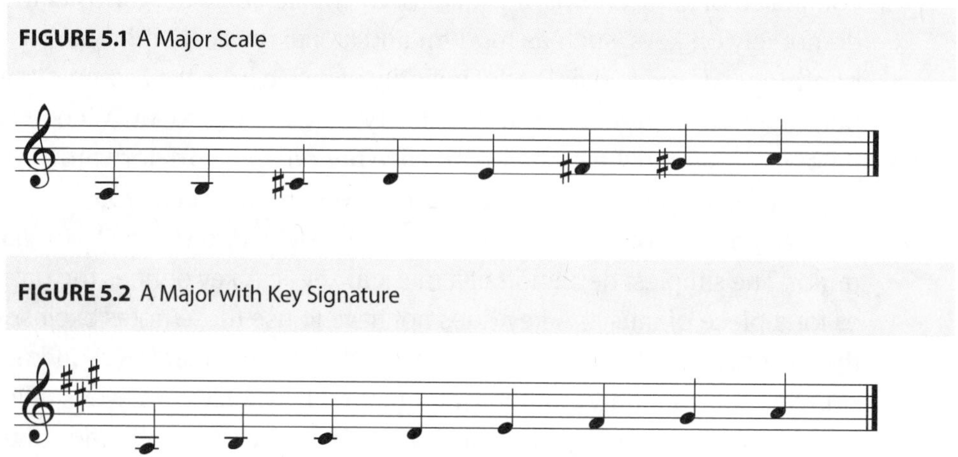

FIGURE 5.1 A Major Scale

FIGURE 5.2 A Major with Key Signature

Simply, a key signature is used to indicate that a certain note or notes is going to be sharp or flat for the entire piece. It cleans up the written music for the reader and eliminates the need for the sharp and flat symbols that would otherwise appear throughout. A good reader will be used to reading in key signatures and prefer them.

The Key Signatures

In Chapters 3 and 4, you saw every possible scale in existence, even the really odd enharmonic keys like F♭ major that you rarely see. Key signatures apply to the common keys/scales and rarely deal with the enharmonic ones. One of the most common things students encounter is the "circle of keys," a graphic representation of all the keys that you typically see. Since every key or scale has its own unique spelling, each of the keys looks different as well. Each single key signature corresponds to one single major key. Here is the circle of keys (**FIGURE 5.3**).

FIGURE 5.3 The Circle of Keys

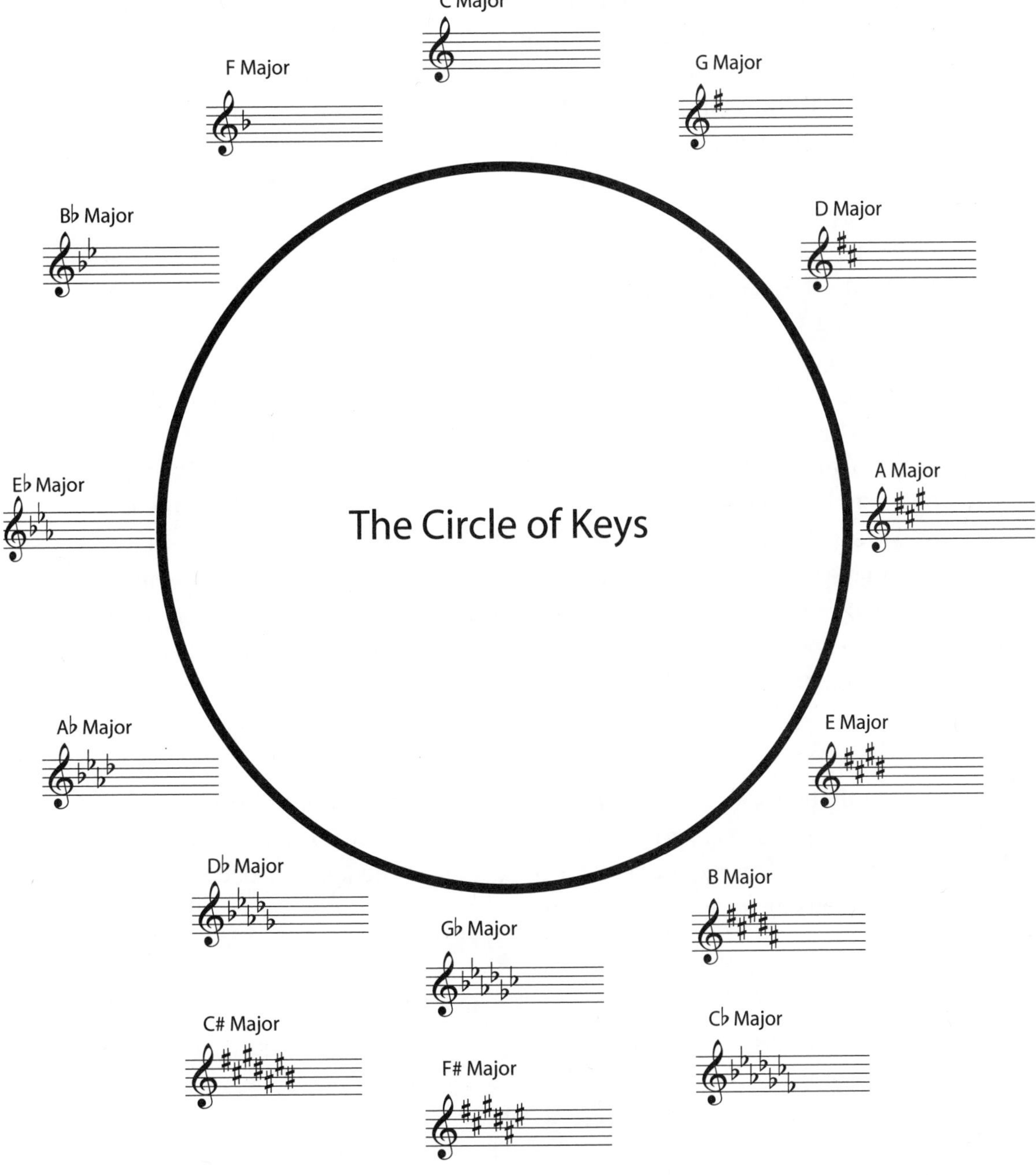

The System of Key Signatures

Key signatures use a specific system. Not just any note can appear in a key signature. There is an order and a logic to key signatures that makes them understandable. Key signatures appear in two varieties: sharp key signatures and flat key signatures (excluding C major, which has no sharps or flats). A key signature will always display only sharps or only flats. You will never see both in the same key signature. Within the groupings of "sharp keys" or "flat keys," there is an order to how individual notes appear. Take a look at sharps and flats separately.

Just like proper scale spellings will result in either sharps or flats, key signatures follow the exact same rule. They do so because scales and key signatures are showing you the same information, which is exactly why they help you understand more about the music.

Sharps appear in key signatures in a specific order. Here is the order of sharps as they appear in key signatures: F♯, C♯, G♯, D♯, A♯, E♯, B♯.

The sharps always follow that order. Also important to note is that sharps appear in the same order. If the key has one sharp, it will be an F♯. If the key has two sharps, it will have F♯ and C♯. It always works through the pattern that way. A great way to remember the order of sharps is to use a little mnemonic device: Father Charles Goes Down And Ends Battle. The first letter of each word corresponds to the sharps as they appear. It's silly, but it might just help you remember.

Point to Consider

Even though key signatures may appear confusing at first, most musicians would have a hard time reading without them. Constant flats and sharps placed throughout music can be more challenging to read than a single key signature.

Just like sharps, flats appear in a specific order as well. Also just like sharps, the order of flats will also appear in the same order every time. Here is the order of flats as they appear: B♭, E♭, A♭, D♭, G♭, C♭, and F♭.

There is also an easy way to help you remember the order of flats: Just reverse the saying for sharps! Battle Ends And Down Goes Charles' Father. One saying gets you both sharps and flats—pretty convenient!

Learning the Key Names

If you stare at the circle of keys long enough, you might memorize what each key represents. There are a few tricks that can help you out. On the flat side, the first key is F, which starts with the same letter as the word *flat*. After that, BEAD the names of the next four flat keys. That's a handy way to learn some of the keys. The sharp side is a bit harder. BEAD appears again on the right side. However, there are two little tricks you can learn for instantly naming a key just by looking at it.

The Sharp Key Trick

For any key that has a sharp in it, naming the key is as simple as following two easy steps. First, find the last sharp (the one all the way to the right). Once you've found and named the note that corresponds to the same line or space the sharp is on, go one note higher, and you've named the key. Look at **FIGURE 5.4**. The last sharp in this key is A♯. Going one note above this is the note B. Five sharps is, indeed, the correct key signature for the key of B major. You can check the trusty circle just to make sure.

FIGURE 5.4 Name This Signature

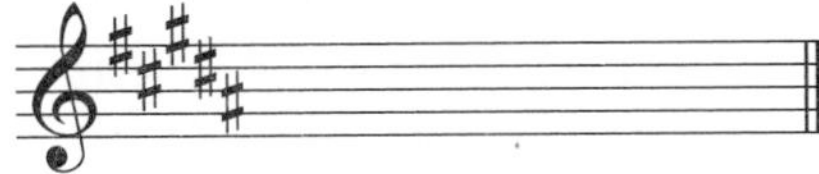

The good news is that this works on every key that has a sharp in it. To find the name of a sharp key:

1. Name the last sharp, the one all the way to the right.
2. Go one note higher than the last sharp, and that's the name!

Easy enough! Unfortunately, it works only when you're looking at a key. If someone asks you, "How many sharps are in the key of E major?" this little trick won't get you very far. For everything else, refer to the circle of keys and the order of sharps and flats.

The Flat Key Trick

The flat keys have their own, different trick for naming them. When you see a piece of music that has flats, find the second-to-last flat. The name of that flat is the name of your key! This is an easy one. Look at the example in **FIGURE 5.5**. This key has two flats and the second-to-last flat is B♭. The name of the key with two flats is B♭! This one is an easy trick.

FIGURE 5.5 Name This Key

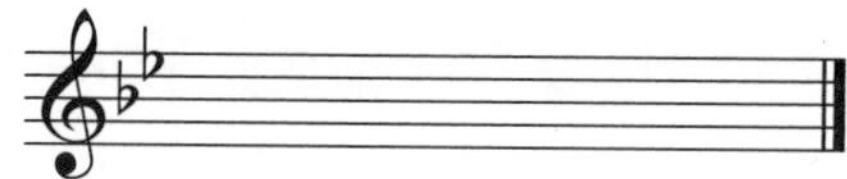

There is one exception, however: the key with one flat, F major. Since this key has only one flat, you can't find the second-to-last flat. In this case, you'll just have to memorize that F has one flat (which is B♭). Shouldn't be too hard! To find the name of a flat key:

1. Find the second-to-last flat (from the right).
2. The name of the flat note you find is the name of the key.

Just remember the exception—the key of F major has one flat and therefore the rule does not work for it. For the other keys, it works like a charm!

The Circle Moves in Fourths and Fifths

The name of this section says it all! The circle of keys is often referred to as the "circle of fifths" or the "circle of fourths." The keys are arranged in the circle in a fairly logical way. The key of C, with no sharps or flats, sits squarely in the center, and the sharp keys move around the right side, each key increasing the number of sharps by one. The flat keys move to the left, increasing their flats by one as they progress.

Extra Credit

Even before you learn the entire circle of fifths by heart, you can construct it using intervals. Draw a C at the top of a piece of paper. Now draw a few fifths to the right to name the sharp keys. To the left, draw a few fourths to get your basic flat keys. Across the bottom of the page, spell the order of sharps from F, in fifths, and the order of flats from B, in fourths. As you move away from the key of C, each key increases by one flat or sharp (depending on which direction you move in). You can match up the flats and sharps from the bottom of the page.

If you move to the right from C, each key is exactly a perfect fifth apart! Not only that, but the order of sharps as they appear in the key signatures are also perfect fifths starting from F♯.

If you move to the left from C, each key is exactly a perfect fourth apart! Conveniently, the flats as they appear in the key signature are also a perfect fourth apart, starting from B♭.

Think about these two points:

- Sharp keys move in fifths around the circle, and the order of sharps are fifths apart.
- Flat keys move in fourths around the circle, and the order of flats are fourths apart.

Note that when you move in one direction in the key circle, you move in fifths, and when you move in the opposite direction, you move in fourths. Remember the explanation in Chapter 2 about interval inversion: A perfect fifth becomes a perfect fourth when inverted. A fifth up is the same as a fourth down. The same applies to the order of sharps and flats. The sharps are spaced a fifth apart starting from F, and the flats are spaced a fourth apart starting from B. Interestingly, when you spell out all the sharps and read them backward (backward = inverted = in fourths), you get the order of flats.

Relative Minor Keys

Up to this point, you have learned solely about major key signatures and their related major scales—the circle of keys and those two tricks for naming the keys have all referred to major keys.

Of course, you know about minor scales, and where there are scales, there are keys. The good news is that all of the minor scales and keys share the same key signatures, which you already know. The bad news is that they aren't the same as the major keys! Never fear, there are some easy ways for you to learn the minor keys as well.

Shared Signatures

Every major key and its corresponding key signature has a dual function. Not only does it indicate a major key, but it also indicates one minor key as well. The concept is called relative keys and related minor. Simply put, every major scale/key has a minor scale/key hiding inside it. For now, you'll learn how to figure out the name of the minor keys. **FIGURE 5.6** shows the key signature for E♭ major. The exact same key signature can also signify the key of C minor.

FIGURE 5.6 Dual Function Key Signature/ Relative Minor

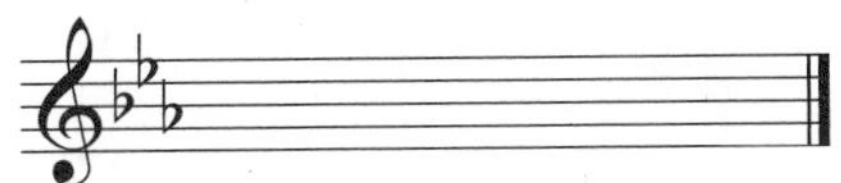

Is this E♭ or C Minor?

How is this possible? Well, simply put, you could spell the E♭ major scale and the C minor scale and see that they share the exact same key signature! The other thing that you are seeing is something called a mode. If you've never heard of modes before, you just learned your first one: The minor scale is a mode of the major scale. Modes come up in the next chapter, so hold tight, but for now, just understand that since they share the same pitches, and even if they are in a different order, they are related.

Point to Consider

Just looking at a key signature won't tell you whether your piece is in the major or the minor key. To find out for sure, you need to investigate the piece itself, not just the signature.

Naming Minor Keys

To name a minor key signature, first name the major key. Once you have found that, you simply count up six notes (up a major sixth) or down three (down a minor third). Either way, you arrive at the same note. In the case of C major, counting up six notes brings you to the note A. C major and A minor share the same key signature. They are referred to as "related keys." When you look at a piece with no sharps or flats in the signature, it may not necessarily be in C major, it could just as easily be in A minor. You won't know for sure by just looking at a key signature because music simply isn't that easy. To really get the answer, you have to look at the harmony of the piece, and harmony and chords come later in this book. For now, just work on being able to name minor keys from major key signatures.

When naming a minor key, be careful to look at the key signature when you are doing so. Simply counting up six notes or down three notes may not give you the correct key. If the note you pick has a sharp or a flat in that key, the name of the minor key needs to reflect that. Simply, you're not just counting up six letters; you have to mind the key signature. It's much easier to use the interval of a major sixth, which has a clear name! Look at **FIGURE 5.7**. In this case, the sixth note was not just C, but C♯, so the name of the key had to reflect that. The key of E major has a relative minor of C♯ minor.

FIGURE 5.7 The Relative Minor of E Major

The 6th note names the relative minor.

FIGURE 5.8 is the full circle of keys with both the major and the minor keys listed.

FIGURE 5.8 Circle of Keys with Minor Keys

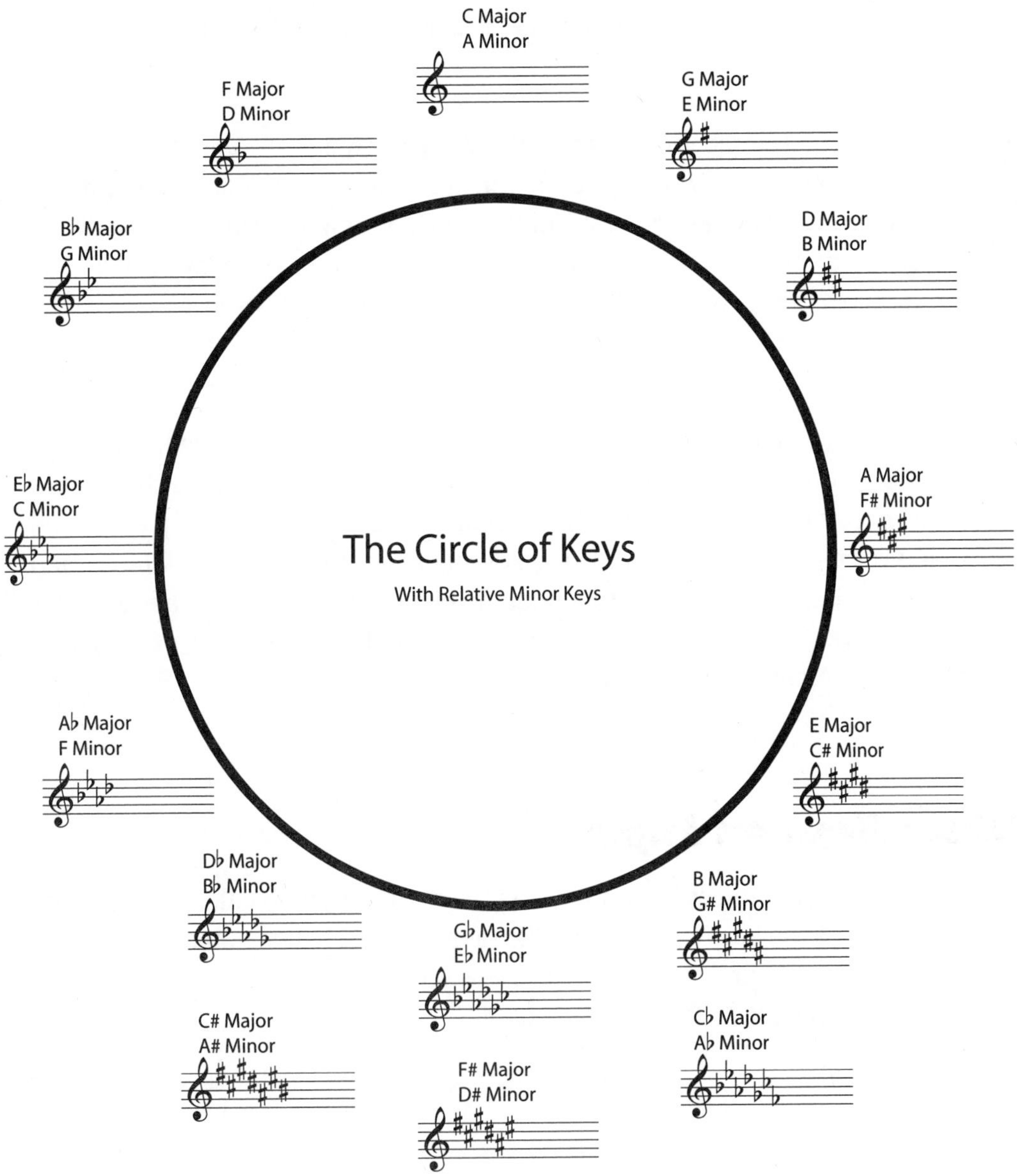

The Circle of Keys

With Relative Minor Keys

C Major
A Minor

G Major
E Minor

D Major
B Minor

A Major
F# Minor

E Major
C# Minor

B Major
G# Minor

C♭ Major
A♭ Minor

F# Major
D# Minor

G♭ Major
E♭ Minor

C# Major
A# Minor

D♭ Major
B♭ Minor

A♭ Major
F Minor

E♭ Major
C Minor

B♭ Major
G Minor

F Major
D Minor

Determining the Key

We know that you can determine the key by looking at the signature and checking your circle of keys. Doing so will give you at least two answers: the major and the relative minor key. In a way, this is your first step toward musical analysis. But musical analysis is more than just looking at a key signature. The answer is rarely that simple. Or isn't it?

An old trick exists that suggests that you can look at the first and last notes of any piece to determine the key of a piece. Now, this rarely works, because music involves so many variables, but sometimes it does work. If you look at a key signature and your choices are either a minor or a major key (C major or A minor, for example), you could scan the piece for Cs or As and that may answer your question. Then again, it may not. While it is true that many pieces conclude on the tonic note of the key, that really gives you only the answer of where the piece ended and ignores the question of where it went in the middle.

IN TIME

Composer Antonio Vivaldi was born in Venice on March 4, 1678, and died in Vienna on July 28, 1741. He was the son of a professional violinist, and was also an accomplished violinist himself. Ordained as a priest in 1703, he soon stopped celebrating Mass on account of his poor health. Today Vivaldi is most famous for his work *Le Quattro Stagioni* (The Four Seasons).

Simply put, if you are trying to decipher what key you're in, the first and last note (or chord) may give you a basic answer. The only true answer that works in every piece can be found only by looking at the details of the piece—and that involves looking at not only the key signature, but also the harmony and per-note changes that exist throughout the piece. Since you know about scales in detail now, you can work on one more aspect of keys based on minor scales and their typical visual patterns.

Minor Keys on Paper

In a great deal of music, you rarely see the natural minor scale; what you see more often is the harmonic or melodic minor scales. When you are looking at a piece of music and the key signature tells you two possible answers, you can look inside the music itself for some clues.

If the piece is in the major key, it won't need any additional accidentals (sharps or flats) to function. That's not to say that pieces in major keys never have accidentals, far from that, but minor keys have very specific accidentals to look for. If you know what to look for, you should have no problem finding out the answer.

Point to Consider

Both the harmonic minor scale and the melodic minor scale have alterations via accidentals. For a minor scale to function in the traditional sense, it will need this alteration. More specifically, it will need its leading tone raised, and this will always cause a subsequent sharp, flat, or natural where it doesn't normally belong.

A leading tone is the seventh note of a scale. In the case of the harmonic and melodic minor scale, it's raised one half step higher than in the natural minor scale. If you take A minor as an example, the leading tone in the natural scale is G, and if you raise it, it becomes a G♯. Now, thinking back to what you know about key signatures, A minor and C major share a key signature that has no sharps or flats.

So, you're looking at a piece with no key signature and scattered throughout the piece are a bunch of G♯s. The final note of the piece is A. Chances are that you are in A minor, or at least you were in A minor for a part of that piece and concluded there.

By the same token, if you see a piece with no key signature and nothing but G♮s, you know that you're in C major, because the G♯ is the leading tone of A minor.

Here is an example (**FIGURE 5.9**); take a look and see what key you think it is.

FIGURE 5.9 What Key Are We In?

TRACK 13

At first glance, the key signature has one sharp, so it could be G major or E Minor. The first thing you want to do is look for accidentals. Do you have any? Yes, you do, you have a D♯ throughout the piece. The next step would be to determine if that is just an accidental or if it is a minor-scale leading tone. In the key of E minor, the leading tone is a raised seventh note, which happens to be D♯. The fact that the piece starts and ends on E surely drives home the point that you are in the key of E minor!

See, that wasn't so hard. It does show you that you cannot judge the key based on the signature alone—you must look at the material within the piece to be absolutely sure. Knowing what your leading tones are will make your job of understanding the differences between key signatures and their relative minor scales much easier.

Extra Credit

To find the leading tones for minor keys, just find the seventh note of the scale. Rather than go seven notes up, simply go one note down. Then make sure it's a half step away. For example, the leading tone for C minor is B♮ because B and C are a half step apart. In D minor, the leading tone is C♯.

Keys Change

Music does not need to stay in one key; key changes happen frequently in pieces of music. The way that you will learn to change keys and identify key changes will become much clearer when you understand harmony more. For now, you can go back to the circle of keys and simply make a few assumptions that will be explained as the book progresses.

Here are the rules:

- When music changes keys, it does so to a closely related key.
- The closest related key is the relative minor.
- The other close keys that you can modulate to are next to the original key on the key circle (either one key to the left or one key to the right).
- The other modulation you can make is from a major to a parallel minor; for example, C major to C minor.

FIGURE 5.10 Circle of Keys with Minor Keys

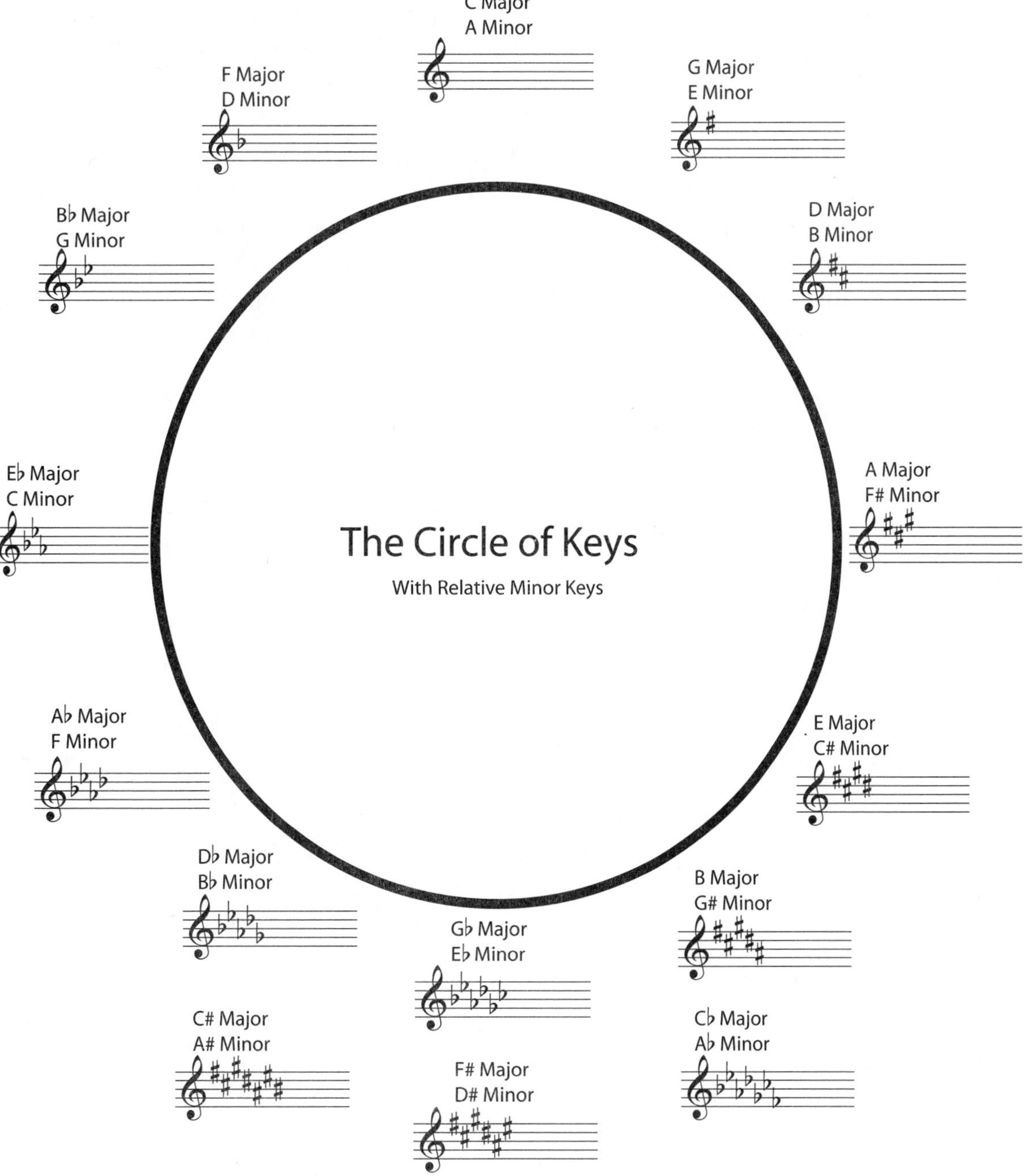

Talking about "common" and "simple" ways to change keys does not mean that the more difficult and uncommon ones are not used; just the opposite is true. Composers love to break the rules and find interesting and musically compelling ways to do so. Part of learning about theory is understanding what the majority of music did when it was written—what were the norms of the times and why did the composers use them? There will always be musicians who push the boundaries of music, bringing music to new levels.

Keys are more than just scales and key signatures, so you really need to keep moving on into the rest of the scales and chords and harmony to fully grasp what keys mean and how you will use them. For now, you have the basic groundwork that you need in order to name and spell keys, which was your goal for this chapter. The next step is to look at the last group of scales and modes that you will deal with in this book, and then on to bigger things: chords and harmony!

Chapter 6

Modes and Other Scales

It is true that major and minor scales make up the majority of the scales that you encounter in everyday life. However, both traditional and modern music theory include other scales besides major and minor. Modes are a term often thrown around as something to learn, and students rarely understand what modes actually are. Besides modes, other scales round out music theory: pentatonic, diminished, and whole-tone scales.

Modes—The Other Side of Scales

The first place to deepen our understanding of scales is right back at the major scale. As a musician, you may or may not have heard the term modes. Many classical musicians don't deal with modes early on in their study. However, jazz and rock players are aware of modes early on. There are several reasons for this musical divide, which will become clear as you learn more about modes.

Defining Modes

The simplest definition of a mode is a displaced major scale. First, you need to examine what *displaced* means. Take the F major scale: F–G–A–B♭–C–D–E–F. As you know, what makes it an F major scale is that the note F has the most weight; the scale wants to stop on the high F when you play it. You could say that the note F (the tonic degree) has the most weight when you are in the key of F major.

Point to Consider

Ever heard the children's sing-along "What Do We Do with the Drunken Sailor"? This familiar old sea chantey (a song sung by sailors) is actually composed using a modal scale: the Dorian mode. Another famous example of modes is the theme to *The Simpsons,* which uses the Lydian mode for its main theme. Modes are all around us; they are often used in film and TV soundtracks as well.

Now, what if you were to use the same vocabulary, that is, use the same F–G–A–B♭–C–D–E–F pitches (the F major scale), but instead, make a different note the root? What if the scale looked like this: D–E–F–G–A–B♭–C–D? If the scale looked like that and D sounded like the root note (which is based on the context of the piece), then you have an official mode. You have a bit more than a mode, actually.

If you reread the last paragraph, you'll notice that an F scale is spelled from D. Is there a special relationship between F and D? Well, they are a sixth apart. Hmm, sixth note of a major scale, where have you heard that before? In Chapter 5, under the heading Naming Minor Keys. Remember the trick you learned there, to find the relative minor by going up six notes. Using the example above, you see that you can spell an F major scale starting from D, its sixth note, and it's called a mode! It's both the D minor scale and also a mode of F major.

So, you see that minor scales are also modes. The notes D–E–F–G–A–B♭–C–D form a D minor scale. A mode is formed when you call any other note besides the original root of the scale the root. The minor scale is just one example of a mode, one that you already know. But wait, there's more! Because a major scale has seven notes, there are seven modes.

Modal History

Modes gained prominence during the golden age of Gregorian chant, circa A.D. 900, when they were used to compose the melodies of vocal plainchant. Modes stayed in use throughout medieval times with some modification. The baroque and prebaroque eras made use of major and minor scales exclusively instead of modes. For all intents and purposes, modes lay dormant throughout the baroque era, the classical era, and most (but not all) of the romantic era.

Even though impressionist composers revived modes, it wasn't until jazz musicians started using modes in improvisation and composition that modes became a useful part of music curricula. Nowadays, all music students learn about modes, but it's the rock and jazz players who tend to utilize them more frequently than anyone else in improvisation and composition.

Seven Modal Scales

Each and every major scale can be looked at from seven different angles—one mode starting from each note in the scale. While modes theoretically come from "parent" major scales, it's easiest to think of them as their own entities.

IN TIME

If you learn about modes in a classical music theory class, they are commonly referred to as the "church modes" because of the widespread use of modes in the sacred music that originated in the church—especially Gregorian chant. Relegating modes to "historical" learning is doing them a disservice! Modes are alive and well in modern music, especially jazz.

Ionian

Ionian is the first mode to learn about and, thankfully, you already know it. The Ionian scale is simply the major scale. It follows the interval pattern WWHWWWH. **FIGURE 6.1** shows an F Ionian mode. Since the Ionian mode is simply the traditional major scale, this example is just a definition of the word *Ionian*. Think of *Ionian* as the "proper" name for a major scale. It's great to know what the proper name is, but you don't have to be caught up in its usage and refer to every major scale as an "Ionian" mode; the terms are interchangeable.

FIGURE 6.1 Mode One: *The Ionian Mode* (Major Scale)

TRACK 14

Dorian

The Dorian mode is the first of the displaced scales. The easiest way to define Dorian is that a Dorian scale is a major scale played from its second note. If you continue to use F major as the parent scale, the Dorian mode in this key starts from the note G and progresses up the same notes. **FIGURE 6.2** shows the G Dorian scale. The G Dorian scale uses the interval pattern WHWWWHW.

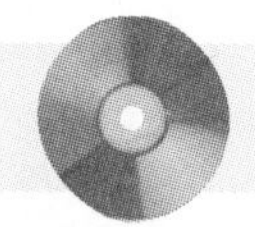

FIGURE 6.2 Mode Two: *The Dorian Mode*

TRACK 15

There is a very important aspect to understand about modes. It is true that the G Dorian scale comes from the F major scale and shares all the same notes. This is an important learning tool. However, all musicians need to learn the modes as "their own thing." The Dorian mode is a scale unto itself, with its own distinct sound. If you look at the notes of G Dorian (G–A–B♭–C–D–E–F–G), you might notice that the G Dorian scale looks a lot like the traditional G minor scale (G–A–B♭–C–D–E♭–F–G). And you're right; it looks a whole lot like it! The only difference is that the G Dorian scale contains an E♮ and the G minor scale contains an E♭.

You could look at the Dorian scale as a minor-type scale, with an altered sixth note. In this case, the sixth note is raised up a half step. It's very much like a "flavored" minor scale. This is how modes are used today—to "spice" up traditional major and minor scales that may sound overused and dated. As you'll see, all of the rest of the modes will closely resemble either a traditional major or a traditional minor scale.

Point to Consider

When you think of the parent scale relationship between each mode, don't fall into the trap of thinking that each mode has to be related to its parent scale. Using the minor scale as an example again, you don't have to think about its related major scale, do you? No, it can stand on its own. The same holds true for all of the modes. Learn to see them on their own if you plan to use them quickly.

Phrygian

Phrygian is the third mode and is the result of forming a scale starting from the third note of the parent major scale. Using F major as the parent scale, the Phrygian scale is an A Phrygian scale. It uses the interval pattern HWWWHWW (see **FIGURE 6.3**). Phrygian has a distinct sound and sometimes recalls the music of Spain, as Spanish composers often use this scale.

FIGURE 6.3 Mode Three: *The Phrygian Mode*

TRACK 16

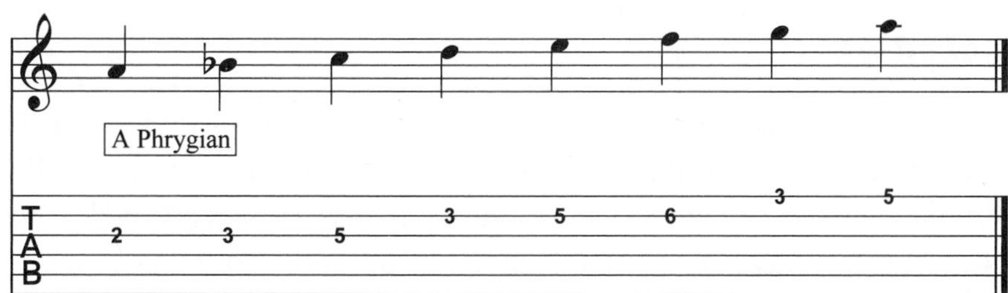

The A Phrygian scale (A–B♭–C–D–E–F–G–A) looks very much like a traditional A minor scale (A–B–C–D–E–F–G–A). The only difference is that the A Phrygian scale lowers the second note a half step down. You could say that Phrygian is just a minor scale with a lowered second note—and you'd be right!

Lydian

The fourth mode of the major scale is the Lydian mode. Using F as a parent scale, you come to the B♭ Lydian scale. Lydian uses the interval pattern WWWHWWH. See **FIGURE 6.4**.

FIGURE 6.4 Mode Four: *The Lydian Mode*

TRACK 17

The Lydian mode is a striking, beautiful, and "bright" sound. It's used by film composers to convey uplifting spirit and is a favorite of jazz and rock composers. The Lydian scale is so bright and happy, it's no surprise that it's closely related to the major scale. The B♭ Lydian scale is spelled B♭–C–D–E–F–G–A–B♭, which resembles a traditional B♭ major scale (B♭–C–D–E♭–F–G–A–B♭). The only difference between B♭ Lydian and B♭ major is that a Lydian scale raises the fourth note of the major scale up a half step. So, B♭ Lydian is a B♭ major scale with a raised fourth note. The raised fourth tone results in a bright and unusual sound and allows the plain major scale to have a unique overall effect.

Mixolydian

The fifth mode of the major scale is called the Mixolydian mode. Using the parent scale of F, our fifth mode is C Mixolydian. C Mixolydian, or "Mixo" as it's commonly abbreviated, uses the interval pattern of WWHWWHW. See **FIGURE 6.5**. The Mixolydian mode is a mainstay of jazz, rock, and blues music.

FIGURE 6.5 Mode Five: *The Mixolydian Mode*

TRACK 18

The Mixolydian mode is closely related to the major scale but is slightly darker sounding. The C Mixolydian scale (C–D–E–F–G–A–B♭–C) closely resembles the C major scale (C–D–E–F–G–A–B–C). The only difference is that the Mixolydian scale lowers the seventh note of the major scale a half step. The lowered seventh note gives the Mixolydian mode a bluesy, dark color, leading away from the overly peppy major scale. Because of this, it's a staple of blues, rock, and jazz players looking to darken up the sound of major scales. It also coincides with one of the principal chords of jazz, blues, and rock music: the dominant seventh chord (C7, which you're going to learn all about in Chapter 9).

Aeolian

The sixth mode of the major scale is the Aeolian mode. If you remember back to the chapter on minor scales earlier in this book, you'll remember that minor scales are derived from the sixth note of a major scale. That's right, the Aeolian mode is the natural minor scale. Thankfully, this is another mode that you already know. Aeolian is the proper name for natural minor. Refer to it as "Aeolian" at parties to make yourself look smarter! Using the parent key of F major, our sixth mode brings us to D Aeolian. You'll also remember that the keys of F major and D minor are related keys—F Ionian and D Aeolian are related modes from the same parent scale. The D Aeolian scale uses the interval formula WHWWHWW. See **FIGURE 6.6**.

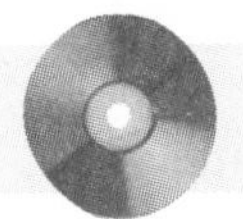

FIGURE 6.6 Mode Six: *The Aeolian Mode* (Minor Scale)

TRACK 19

Since the Aeolian scale is an exact minor scale, no comparison to another major or minor scale is needed. Even with that, some players are more comfortable with major scales; Aeolian can be looked at as a major scale with a lowered third, sixth, and seventh note. This way of looking at minor scales is useful to some.

Locrian

The seventh and final mode is called the Locrian mode. In our parent scale of F major, the seventh mode is E Locrian. E Locrian mode uses the interval pattern HWWHWWW. See **FIGURE 6.7**. The Locrian mode has a very distinct sound. You're not going to encounter this mode often. Actually, you may go your whole life without ever hearing it or using it. Nevertheless, it completes your knowledge of modes, so it's good to know it.

FIGURE 6.7 Mode Seven: *The Locrian Mode*

TRACK 20

The E Locrian scale (E–F–G–A–B♭–C–D–E) looks a lot like an E minor scale (E–F♯–G–A–B–C–D–E). The only difference between the two scales is that the Locrian scale has a lowered second and a lowered fifth note.

Looking at Modes on Their Own

The modes that you know, you know in relation to a parent scale. If someone were to ask you to spell a C♯ Lydian scale, you might have to go through quite an ordeal. First, you have to remember which number mode it is, then you have to backtrack and find the parent scale, and then you can spell the scale correctly. It's much more convenient to think of the modes on their own, which is how they are usually used. It's much easier to make an effort to understand modes than to always have to take several steps to puzzle them out. Looking at modes as "almost" major or minor scales will help you understand them.

Here is a recap of the modes, their interval formulas, and easy ways to relate the scales:

Modes, Scales, and Interval Formulas

Mode	Scale	Interval Formula	Description
Mode 1	Ionian	(WWHWWWH)	Ionian is the major scale.
Mode 2	Dorian	(WHWWWHW)	Dorian is a minor scale with a raised sixth note.
Mode 3	Phrygian	(HWWWHWW)	Phrygian is a minor scale with a lowered second note.
Mode 4	Lydian	(WWWHWWH)	Lydian is a major scale with a raised fourth note.
Mode 5	Mixolydian	(WWHWWHW)	Mixolydian is a major scale with a lowered seventh note.
Mode 6	Aeolian	(WHWWHWW)	Aeolian is the minor scale.
Mode 7	Locrian	(HWWHWWW)	Locrian is a minor scale with lowered second and fifth notes.

By learning these formulas, you will be able to learn modes as their own scales and spell and relate them quickly and easily. Here is each mode spelled from the same root (good old C, which is so easy to think and work with) so you can see how each mode differs from each other.

FIGURE 6.8 All Seven Modes from a C Root

Modal Practice

Here's some practice spelling some modal scales. In the following example, use this process:

- If your mode is a major-type mode, spell the major scale first.
- If your scale is a minor-type mode, spell the minor scale first.
- Alter the scale as prescribed in the list for modal formulas.

If you work this way, you won't need to figure out the parent scale, and it will further reinforce your knowledge of common major and minor scales. See the next two figures for reference.

FIGURE 6.9 Major-Type Mode Practice

To spell an E Mixolydian scale, start by spelling E Major.

To make the scale Mixolydian, simply lower the 7th note ½ step.

E Mixolydian!

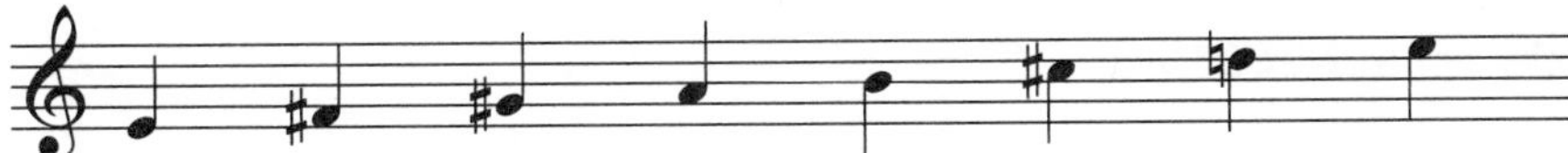

FIGURE 6.10 Minor-Type Mode Practice

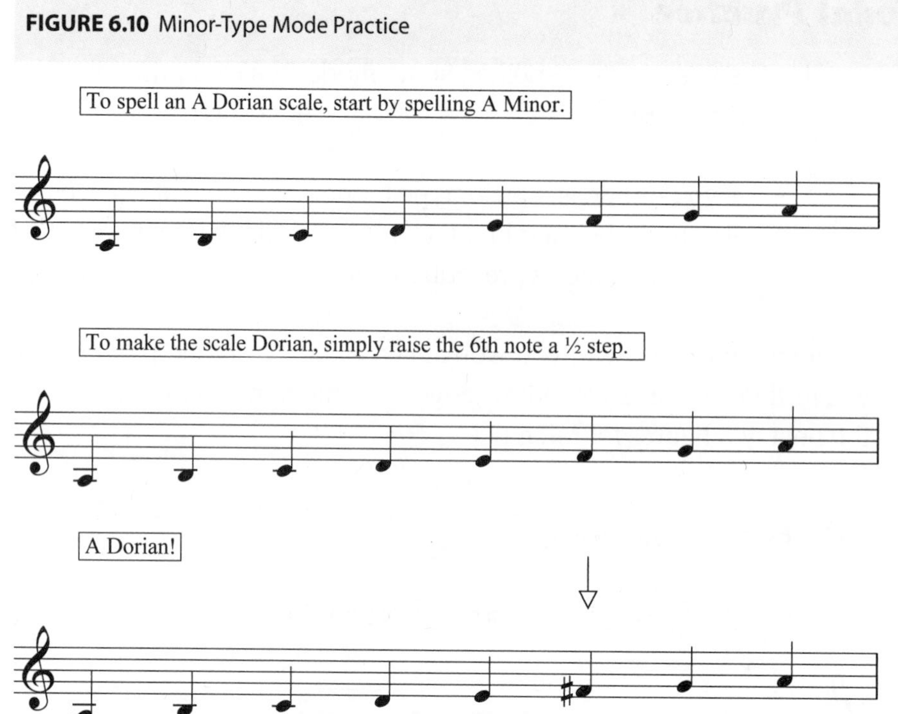

Other Important Scales

Major scales, minor scales, and modes make up the majority of the scales encountered in Western music. However, they are not the only important scales; scales come in many different shapes and sizes, especially as you move throughout history.

Major Pentatonic

Pentatonic scales differ from traditional major and minor scales in that they contain only five notes per octave as opposed to major and minor scales, which contain seven. The name *pentatonic* reflects this distinction as the prefix of *pentatonic* is *penta*, Greek for "five"—*tonic* means "tones" or "notes." The pentatonic scales are widely used in folk, liturgical, rock, and jazz music. Pentatonic scales come in two varieties: major and minor.

The major pentatonic is a five-note scale that is derived from the major scale. It simply omits two notes—the fourth and seventh tones—from the major scale. In the key of G, the major pentatonic scale is G–A–B–D–E. Stated another way, the G major pentatonic is the first, second, third, fifth, and sixth notes of a major scale.

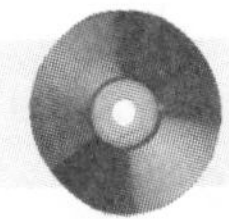

FIGURE 6.11 The Major Pentatonic Scale

TRACK 21

The major pentatonic is a mainstay of folk, blues, rock, and country music. Famous melodies such as "Mary Had a Little Lamb" and "London Bridge" were composed solely using the major pentatonic scale. If you like to improvise solos, the major pentatonic is a basic and essential scale for improvisation over major tonalities found in music genres such as rock, jazz, and blues.

Minor Pentatonic

Like its relative the major pentatonic scale, the minor pentatonic scale is also derived from a scale with two notes omitted (just not the same ones). To form a minor pentatonic scale, simply leave out the second and sixth tones from a natural (or more formally, Aeolian) minor scale. In the key of D, a minor pentatonic scale is (D–F–G–A–C). You could also say that the scale is the first, third, fourth, fifth, and seventh notes of a natural minor scale.

FIGURE 6.12 The Minor Pentatonic Scale

TRACK 22

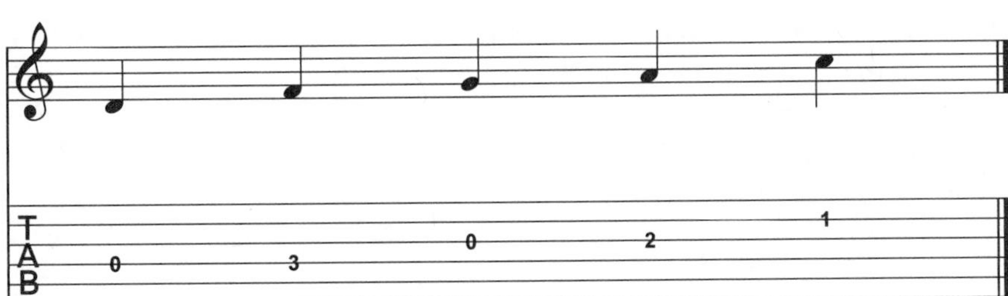

Whole Tone

The whole tone scale is a particular type of scale called a symmetric scale. The whole tone scale is built entirely with whole steps. Because it uses the same intervals, the whole tone scale is considered a symmetric scale. Using whole steps from C, a C whole tone scale is C–D–E–F♯–G♯–A♯. It's very important to note that the whole tone scale is a six-note scale. Not five notes like our pentatonic scales, or seven notes like major and minor scales, but six!

FIGURE 6.13 The Whole Tone Scales: *C and D♭*

TRACK 23

Of particular interest is that there are only two different whole tone scales. Forming whole tone scales from anywhere other than C or D♭ will yield the exact same notes as the C or D♭ whole tone scales. See for yourself:

FIGURE 6.14 C and D Whole Tone Scales

Notice how both the C and D whole tone scales contain the exact same notes. This makes them very easy to learn and play. You see whole tone scales in romantic music and jazz music.

IN TIME

Jazz pianist Thelonious Monk loved the whole tone scale, and you can find it in virtually all of his recorded improvised jazz solos. The whole tone scale was a trademark for him. He wasn't the first to use it, but boy, did he like it!

Diminished/Octatonic Scales

The last scale is another symmetric scale and is built using repeating intervals. The diminished scale is based on repeating intervals, always half steps and whole steps. There are two varieties of diminished scales: one that starts with the pattern of whole step, half step intervals, and one that uses a half step, whole step interval pattern. **FIGURE 6.15** shows the two varieties of diminished scales, both starting from C. The other name that diminished scales go by is *octatonic*, which is Greek for "eight-note scale." This is the first scale that exceeds seven individual notes.

FIGURE 6.15 The Two Types of Octatonic/Diminished Scales

TRACK 24

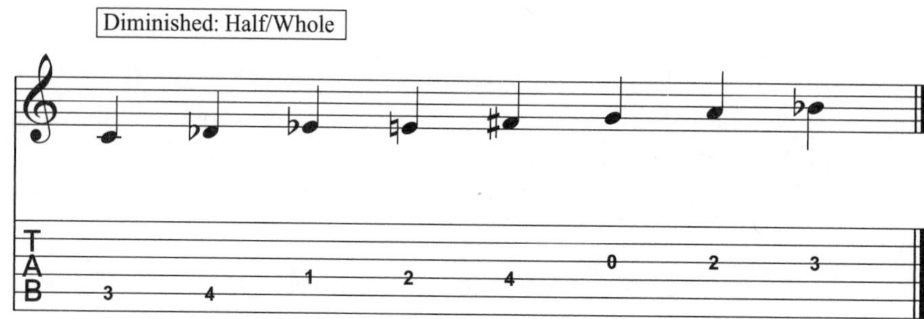

Another interesting fact is that there are only three unique diminished scales. Diminished scales spelled from C, C♯, and D are the only diminished scales that utilize unique tone sets. Spelling diminished scales from other roots will yield repeating scales, with the identical tones from C, C♯, or D diminished. Composers, theorists, and jazz players use diminished scales primarily.

Time for Etudes

Next, you will start a unique part of this book: the etudes. *Etude* comes from the French term meaning "to study." The etude is a widely used moniker for pieces that you might learn as a student of an instrument. For example, Chopin's piano etudes are famous not only for their teaching ability, but for their musical content as well. In this book, the etudes will give you a space not only to practice what you have learned so far, but more importantly, to put it to musical use by composing some music with what you have learned. You will encounter two other etude chapters where you will be able to turn this information from "theory" into music—and isn't that the whole point of this? Indeed it is.

Chapter 7

Etude One: Scales and Keys

Name the Following Intervals

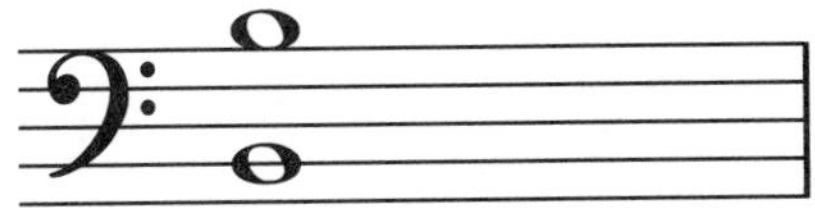

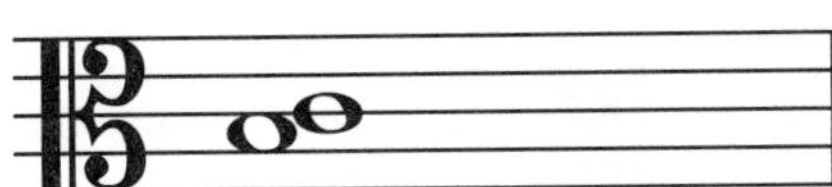

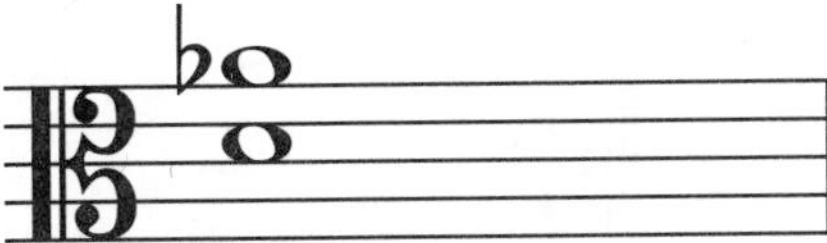

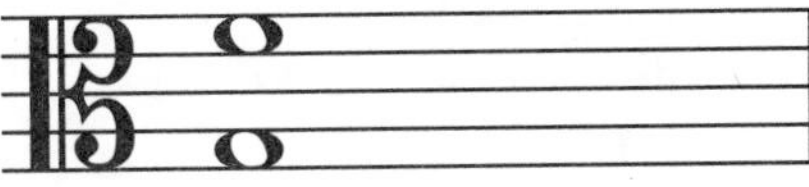

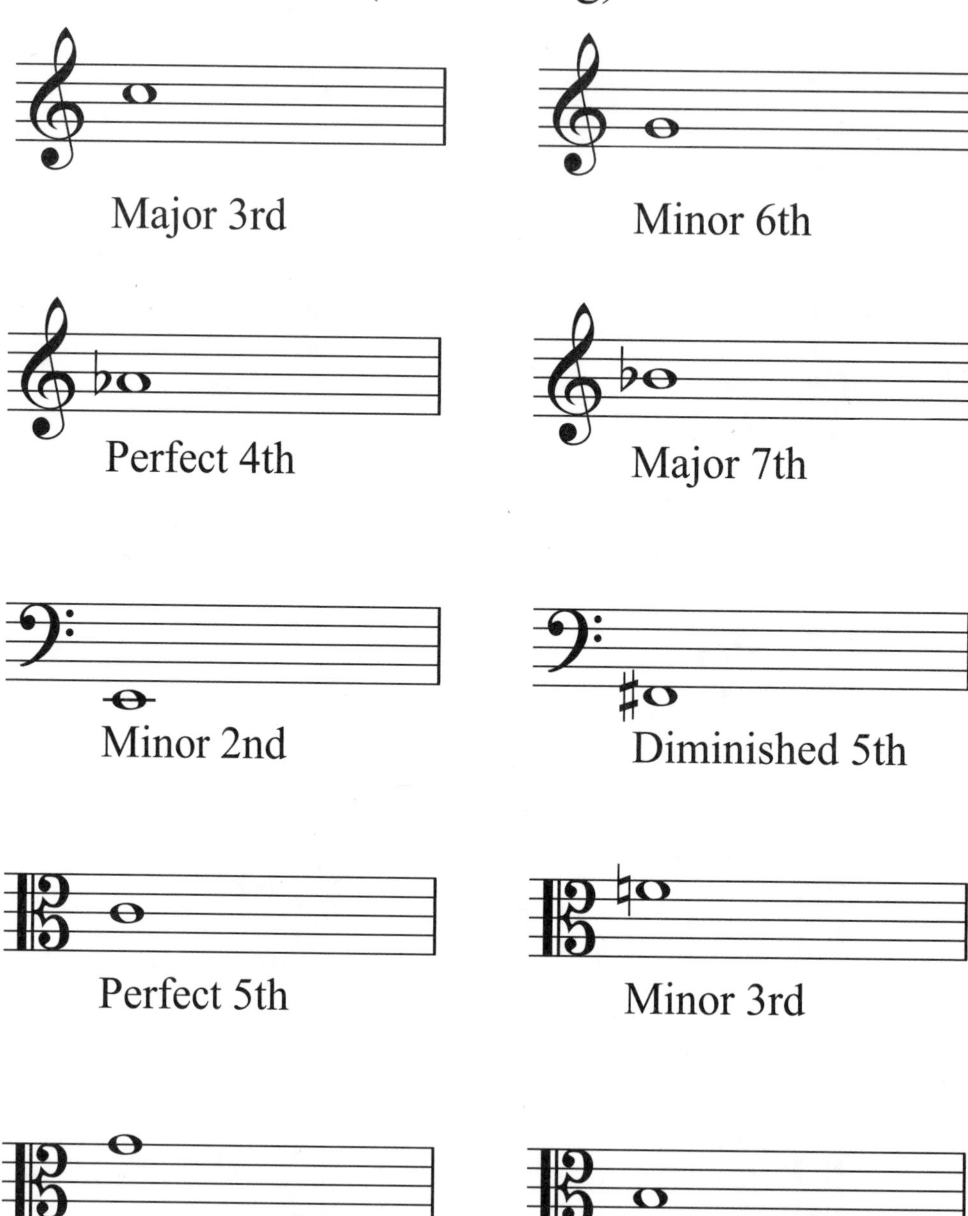
Write the Following Intervals
(Ascending)
Major 3rd
Minor 6th
Perfect 4th
Major 7th
Minor 2nd
Diminished 5th
Perfect 5th
Minor 3rd
Major 2nd
Octave

Write the Following Intervals (Descending)

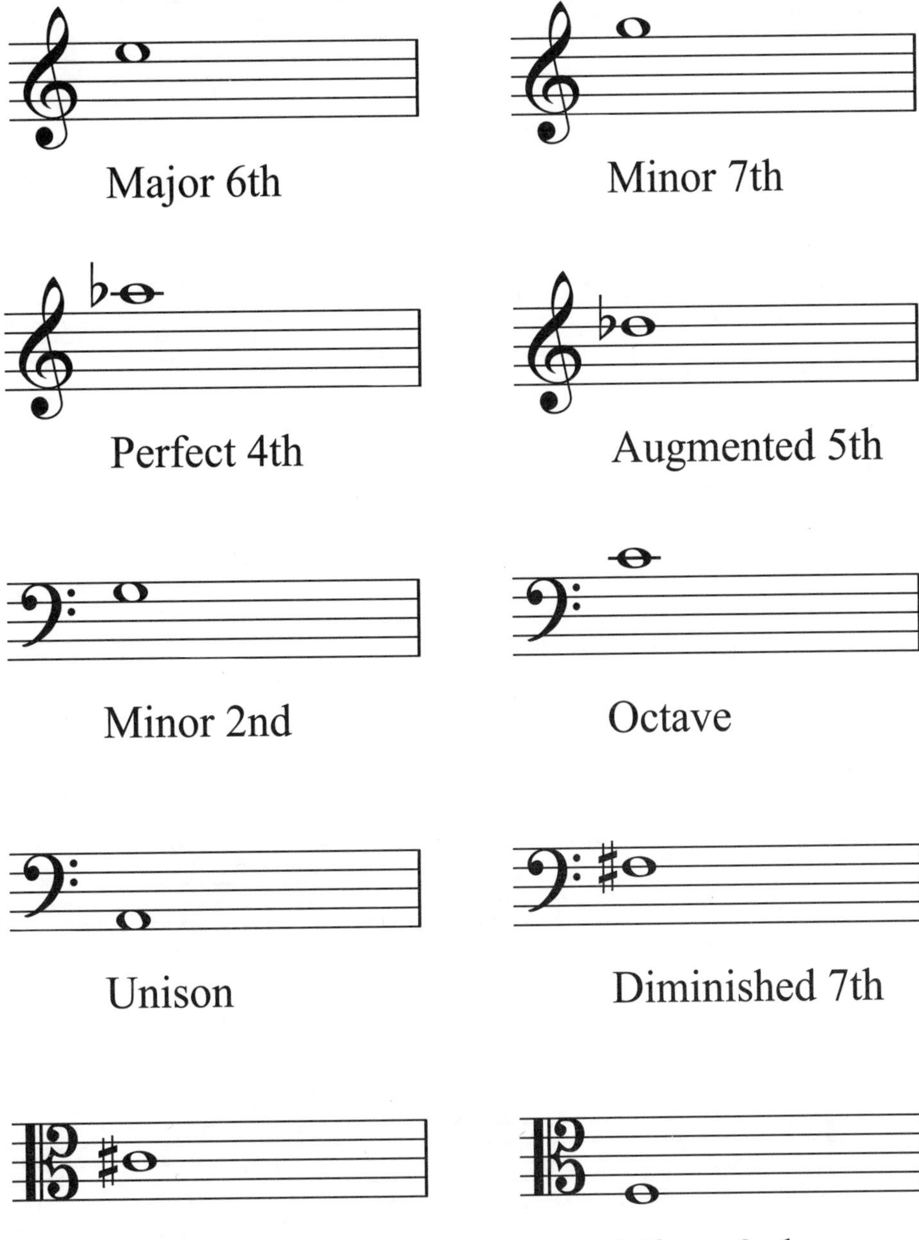

Write Major Scales from the Following Notes

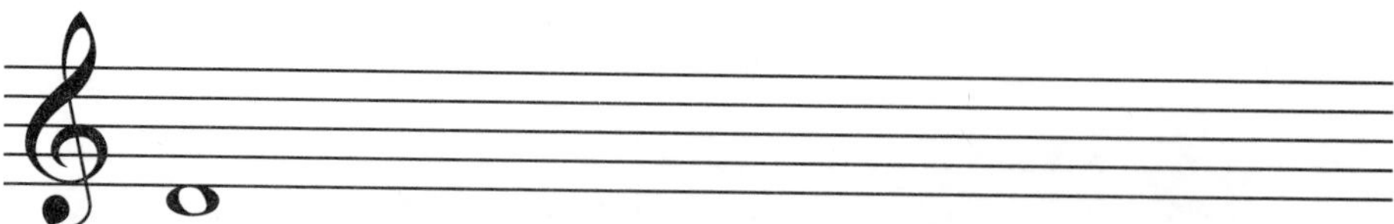

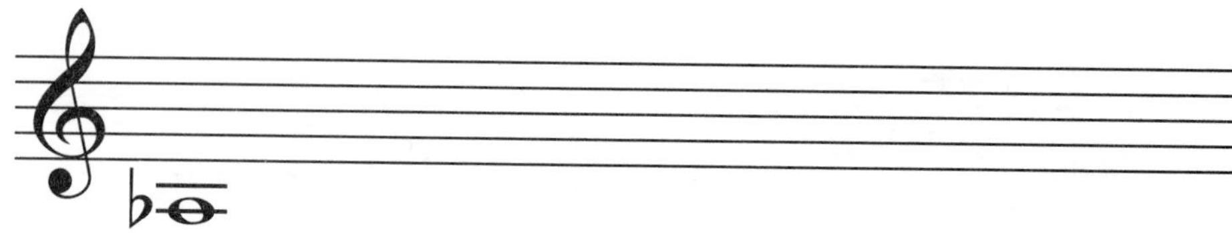

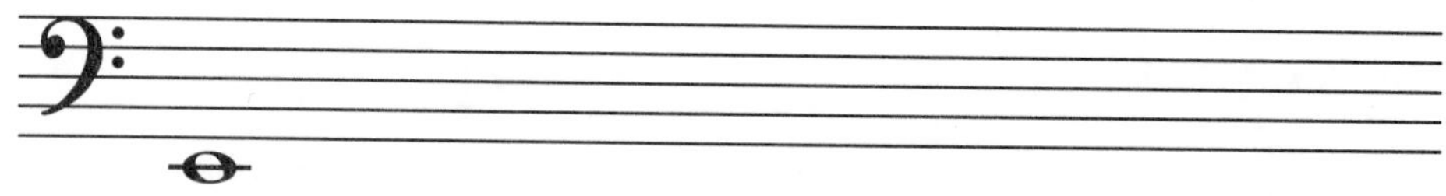

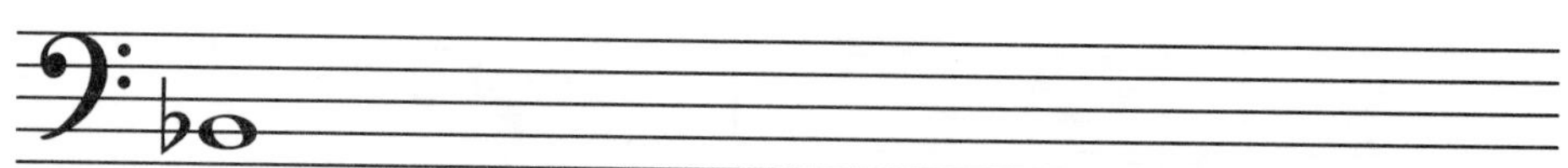

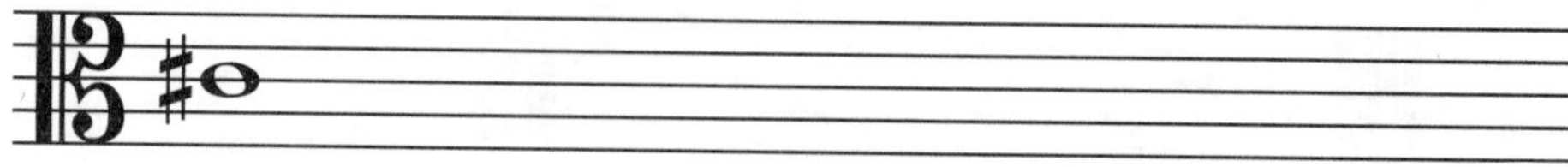

Write Minor Scales from the Following Notes

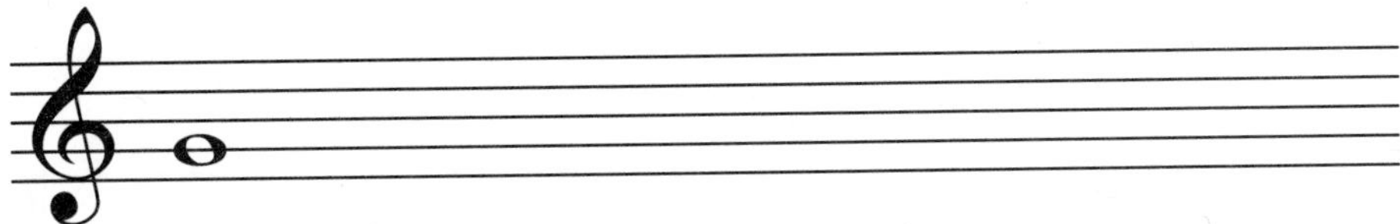

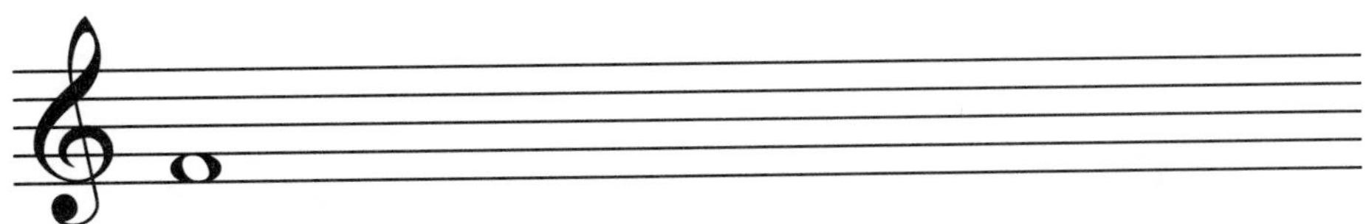

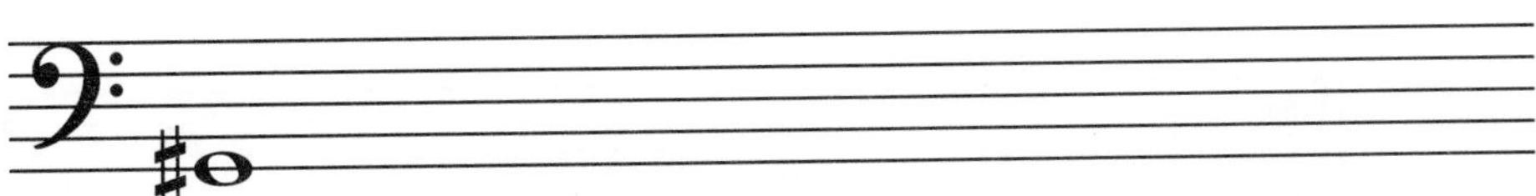

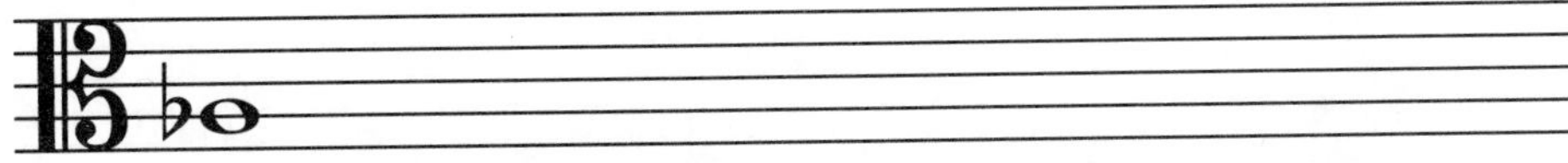

Name the Following Scales (Major or Minor)

Name the Following Scales
(Major or Minor)

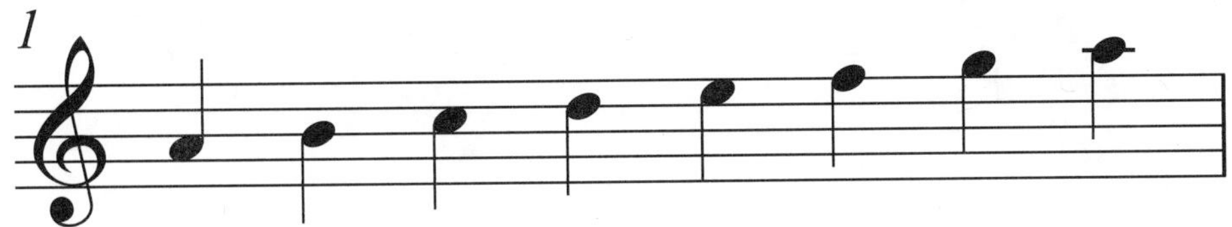

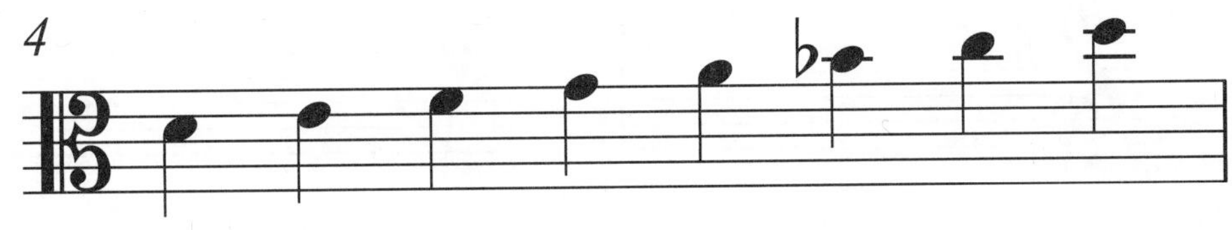

Name The Following Key Signatures (Major and Relative Minor)

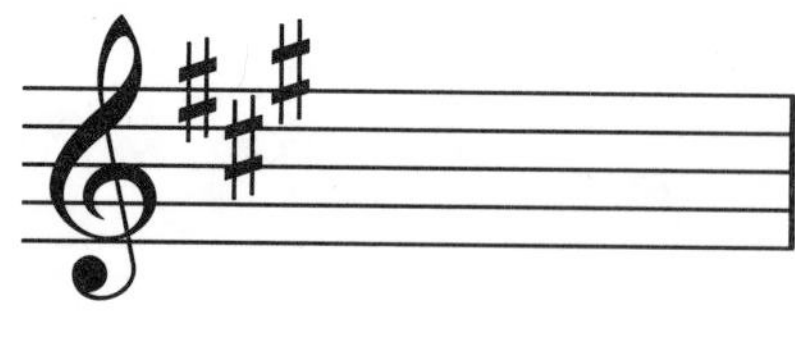

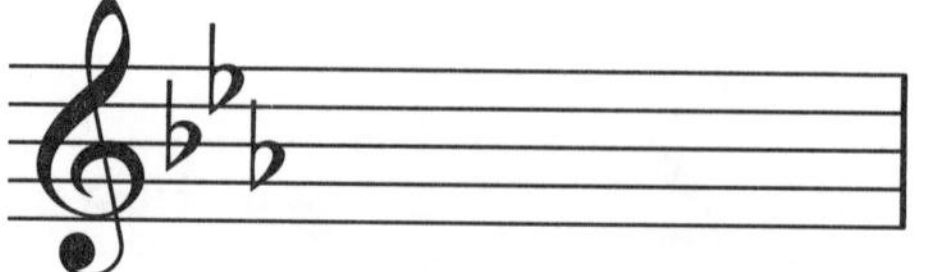

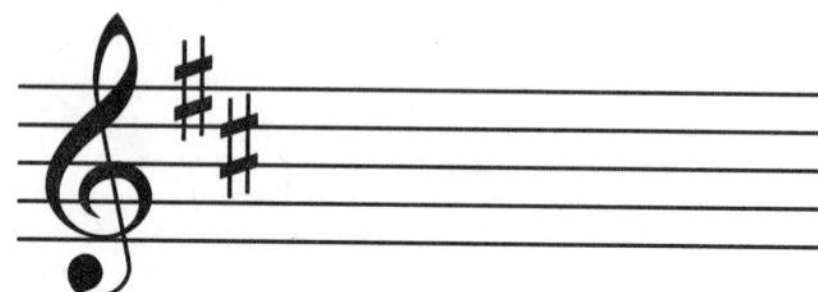

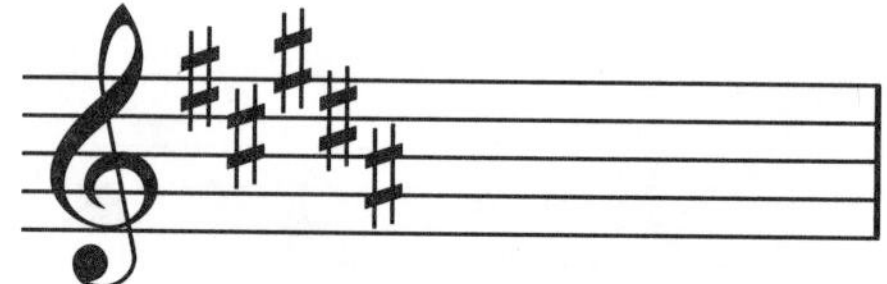

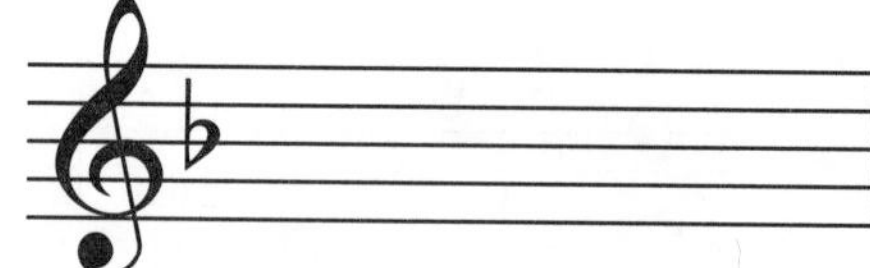

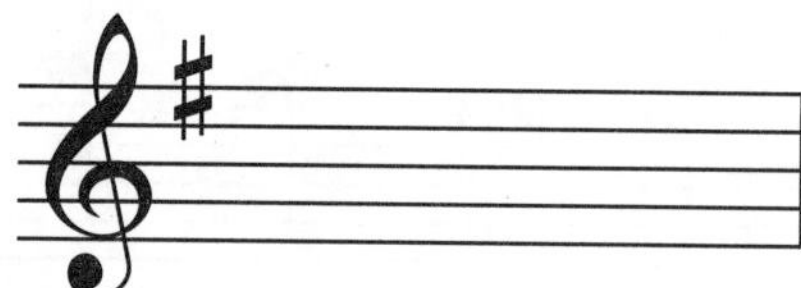

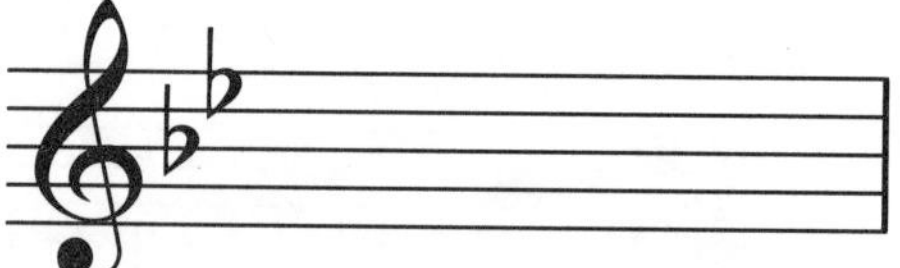

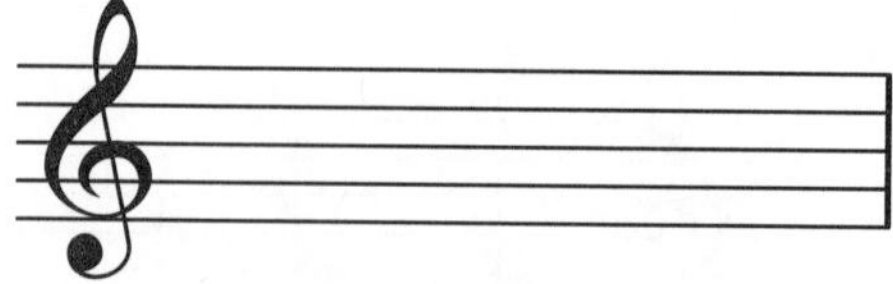

Write Modal Scales From The Following Notes

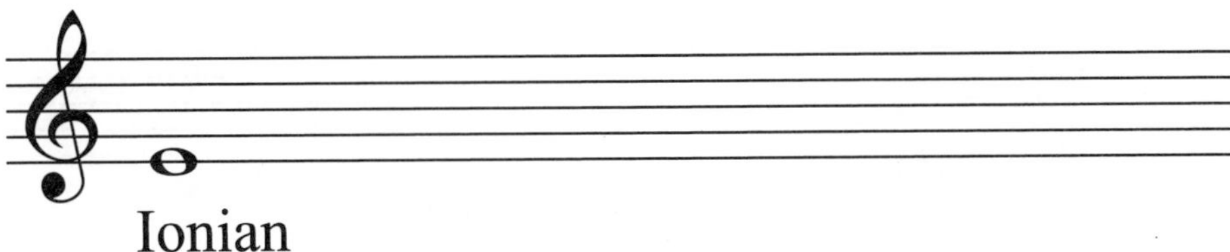

Ionian

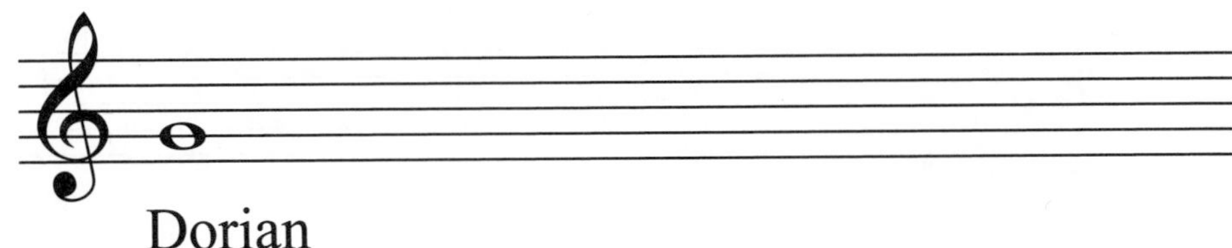

Dorian

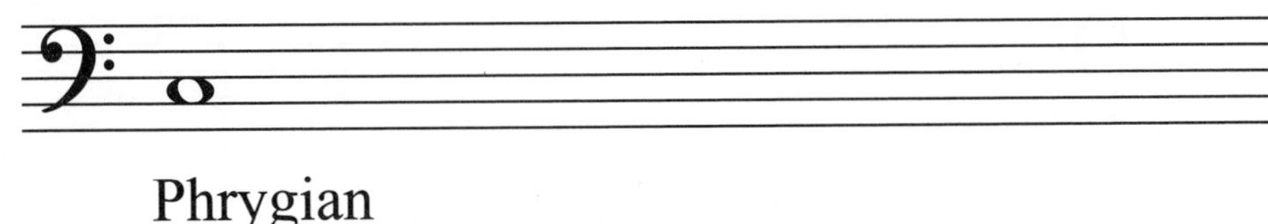

Phrygian

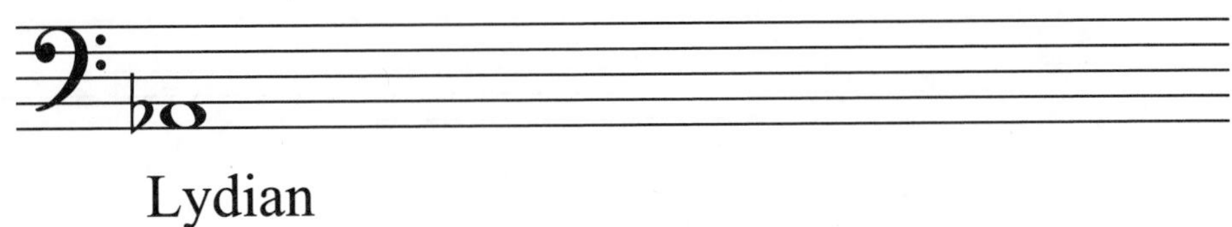

Lydian

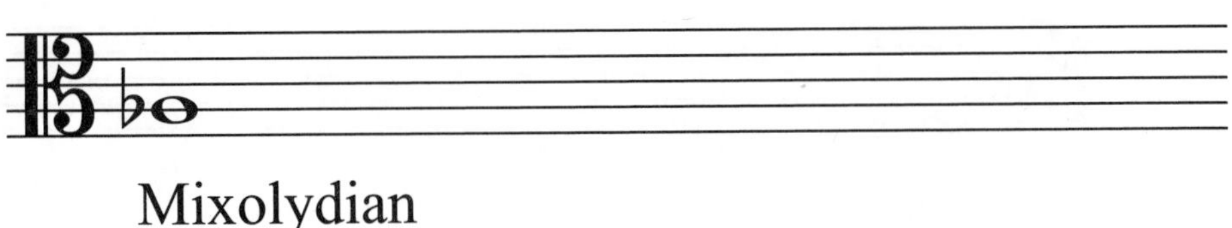

Mixolydian

Write Modal Scales from the Following Notes

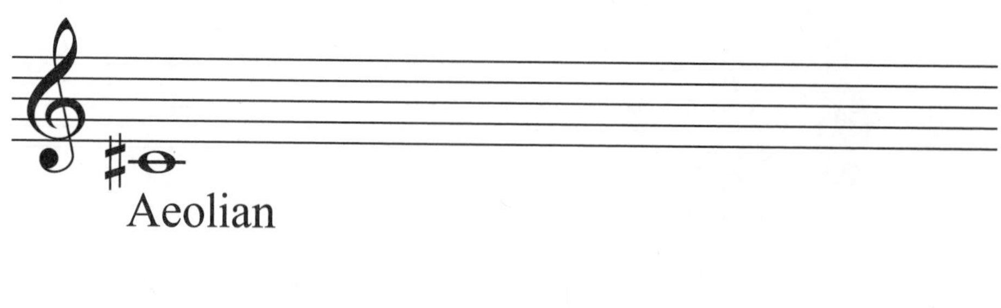

Aeolian

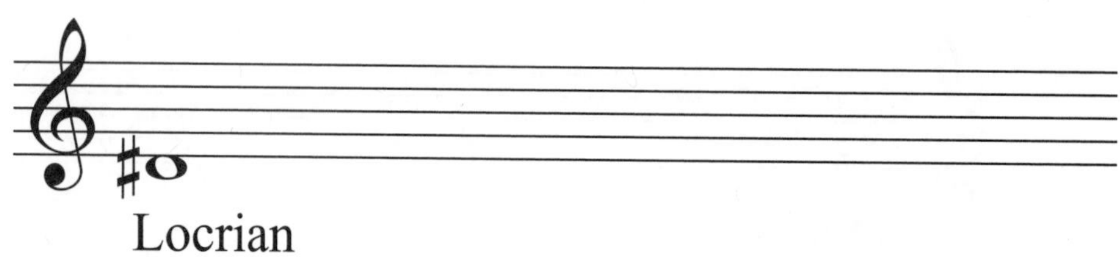

Locrian

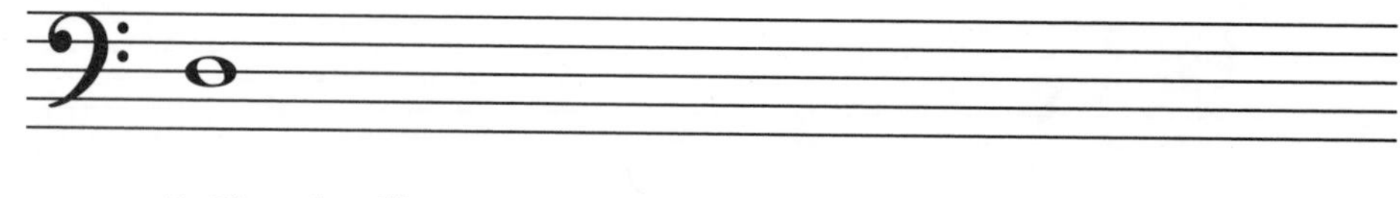

Mixolydian

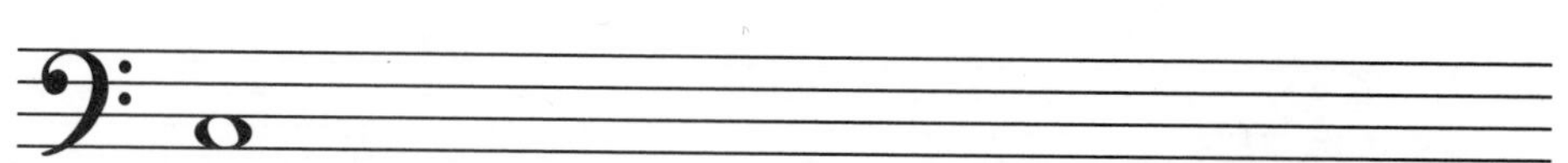

Dorian

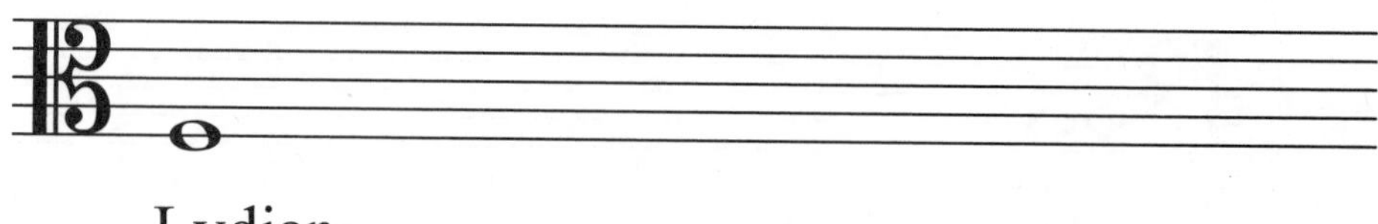

Lydian

Write "Special" Scales from the Following Notes

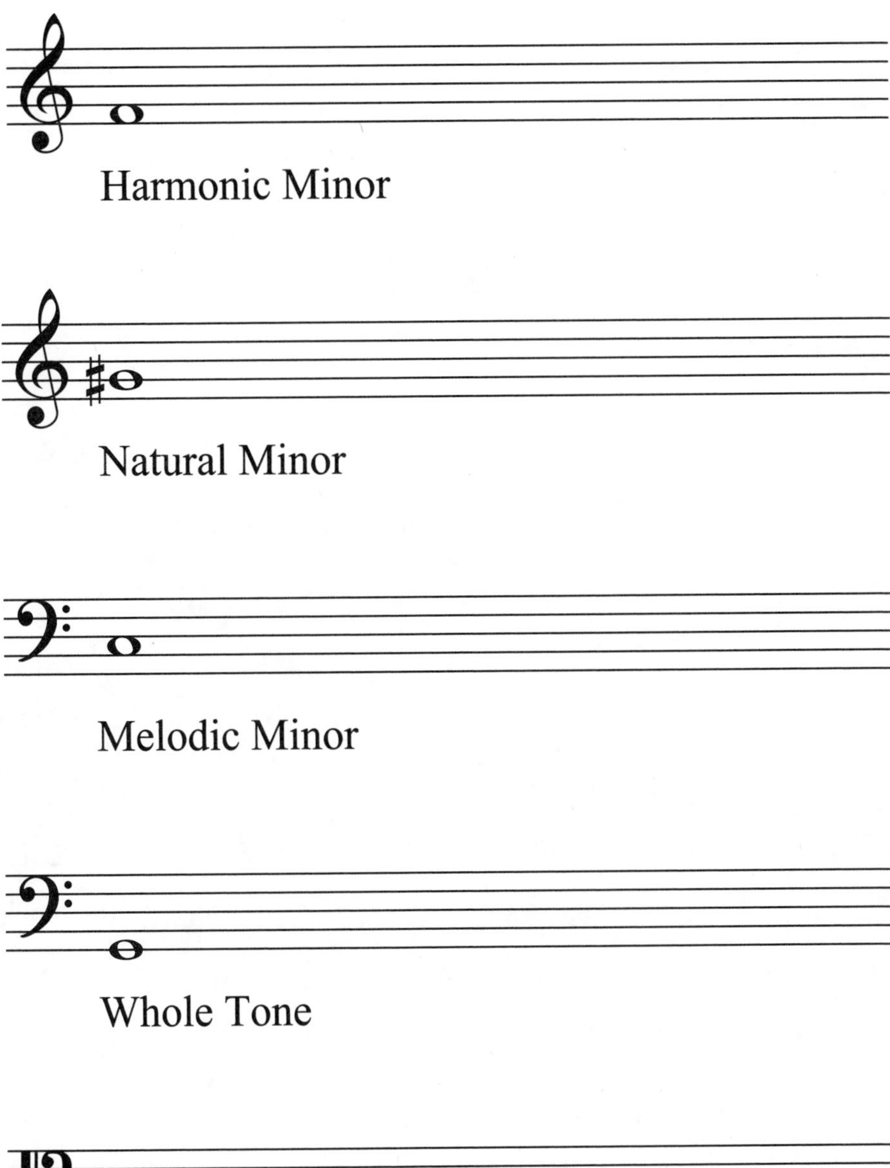

Chapter 8

Chords

Thus far, you have dealt with, at maximum, two notes at a time, when working with intervals. You have learned all about scales and key signatures, which give you all the possible arrangements of notes in a line, but you have been waiting for one more piece to complete your knowledge. The next step is to look at chords and the basic foundations of harmony. Intervals combine into chords, and harmonies emerge from those chords, providing the foundation of tonality, which is the language spoken by the music you hear.

What Is a Chord?

What's a chord? To start, a chord is essentially defined as three or more notes sounded simultaneously. Chords can, of course, be a whole lot more than three notes, so a few things need to be clarified. First, the simplest kind of chord is a triad, which begins with the prefix of *tri*, meaning "three." A triad is a three-note chord, and the intervals between the notes (as you will get into soon) are always thirds apart—yet another use of the prefix *tri*.

Just like intervals, chords come in different qualities. The quality refers to the type of chord it is, which is always based on some sort of construction rule. The basic chord qualities for triads are major, minor, augmented, and diminished. Those are the same qualities that the intervals had (excluding perfect). So to recap, a chord at its simplest is a three-note triad with intervals that are thirds apart and notes that ring together. Before you go any further, here is what a simple C major triad looks like.

TRACK 25

FIGURE 8.1 A Simple C Major Triad

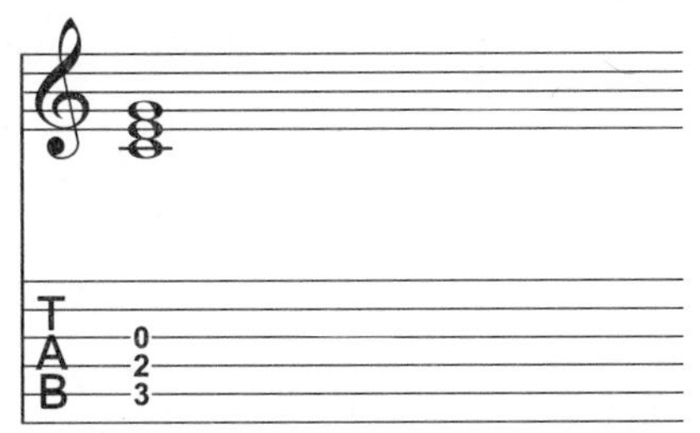

That is the simplest way to look at a chord, essentially the model or "prototype" voicing, but rarely do you see chords in such clear order. What you do see are chord voicings.

You should think about triads as being "model" chords. They are the absolute simplest way for you to have a chord spelled out. Unfortunately, rarely do you ever see such models of perfection in music. What you do see are chord voicings. What's a voicing? Simply, it's a sort of rearrangement of the notes of the triad in some way without adding or taking away from the essential ingredients (in the case of C major: C–E–G).

FIGURE 8.2 shows what a guitarist plays when asked to play a C major chord.

FIGURE 8.2 A Guitarist's Version of C Major

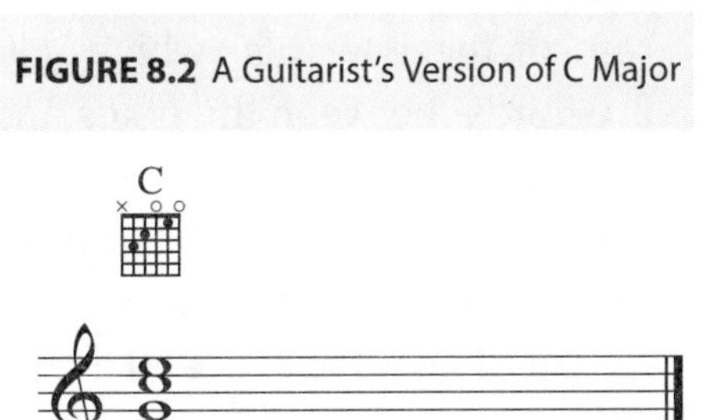

If you compare this with the "pure" triad in **FIGURE 8.1**, you see that while they appear visually different on the page, in fact, they contain the same stuff. Both chords contain the principal notes C, E, and G, but the guitar voicing repeats the notes C and E again. This simply fills out the chord and makes it sound more full. Either way, it's still C–E–G no matter how you slice it. When you analyze chords, you look for the basic notes that define it, and typically, you don't see them all in a pretty little row, right in triadic order; many times you have to hunt around, but you can address that during analysis later on. Now you need to define exactly what makes each of the chords what they are.

IN TIME

The son of a schoolmaster, Franz Schubert was born in Vienna on January 31, 1797, and died in Vienna on November 19, 1828, at the age of thirty-one. Even as a child he showed an extraordinary aptitude for music and studied the violin as well as the piano. His fame increased markedly after his death, and today he is perhaps most noted for his piano sonatas.

Building Chords

If you understand your intervals well, building chords is no big deal. Of the four triad qualities (major, minor, diminished, and augmented), each has its own distinct building patterns, much like all the scales did: Once you learn them, it's very hard to get them confused as they are different from one another. Start by detailing the structure of the four basic triads in music, beginning with major.

Major Triads/Chords

The formations of each chord and triad are going to be described differently than in the past. Previously, it was formula first and then application. This time, you know enough to look at a chord first and deduce the formula (with a bit of guidance) afterward.

Start by looking at a plain C major triad:

FIGURE 8.3 The C Major Triad

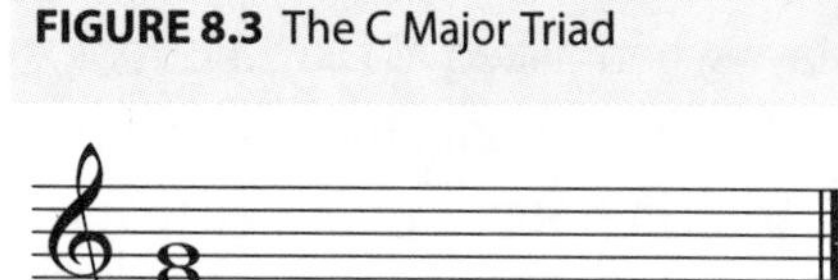

Here's what you know about triads: They are three-note chords built in thirds. So, you should look at the structure of the intervals (which you know are thirds) between the notes and figure out the pattern.

First up is the interval of C to E, which is a major third. Next up is E to G, which is a minor third. You can now form formulas for major triads: Start with a root, any root you want, and add a major third from the root and a minor third from the resultant note. You can think of it as major3/minor3 for short, knowing that with triads, you are always dealing with third intervals, and this will give you the fast way to spell this triad.

Alternative View of Major Triads

Besides looking at the intervals in thirds, it is very helpful to see a few other relationships that are present in the simple C major triad. First thing to look at: C to E, which is clearly a major third interval. But how about the interval from C to G? Intervals measure distance, and while the chord is composed of thirds, that's looking at the relationship from only one note to its adjacent note in the triad. What if you measured each interval from the root of the chord? Well, if you did that, you would need to look at the distance from the first note (C) to the last note (G). The interval from C to G is a perfect fifth. To construct triads solely from the root, you have to do the following:

1. Form a major third interval from the root of the chord.
2. Form a perfect fifth interval from the root of the chord.

It's really important to know both ways to form your triads, but it's beneficial to learn intervals from the root because it makes you aware of something new: Triads have roots, thirds, and fifths!

Extra Credit

Just like scales have to have seven notes and those seven notes have to use one letter from the musical alphabet each time they are spelled, triads must contain a root, a third, and a fifth. All of the basic triads from C will contain some form of C–E–G (with different accidentals, of course), but all C triads will have C–E–G. Knowing this makes spelling triads much faster—especially when you learn the derivative approach to forming triads from each other (which you will get to very soon).

The other thing to know about major triads is that not only do they have a root, a third, and a fifth, but they also have the root third and fifth from the major scale that they come from! This is great to know. If you're spelling a D major chord, just take the first, third, and fifth notes from the D major scale (which you know how to spell so well now)—D–F♯–A— and bingo, you have an instant major triad. There's much more to this, and you will get into the whole range of what you can do with scales and their relations to chords in the section entitled Diatonic Chords later in this chapter. Now, on to minor chords!

Minor Triads/Chords

To further drive home the derivative approach, take a look at all the chords in the chapter from a C root. This way, you can look at each possible variant and learn the differences among them. Sometimes, learning what stays the same and what small elements change helps you acquire the knowledge faster. Start with a C minor triad:

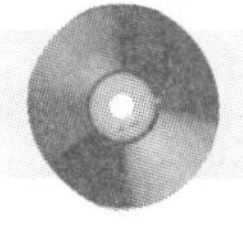

TRACK 26

FIGURE 8.4 A C Minor Triad

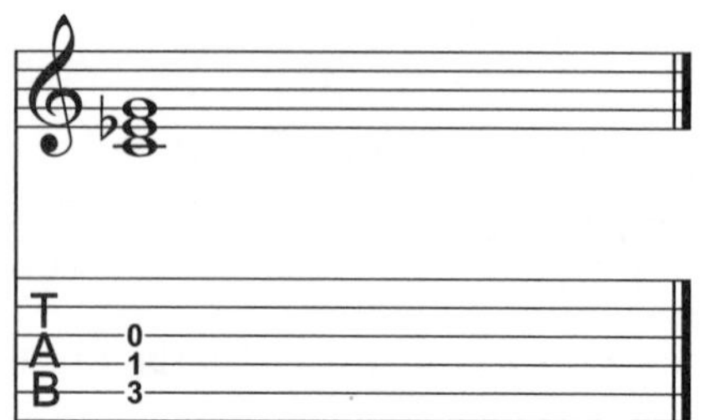

Based on what you know about intervals, look at the distance between each of the third intervals to deduce a formula for this triad. Start with C to E♭, which is an interval of a minor third. E♭ to G is an interval of a major third. So the formula would go as follows: minor third, major third. If you compare that with the formula for a major triad (major third, minor third), you see that both the major triad and the minor triad contain a major third and a minor third. What's unique is that both of the triads contain one of each quality of third, but they are backward! The major triad is major3/minor3 whereas the minor triad is minor3/major3.

Extra Credit

Here's a great way to remember the order of your thirds in simple major and minor triads: The name of the triad will tell you the quality of the first third. Major triads start with major thirds, and minor triads start with minor thirds. Both triads conclude with the opposite interval; that is, major triads start with major thirds but conclude with minor thirds, and minor triads start with minor thirds but conclude with major thirds. Memorize this!

Alternative View of Minor Triads

As with the major triads above, you can look at the minor triads in a few other ways to aid your understanding. The first would be to look at all the intervals from the root of C. Look at what you get:

- The interval from C to E♭ is a minor third.
- The interval from C to G is a perfect fifth.

If you remember from the major triad, it also had a perfect fifth! This is yet another reason that it is called a perfect interval. As for the differences between major and minor, since the fifths don't change, you have to look at the thirds. Major triads have major thirds, and minor triads have minor thirds, and both have perfect fifths from their roots. It's amazing that the difference between a C major triad and a C minor triad is just one note, yet they sound so different. Use **FIGURE 8.5** as a sound example—change one note and the whole game changes!

TRACK 27

FIGURE 8.5 C Major Versus C Minor: *A Sound Battle*

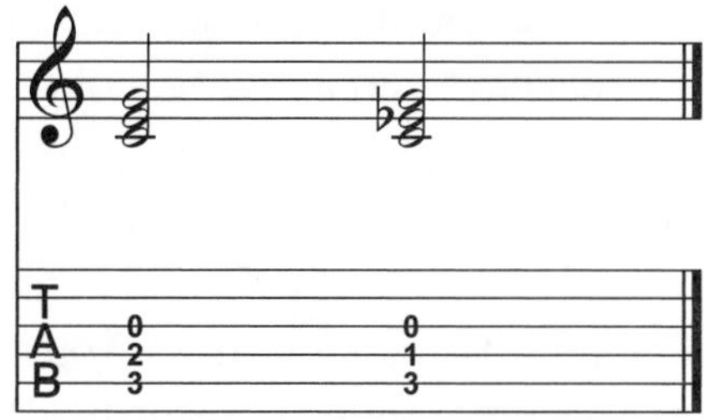

Another look at the derivative approach to music: If you can spell any major triad, all you have to do to make it into a minor triad is simply lower the third of the major triad one half step down. It's a trick that always works! Many times, your speed at working with theory can come from changing things you already know, and most people find that the major scale and the major triad are memorized early on, before really memorizing the other aspects of theory. So, if you have those scales and triads memorized, changing one note to make them major or minor isn't such a big deal. With music theory, you have to be very quick, and these things enhance your speed.

IN TIME

Historically, the major scale has been the basis for music theory. Many formulas and the entire idea of a derivative approach to theory exist because theorists are constantly deriving method and relationships from the major scale. As you will see as this book rolls on, just about everything is some form of an altered major scale, or in the case of this chapter, a major chord!

The other way to look at a minor triad is to relate it to its corresponding minor scale. Just like the major triad took the first, third, and fifth note from the C major scale, the C minor triad does the same thing, just from its corresponding minor scale. To spell a C minor triad, spell the C minor scale and select its first, third, and fifth notes: C–E♭–G. This may or may not be the fastest way for you to work.

Diminished Triads

Next up on your look at triads is the diminished triad. **FIGURE 8.6** shows a C diminished triad.

FIGURE 8.6 The C Diminished Triad

Break the intervals in the C diminished chord down. Start with the interval from C to E♭, which is a minor third. The next interval is from E♭ to G♭, which is also a minor third. The intervallic pattern of this triad is minor3/minor3. This is important to note, because both intervals are minor thirds. Both the major and minor triads have contained one of each third (one major third, one minor third), albeit each triad had the thirds in different order. In the diminished triad, you have the same thirds (both minor). Think of it this way: Each triad contains two thirds, and there are only major and minor thirds to choose from. You can have two triads that use one major third and one minor third (in reverse order), and that gives you two possible triads (major and minor). If you use the same third twice, you can get two more triads. In the case of using two minor thirds, you get a diminished triad. You will see shortly what happens when you use two major thirds.

The diminished triad is used more in classical music than in popular music, although it is found in certain popular songs. A great example is "Michelle" by the Beatles, which uses a diminished chord in its harmony (you should check out the sheet music to see where it is).

Our naturally occurring scales are the major and minor scales. The other scales you have learned are either "man-made" or outgrowths of the major scale. Chords can be constructed solely on intervals, or they can be related to scales, and as you will see shortly, they also can be derived from scales. The three triads you have explored thus far—major, minor, and diminished—are all "natural" triads that occur naturally in music because of their relationship to scales. The final triad, augmented, is not a naturally occurring triad from any major or minor scale.

Alternative View for Diminished Triads

Start off by looking at all the intervals in the C diminished triad all measured from C.

- The interval from C to E♭ is a minor third.
- The interval from C to G♭ is a diminished fifth.

It's important to note that the diminished triad is the first time you see a fifth in a chord that isn't perfect! That could explain why the diminished triad has an unusual sound when compared to the major and minor triads.

While there is a diminished scale, most musicians don't correlate the spelling of a diminished triad to that of the diminished scale even though you can still take the first, third, and fifth tones of that scale to form the chord. The reality is that unless you are a jazz improviser, you probably won't deal with the diminished scale except in theoretical understanding. For most of us, the derivative approach makes the most sense. If a C major triad is C–E–G and a C diminished chord is spelled C–E♭–G♭, then you can derive the following rule: To turn any major triad into a diminished triad, lower the third and fifth one half step down.

You could alternatively derive the answer from the minor triad (1, ♭3, 5): To turn any minor triad into a diminished triad, lower the fifth one half step down.

Augmented Triads

The last triad to examine is the augmented triad. At this point, you have seen triads formed from almost every possible combination of thirds—you're only missing one combination! A quick look at **FIGURE 8.7** will show you the intervallic formula of a C augmented triad:

FIGURE 8.7 The C Augmented Triad

TRACK 29

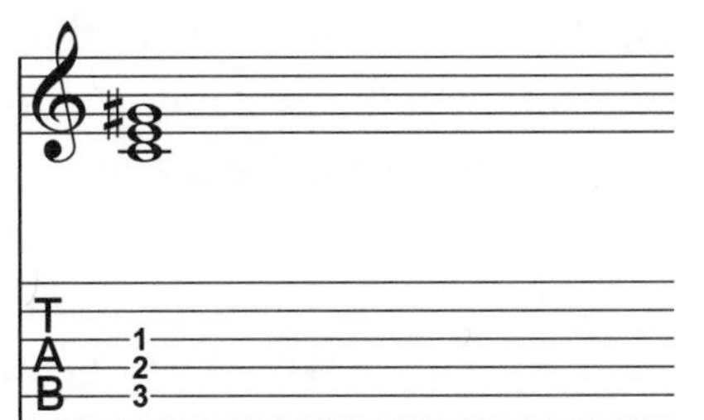

If you break down the chord by its third intervals, you get from C to E, a major third interval, and from E to G♯ is a major third. At last, you have every possible combination of thirds! The table below will explain what you can do with three notes and two thirds!

Table of Triad Formulas	
Triad	**Formula**
Major	Major third, Minor third
Minor	Minor third, Major third
Diminished	Minor third, Minor third
Augmented	Major third, Major third

As you can see, that's all the possible permutations of combinations of major and minor thirds in a triad; those combinations yield the four triads that music deals with!

Symmetry relates to intervals being consistent throughout a musical idea or form. Diminished and whole tone scales are considered symmetrical because they contain either the exact same intervals (whole tone) or the same repeating interval pattern (diminished). With the introduction of diminished and augmented triads, you extend your understanding of symmetry to the world of triads. Since diminished triads are composed solely of minor third intervals, they are symmetric triads. Also, since the augmented triad is composed solely of major thirds, it is also considered a symmetric triad.

Point to Consider

If diminished triads are rare in popular music, then augmented triads are even more sparsely used! But as always, learn as much as you can, and hey, you just may be the one to use an augmented triad in popular music. (Pink Floyd uses an augmented triad in "Us and Them.")

Alternative View of Augmented Triads

Take another look at the augmented triad, this time looking at all the intervals from the root of C.

The interval from C to E is a major third. The interval from C to G♯ is an augmented fifth. This is the second triad that has a nonperfect fifth (the other was diminished). It's also not a coincidence that the fifth is an augmented fifth and the triad is called an augmented triad (the same with the diminished chords, diminished fifth interval).

Looking at the derivative approach for forming augmented triads, if you start with the C major triad (C–E–G) and compare it with the C augmented triad (C–E–G♯), you come to the following conclusion: To make any major triad into an augmented triad, simply raise the fifth note one half step.

Now, here's a recap of the derivative approach for all of the triads so you can become a triad speller in no time!

The Full Derivative Approach for Forming Triads

The derivative approach simply presupposes that you can spell a major triad easily. Since major scales are so commonly used and practiced, it's fairly easy to spell them. If you can't do that as easily as you want to, work hard on major scales because much of the theory remaining in this book will derive from the major scale in some way; it's simply an excellent base to start with.

The first slight change you are going to make is to use only numbers now. So, instead of talking about the root, third, and fifth, you will simply say 1–3–5.

Here is the full listing of all the triads and how they derive from the major triad:

Major	1–3–5
Minor	1–♭3–5
Diminished	1–♭3–♭5
Augmented	1–3–♯5

Since this is a music book, take a look at all the triads side by side so you can see what's happening musically.

FIGURE 8.8 All Triads

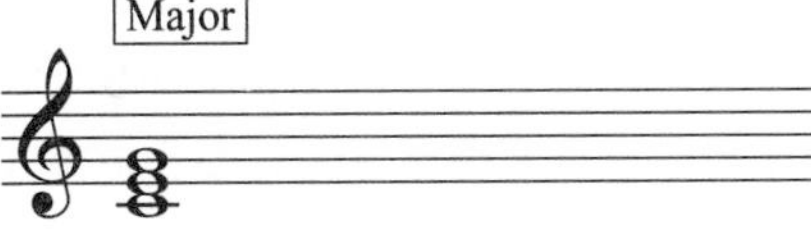

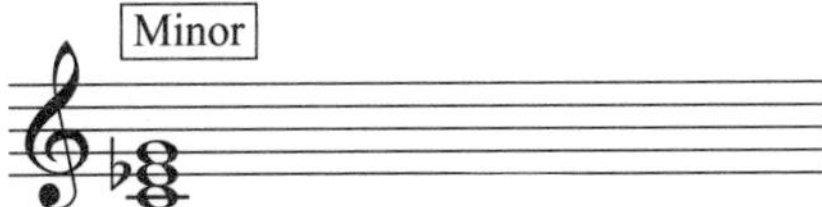

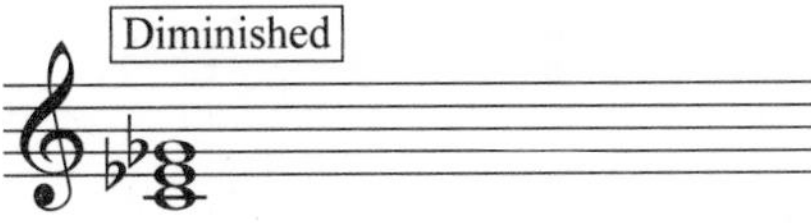

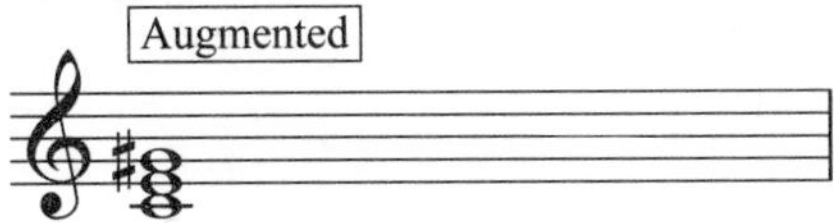

Knowing how to build triads on pure interval, from intervals from the root, and deriving them from the basic major triad are all approaches that you should be familiar with.

Chords in Scales

Scales are very important. This cannot be overstated. They are nothing short of musical DNA—an essential building block. Now, it's time to revisit the C major triad.

FIGURE 8.9 Your Old Friend: *The C Major Triad*

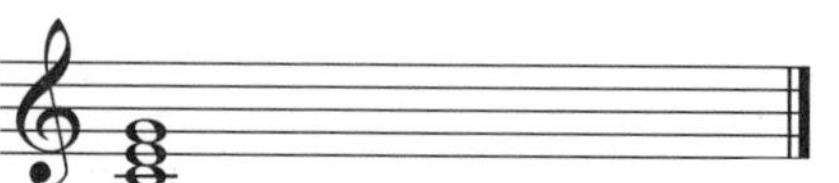

This triad can be constructed a few different ways. One of the ways is to take the first, third, and fifth notes of the C major scale and stack them together. By doing this, you are able to build a quick C major triad. This trick works in every major and minor scale, so in theory, you could build any major or minor chord you need to. Since chords are built from third intervals, it would make sense that you could do more than just stack the first, third, and fifth notes together. There are a whole bunch of possible third combinations in a scale if you start on each note in the scale and build triads. What would happen if you stacked these different combinations from each note? You'd get a whole bunch of different chords, seven to be exact—one from each degree of the scale.

You are going to learn how to make triads from every note in a C major scale. To do this, start out with a C major scale and simply add triads (roots, thirds, and fifths) from each note in the scale. What you've just done is created all of the basic harmonies (and chords) in the key of C major by creating triads off of each note.

FIGURE 8.10 Harmonizing the C Major Scale

TRACK 30

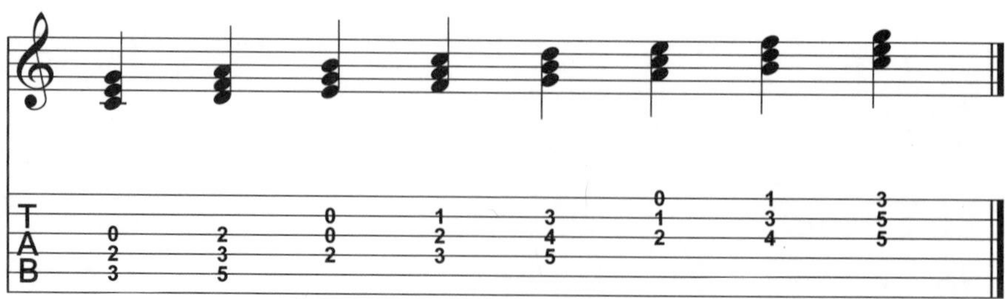

Don't downplay the significance of this. You've just learned the basis for understanding harmony and chord progressions. Contained within those triads are seven different chords and endless possibilities for creating music. When you create triads from a scale and use only those notes to do so, you use a technique called "diatonic" harmony. Diatonic means using the notes from only one scale/key to make chords.

Diatonic Chords

In the last section, you took a C major scale and added triads to each note in the scale, creating seven diatonic triads in that key. Now look at exactly what chords are created from making these triads.

FIGURE 8.11 Name Those Triads

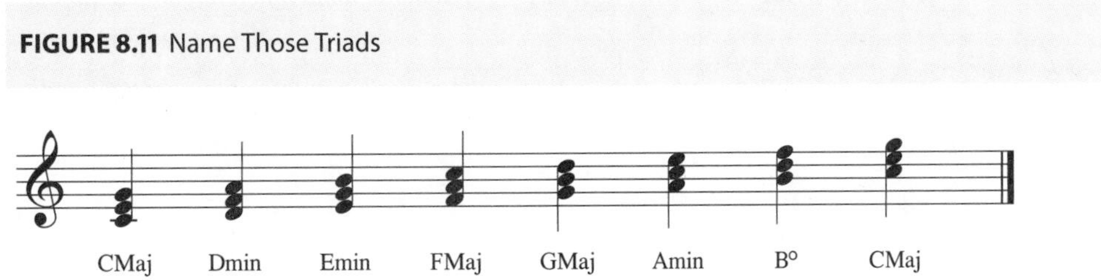

You can see from the example that there are a variety of triads created. You see a major chord, minor chords, and a diminished chord. Strangely, augmented triads are missing!

The Order of Triads

The order of triads in the scale is important. In a major scale/key, the triads always progress in this order: major, minor, minor, major, major, minor, and diminished. Memorize this; it's going to serve you quite well in the future. And the best part is that what you've just done in the key of C major holds true in every major key. Since all major scales are constructed in the exact same fashion, with the exact same intervals, when you stack triads in any major scale, you always get the same order of triads/chords. This is a huge time-saver! The only thing that changes are the names of the notes themselves, as no two keys have the exact same pitches. The chords and their order will always be the same.

FIGURE 8.12 shows an example in the key of D major, E major, and B♭ major to show you that no matter what the scale is, the same order of triads always exists. Just like major scales have formulas for their construction that allow you to spell any scale easily, knowing that the triad order holds true to all the keys is something you can depend on!

FIGURE 8.12 Different Keys, Same Triad Order

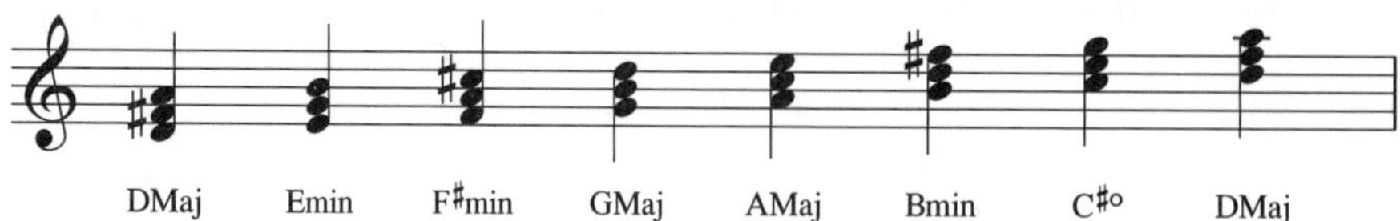

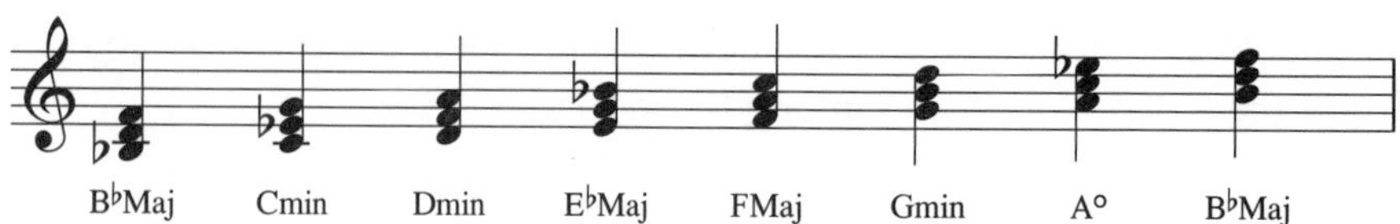

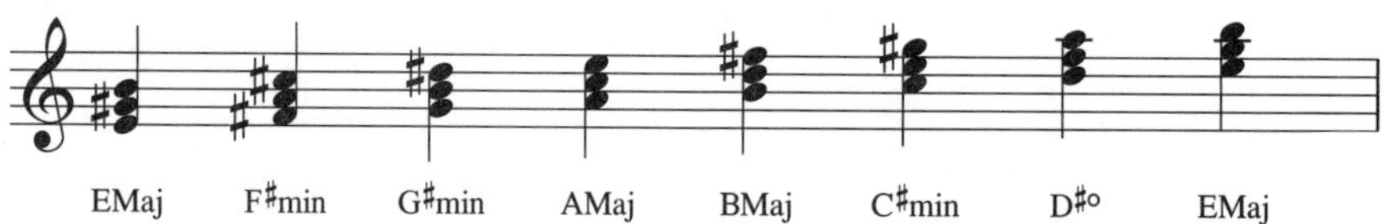

Notice that the notes in the scales are in different keys, but the order of chords (major, minor, minor, major, major, minor, and diminished) stays the same. This holds true for every major scale/key.

Roman Numerals

To music theorists, there isn't any real difference between any major key. Unless you possess the ability of "perfect pitch," where you can name a note just by listening to it, you won't be able to hear a difference between C major and D major scales. Since there is such equality in the keys, music theory has a system of naming chords relative to what note of the scale they are built from. If you were to number the notes and their corresponding triads from the G major scale, you'd end up with:

FIGURE 8.13 Numerals with Triads

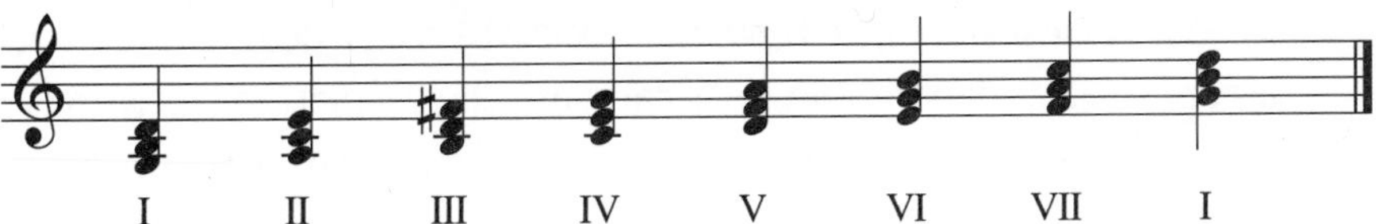

As triads are built off of the notes, they can now be referred to by number and or Roman numeral. For example, a one chord in the key of C major is the chord built off of the first note in the scale, which is C major. Since every major scale starts with a major triad, you could say that the one chord in any major key is major.

In Chapter 3, you learned the names of the scale degrees. When discussing chords, the scale degree names are used as well. I (one) chords are referred to as tonic chords, while V (five) chords are referred to as dominant chords corresponding with the information in Chapter 3 on the proper names for scale degrees.

The only limitation with using numbers this way is that there is no way to convey whether that chord is major or minor simply by using the number 1, 2, or 3. Musicians use Roman numerals instead of Arabic numbers for this very reason. You may remember from math class that Roman numerals have lowercase equivalents. By using uppercase Roman numerals for major chords and lowercase Roman numerals for minor chords, musicians have a system that makes sense in every key and conveys a lot of information about a chord.

FIGURE 8.14 shows the harmonized major scale with all of the corresponding Roman numerals. You'll also notice that the diminished chord is denoted by a lowercase Roman numeral and a small degree symbol next to it. That's the standard way to indicate diminished chords.

FIGURE 8.14 Major Scale with Roman Numerals to Indicate Chord Quality

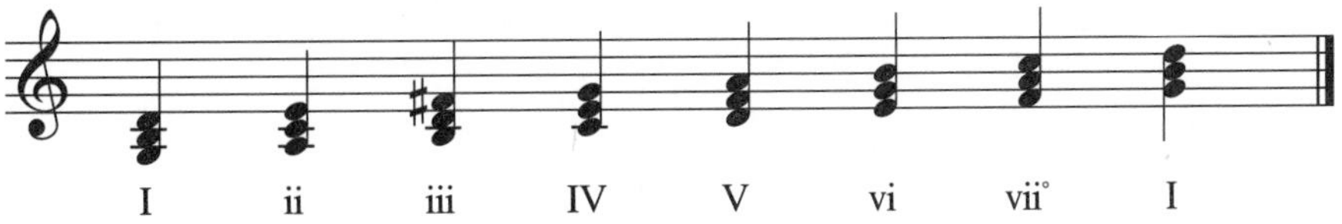

Roman numerals are a standard way for music theorists not only to name chords, but also to analyze choral structures in pre-existing music in order to gain some insight into how the music was constructed. Roman numerals are still a convention in classical music. If you plan to study music formally, becoming more familiar with Roman numerals is essential.

Minor Scale Harmony

The minor scale has a few peculiarities. The minor scale has the exact same notes as the major scale and accordingly should have the exact same resulting chords, just in a different order, but the minor scale has some quirks when it comes to harmony. You may recall the harmonic minor scale, a minor scale with a raised seventh tone, from Chapter 4. The harmonic minor scale exists solely to correct the harmony of the minor scale and make it more useful. Take a look at a "normal" minor scale harmonized with triads to see what you get.

TRACK 31

FIGURE 8.15 All Triads in A Minor

By harmonizing the A natural minor scale like this, you get the same chords as you did in C major, but they are just in a different order. There is nothing wrong with the natural minor scale. However, in tonal music, that minor scale is not harmonized, because it's lacking what is known as a proper dominant chord. You will get a chance to examine functional chord progressions in Chapter 10 to see how the minor scale is actually used in practice.

Chapter 9

Seventh Chords and Chord Inversions

Chords are more than just a collection of intervals! You know from Chapter 8 that chords have their origins in scales and melodies. You need to look at two more aspects in order to understand chords in their entirety: seventh chords and chord inversions. Seventh chords are the next logical step after you understand triads and are used extensively in music throughout the ages. Inversions allow your chords to move smoothly and efficiently from one chord to the next; this is the foundation for voice leading.

Seventh Chords

A triad is a three-note chord; this much you know. Triads take care of most of the basic harmony, but not all of it! You build all of your chords in thirds. When you derived diatonic harmony from major and minor scales, you simply stacked thirds from each root and came up with seven triads—all built in thirds. Your knowledge of intervals allowed you to decode what the triads were and what order they appear in.

FIGURE 9.1 Diatonic Triads in F Major

Now, what would happen if you added another third to your triads? Well, simply, you'd form seventh chords, which are named so because the last interval you add is seven notes away from the root. You could call them quad-ads, but it doesn't have the same ring to it as "seventh chord" does—plus it sounds like a form of sit-ups!

The majority of the harmony you deal with is built in intervals of thirds. This type of harmony is called tertian harmony and is the basis for "common practice" or "tonal" harmony that is studied and still utilized today.

Diatonic Seventh Chords

Remember the term *diatonic*? It means "from the key." You first learned about diatonic when you formed simple triads within a scale. Do it again in F major!

Now, to make them into seventh chords, you simply need to add another third on top of each triad, adding an interval of a seventh if you measure from the root. Remember to use only the notes from the F scale (F–G–A–B♭–C–D–E–F) when adding your thirds to keep this example diatonic. Doing so will leave you with these seventh chords:

FIGURE 9.2 Diatonic Seventh Chords in F Major

TRACK 32

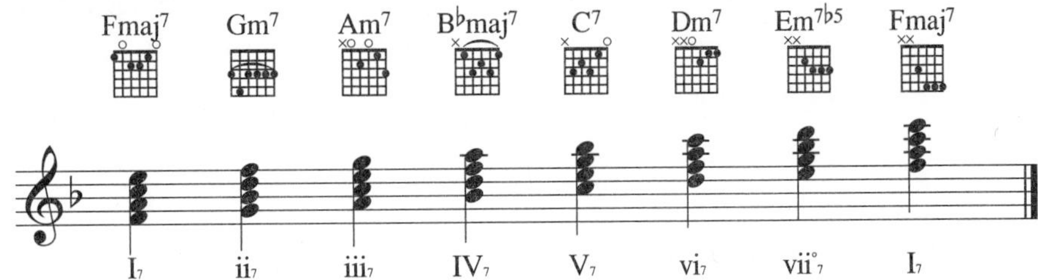

From this list of chords, you see four different types of seventh chords: major seventh, minor seventh, dominant seventh, and half diminished seventh.

Notice that in **FIGURE 9.2**, the Roman numerals used to analyze the chords did not identify which kind of seventh chord you were encountering. They simply added "7" next to each Roman numeral. The answer had to be spelled out. Because of this, you need to understand what makes a major seventh different from a dominant seventh, even though both use uppercase Roman numerals (signifying major chords) with sevenths attached to them.

Point to Consider

Typically, even if your experience with theory is limited, you've come across, played, or heard about a G7 chord (or any other root). That is one kind of seventh chord (as you will learn about). This book uses the term seventh chord as a broad category. Seventh chords come in many different types, and G7 is simply one type.

Diatonic seventh chords are definitely useful, and in Chapter 10, you will see just how useful they are, when the focus is on chord progressions. For now, you need to understand the structure of the seventh chords, because there are more than just the four diatonic seventh chords used in modern music!

Seventh Chord Construction

Here, you will explore all the different seventh chords that are available to you. You should begin to think like this: A seventh chord is nothing more than a triad with an added seventh interval (when measured from the root). Doing so will give you at least eight seventh chords (four possible triads and two sevenths), although there is one more that breaks the rules a touch (more on that soon). Go through them one by one so you can see how they are put together and how they are named.

Major Triads with Sevenths

If you take a major triad and make it into a seventh chord, you can come up with only two possibilities: a major triad with a major seventh on top, and a major triad with a minor seventh on top.

Start with **FIGURE 9.3**.

FIGURE 9.3 Major Triad with Major Seventh

TRACK 33

When you look at that chord, you can look at two things: first, you have your major triad, D (D–F♯–A), and you have an added C♯. The interval from the root of the chord to the seventh (D to C♯) is a major seventh. Call this chord a major/major seventh chord for a second because it tells you exactly what you have: a major triad with a major seventh interval added. Now, the rest of the world will simply call this chord a major seventh, as in D major seventh, or Dmaj7 for short. Many theorists will use "major/major seventh" to be more specific, but if you say "D major seventh," you're saying exactly the same thing. The major seventh chord is found on the first (tonic) and fourth (subdominant) degrees of a harmonized major scale.

You could think of the formula for a major seventh chord as being:

1, 3, 5, 7

(This is if you take the scale degrees from a major scale.)

Extra Credit

The major seventh chord is interesting for two reasons: First, you can spell it simply by choosing the first, third, fifth, and seventh notes from any major scale. This is because a major seventh chord is the tonic seventh chord in a major key. It's also interesting that its proper name of "major/major seventh" shortens to simply "major seventh."

FIGURE 9.4 Major Triad with Minor Seventh

TRACK 34

The next possible seventh chord would be **FIGURE 9.4**.

Looking at this chord, you see another D major triad (D–F♯–A) and an added seventh of C. The interval between D and C is a minor seventh. This chord is fully called a major/minor seventh chord. When it's shortened, it's simply called a seventh chord, as in G7, or D7 in this case. Since the term *seventh chord* is far too general for music theory, theorists and many musicians call this chord a dominant seventh chord because, as illustrated in **FIGURE 9.1**, this chord occurs only on the fifth scale degree, which has the proper name of the dominant scale degree. Whichever you call it, G7 or G dominant seventh, both are acceptable and correct.

The formula for a dominant seventh chord is: 1, 3, 5, ♭7 (if you take the scale degrees from the major scale). Dominant seventh chords are *really* important! It's awfully hard to have harmony without dominant (V) chords.

Minor Triads with Sevenths

When it comes to minor triads with sevenths, there are also two varieties! Start with **FIGURE 9.5**.

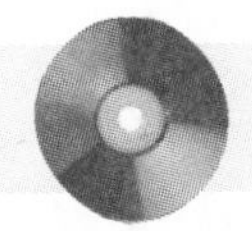

FIGURE 9.5 Minor Triad with Minor Seventh

TRACK 35

Start with a C minor triad (C–E♭–G) and add the note B♭. The interval from C to B♭ is a minor seventh, so this chord is called a C minor/minor seventh chord. It's shortened to simply C minor seventh or Cm7 or C-7. This is the basic minor seventh chord that is found on the second, third, and sixth scale degrees of a harmonized major scale. Also worth mentioning is that again, just like the major seventh, when both the triad and the seventh are the same (both minor), the name of the chord is simply minor seventh. The minor seventh chord is also the chord you can form by taking the first, third, fifth, and seventh notes from a pure minor scale (Aeolian).

If you wanted to relate the scale to major, its formula would be: 1, ♭3, 5, ♭7 (relating the scale degrees to the major scale).

The next seventh chord that you come to is your first "unnatural" seventh chord in that it's not formed in the diatonic major or minor scales. Take a look at **FIGURE 9.6.**

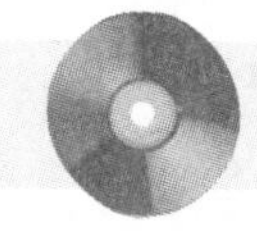

TRACK 36

FIGURE 9.6 Minor Triad with Major Seventh

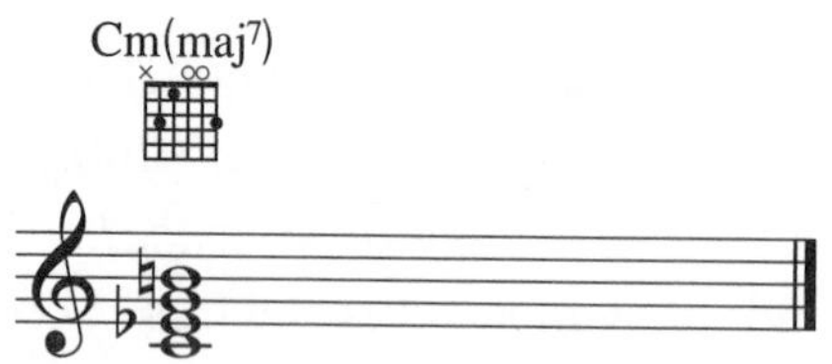

This C minor triad with an added B natural gives us a very unusual sound—unnatural, even! The interval from C to B is a major seventh, so the full name for this chord would be a C minor/major seventh chord. There actually is no shortening for this chord; it is always referred to as a minor/major seventh chord. The only shorthand you may see is in the chord symbols in popular music: Cm(maj7), C-(maj7) or Cmin(maj7). While these chords have an unusual sound, they can be quite striking and beautiful when used in the proper context. Again, this triad does not occur anywhere in the natural major or minor scales.

Point to Consider

If you were to harmonize the harmonic or melodic minor scales, you would spell a minor/major seventh from the tonic scale degree. This is where modern theorists see the chord coming from. Others think that it is simply the natural extension of trying a minor triad with a major seventh interval added to it. Either way, it exists in jazz and popular music, most famously in "Us and Them" by Pink Floyd, on their legendary *Dark Side of the Moon* album.

If you were to derive a formula for a minor/major seventh chord, it would appear as follows: 1, ♭3, 5, 7 (if you take the scales degrees from the major scale).

That's all you can do to minor triads and sevenths! That brings your grand total up to four seventh chords, and you're through only major and minor! Next up: diminished.

Diminished Triads with Sevenths

Diminished chords are a bit tricky, especially when it comes to naming them. Start with the diatonic diminished seventh chord, built from the leading tone of a major scale.

FIGURE 9.7 Diminished Triad with a Minor Seventh

TRACK 37

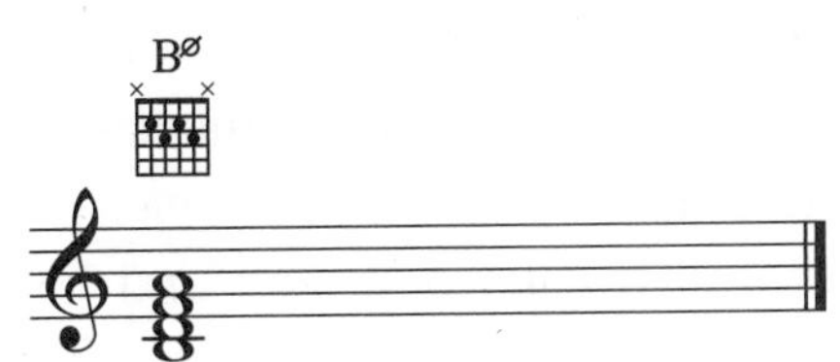

What you have is a B diminished triad with an added A. The interval from B to A is a minor seventh, so the full name for this chord is a diminished/minor seventh. However, here's where it gets tricky. This chord is called a half diminished chord. Half diminished chords use this symbol: Bø7.

If you wanted to derive a formula for the half diminished seventh chord, it would look like this: 1, ♭3, ♭5, ♭7 (if you take these from the major scale degrees).

This chord, while it may be the "diatonic" chord, is not the typical diminished seventh chord you see. Take a look at another diminished seventh chord, which will explain why that particular chord is called half diminished.

FIGURE 9.8 Diminished Triad with a Diminished Seventh

TRACK 38

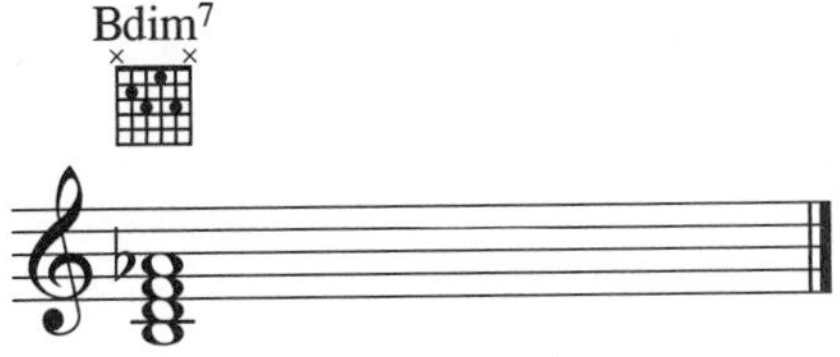

We start with a diminished triad and add an A♭. The interval from B to A♭ is a diminished seventh. The full name for this chord would be a diminished/diminished seventh. Just like major and minor seventh chords that share the same name and type of seventh, this is the diminished seventh chord. It's also called a fully diminished seventh chord, but for most people, "diminished seventh" will do. The symbol for a fully diminished seventh chord is B°7.

If you wanted to derive a formula for the diminished seventh chord, it would look like this: 1, ♭3, ♭5, ♭♭7 (if you take these from major scale degrees).

Note: This is the first time you've seen a double flat in a chord formula! That's because fully diminished seventh chords don't occur in major or minor scales naturally. They are the result of stacking of minor third intervals. You can also derive this chord if you harmonize the harmonic minor scale at the leading tone degree.

Half and Whole Diminished

It's a bit confusing—why is one diminished chord half diminished and another whole diminished? Well, for starters, part of this is simply a name. But there's more to it than that. The diminished triad is a symmetric chord in that it uses all minor third intervals. When you spell a diminished seventh chord, you actually use all minor thirds again (B–D–F–A♭). It is called "fully" diminished because it follows the pattern of all minor thirds and becomes perfectly symmetrical at that point. A half diminished chord (B–D–F–A) has a major third between the fifth and the seventh and isn't fully diminished because it loses the pattern of all minor thirds. That's where the difference comes from. In music, when you see diminished chords with sevenths, 90 percent of the time, they are fully diminished seventh chords. You do see half diminished chords, mostly in jazz but sometimes in classical and popular music as well.

Since the diminished chord comes in two flavors—half and full diminished—modern musicians, especially jazz musicians, help to differentiate these two chords. One way that they differentiate them is simply by not calling a half diminished chord a half diminished! If you look at a half diminished chord, you could look at it as a minor seventh chord with a ♭5. To avoid confusion, most modern music uses min7♭5 instead of the half diminished symbol (ø) to avoid confusion. This way, when you see a diminished symbol (°), you can infer that it's a fully diminished chord.

Augmented Triads with Sevenths

Augmented triads are weird chords to begin with. They have a particular sound that simply isn't used very much. Nonetheless, modern music, especially jazz, makes use of augmented seventh chords, which come in two varieties.

Start with **FIGURE 9.9.**

Start with the G augmented triad of (G–B–D♯) and add an F♯. The interval from G to F♯ is a major seventh, so this chord would be called an augmented major seventh. For short, you see the symbol G+(maj7) or Gaug(maj7).

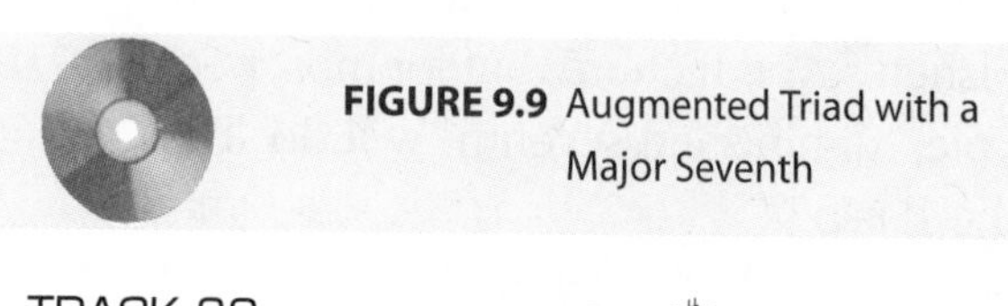

FIGURE 9.9 Augmented Triad with a Major Seventh

TRACK 39

Gmaj7♯5

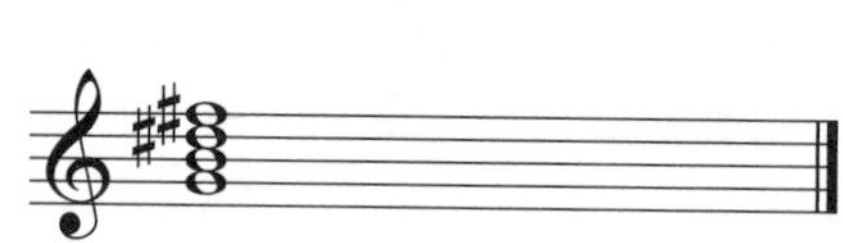

If you wanted to derive a formula for this chord, it would look like this: 1, 3, ♯5, 7 (if you derive this from the degrees of a major scale).

This chord does not occur in natural major or minor scales, but you can find it on the third degree (submedian) of the harmonized harmonic and melodic minor scales. It's a very strong musical sound and it's used in modern jazz quite a bit as well as late romantic and twentieth-century music.

The other augmented chord is shown in **FIGURE 9.10.**

We start again with the G augmented triad and add the note F. The interval from G to F is a minor seventh, so the full name for this chord would be an augmented minor seventh. Typically, you'll see this shortened to G+7, Gaug7, or G7♯5—all are synonymous. The G+7 chord is closely related to a G7 chord. The

FIGURE 9.10 Augmented Triad with a Minor Seventh

TRACK 40

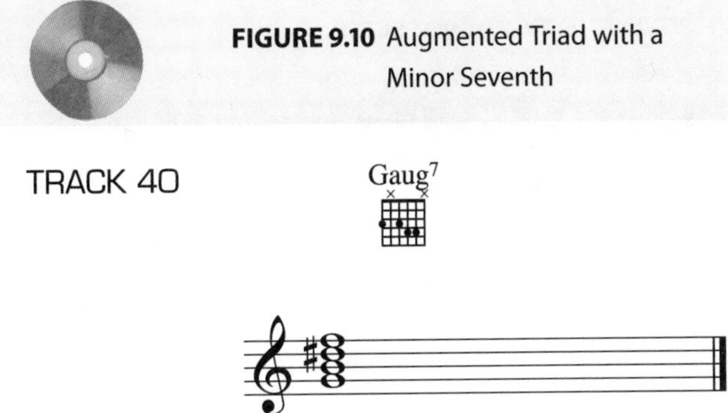

augmented nature of the raised fifth is simply seen as an alteration. Typically, when you see this chord, it functions much the same way that a dominant V chord does. More in the next chapters on usage.

If you wanted to see the formula for this chord, it would look like this: 1, 3, ♯5, ♭7 (if you derive the formula from major scale degrees).

Well, as far as seventh chords go, that's all you have! As you will see from the music looked at later in the book, out of the eight chords, you typically see four or five of these chords in everyday usage, but if you want to understand everything there is to know about chords and how they are formed, then you'll want to at least understand how to form them from their intervallic relationships.

Seventh Chord Recap

You just spent a fair amount of time going over all eight seventh chords, so it would be a good idea to codify all that information into one section where you can see all the chords from the same root and, also, all the formulas side by side. First up is a chart of every possible seventh chord from the root of C in notation.

FIGURE 9.11 All Possible Seventh Chords from C

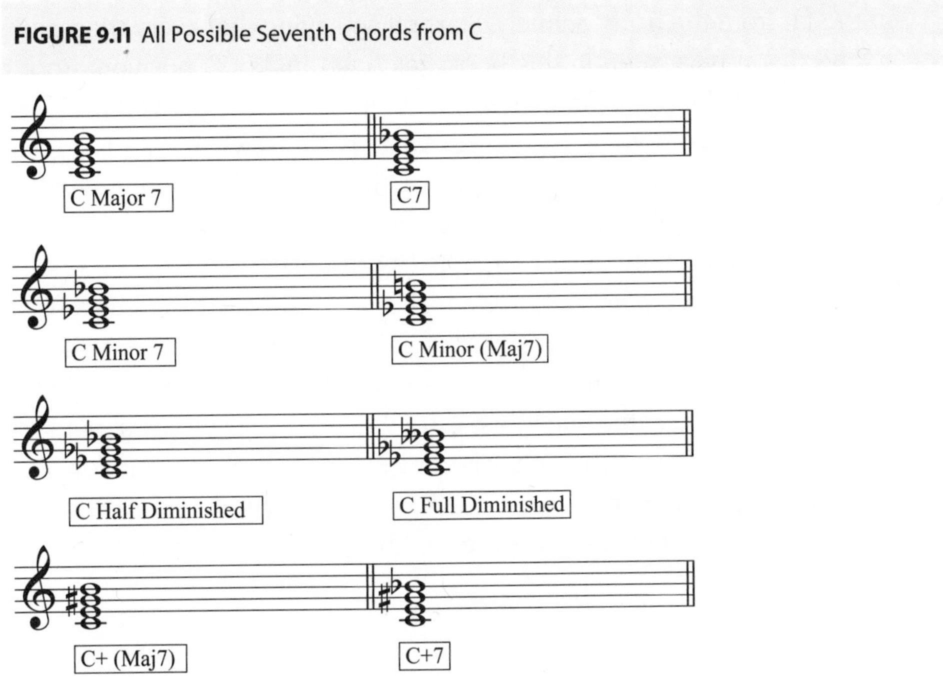

Now, look at all the formulas as derived from a major scale.

Formulas Derived from a Major Scale
Major Seventh—CMaj7: 1, 3, 5, 7
Dominant Seventh—C7: 1, 3, 5, ♭7
Minor Seventh—CMin7: 1, ♭3, 5, ♭7
Minor/Major Seventh—CMin(Maj7): 1, ♭3, 5, 7
Half Diminished Seven—Cø: 1, ♭3, ♭5, ♭7
Fully Diminished Seven—C°7: 1, ♭3, ♭5, ♭♭7
Augmented Major Seventh—C+(Maj7): 1, 3, ♯5, 7
Augmented Seventh—C+7: 1, 3, ♯5, ♭7

You have almost completed your understanding of chords! Now, you will learn about chord inversions.

Inverted Chords

When you think of the word *inverted,* what comes to mind? Most people think "upside down" or "backward." When it comes to inverted chords, this is not too far from the truth, actually. Start off by saying that every triad and seventh chord you have seen in this book has been in "root" position. Root position means that the root of the chord (the tone its name is derived from) is the lowest note in the chord. Now, there are a lot of times when chords appear in root position; however, it's not the only way that chords function. Any other note in the chord can take the lowest voice, and that is exactly what an inversion is: when the third, fifth, or seventh note (if present) is in the bass voice.

Inversions can make chords a bit harder to spot on paper because you lose that wonderful "third order" that you get used to when you start to memorize the triad names. Regardless, inverted chords are found in all styles of music throughout almost the entire history of written music, so you should know a lot about them. With inverted chords comes a new set of symbols you also have to learn when you analyze music. Start with triads and their inversions and then move on to seventh chords as they are treated a bit differently.

Inverted Triads

Okay, start off with your friend, your old pal, the root position C Major triad. By now, you should be able to identify this chord quickly as a root position C triad. If you were to go a step further and analyze it with a Roman numeral, you would give it the Roman numeral I, because in the key of C, C is the tonic or I chord!

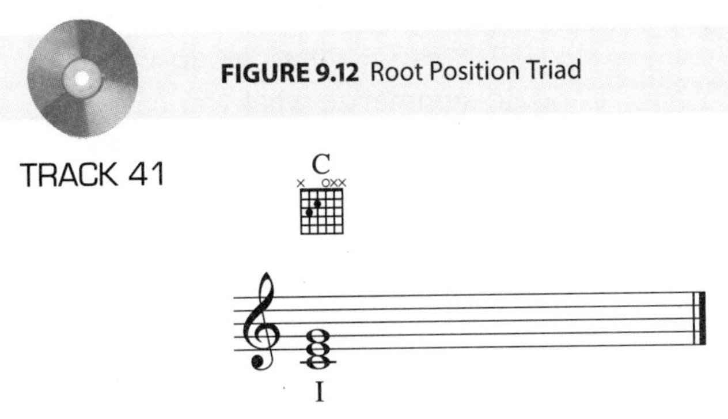

FIGURE 9.12 Root Position Triad

TRACK 41

Now, if you want to start inverting this triad, all you have to do is raise the bass note (which is C) one octave. The result is **FIGURE 9.13**.

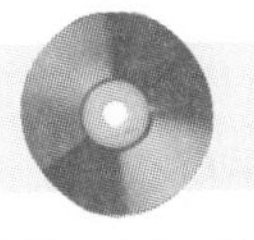

FIGURE 9.13 First Inversion C Triad

TRACK 42

With the C raised up an octave, the third of the chord (E) takes the place as the lowest-sounding note in the chord. Whenever the third of the chord is in the bass (the lowest-sounding voice), that triad is said to be in first inversion. Now, in terms of naming this chord, there are two ways: the classical way and the modern way. You will be given both.

The classical way of naming this triad would be to call it a I_6. Why is it called a I_6? If you look at the interval between the lowest note in the chord (E) to the C, the interval is a sixth, so that's where the six comes from. If you're wondering why the interval from the E to the G is disregarded, it's because it's a third and it's accepted that you'd have a third. It's just the way it's evolved.

When analyzing this chord in classical style, every first inversion chord will have a small 6 subscripted next to its Roman numeral. This is true no matter what kind of triad it is; major, minor, diminished, and augmented in first inversion are all "6" chords. It also doesn't matter which Roman numeral they are functioning as. All seven chords in the harmonized scale can be in first inversion with the marking of a subscripted 6.

Now, as to the modern notation, this one is easy: The triad is simply called C/E, which translates to C chord with an E in the bass. The slash (/) is commonly referred to as "over," as in "triad over bass note." Regardless of which is easier, it's really good to know both—if you want to learn traditional theory at some point, you'll need to know these figured bass symbols. On to the next inversion!

Remember how the first inversion was made? You simply took the lowest note and popped it up one octave. Well, to get to a second inversion, you are going to do exactly the same thing. This time, you start with a first inversion triad and move the E up an octave. The result is shown in **FIGURE 9.14**.

TRACK 43

FIGURE 9.14 Second Inversion C Triad

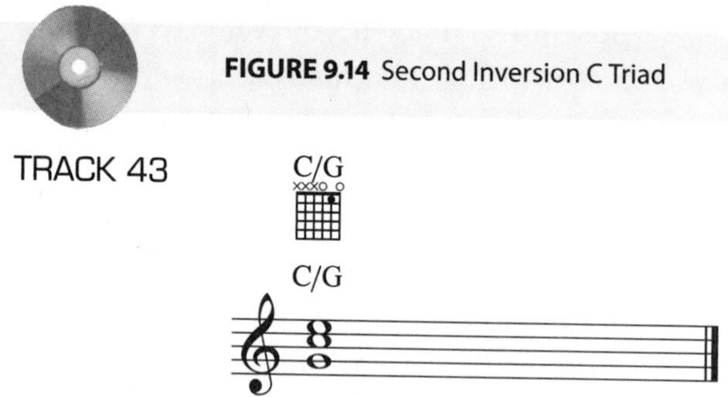

That wasn't so hard to do was it? So, to summarize what you have now: You still have a C triad and the notes C–E–G—those elements never change; what has changed is that the lowest note in the chord is now the fifth of the chord (G). Whenever the fifth of the chord is in the bass of any triad, it becomes a second inversion triad.

The classical way of naming this triad would be to call it a I_4^6. It's a I_4^6 triad because the intervals from the lowest note (G) are as follows: G to E is a sixth and G to C is a fourth, so that's where $^6_4$ comes from.

IN TIME

In baroque times, harpsichordists read inverted chords written as "figured bass." Figured bass was basically a bass note and a bunch of numbers under the notes. The player would know based on the numbers present what chord to play and in what inversion—this is very much like the modern jazz guitarist or pianist who reads off a lead sheet.

A modern musician would see that chord as C/G, which is defined as a C triad with G as its lowest note.

Since triads have only three notes, you are all out of inversions!

To recap:

- If a chord is in root position, no further action is necessary.
- If a chord is in first inversion (the third of the chord is in the bass), it would be called a I_6 or C/E (depending on the triad; C is just an example).
- If a chord is in second inversion (the fifth of the chord is in the bass), it would be called a I_4^6 or C/G (if C triads are used as examples).
- Any triad, regardless of its type—major, minor, augmented, or diminished—can be inverted.

- Every chord in the harmonized scale can be inverted, so every Roman numeral from I to VII can be inverted using the figured bass symbols for first and second inversion.
- If you see a Roman numeral with nothing after it, it is in root position.

Now, on to seventh chords, which invert the same way, except they have one more note in them and that changes how they are named.

Inverted Seventh Chords

In theory, inverted seventh chords are no different from the inversion you just learned about with triadic inversions. The only difference is that for starters, a seventh chord has one extra note, so you get one more possible inversion: the third inversion. The other difference is that the classical music theory figurations that name the inversions are completely different for seventh chords. Other than that, the same rules apply, and you can shoot through these pretty quickly.

You're going to use the G7 (G–B–D–F) chord in our example in the key of C, so this chord would function as a dominant, or V, chord.

In root position, nothing changes, so there's nothing to show, it's simply G7 or V.

The first inversion of a G7 chord moves the G up an octave, placing the B in the lowest voice. This inversion is specified with the symbol V^6_5. You could also call this chord G7/B, or G seventh with B in the bass.

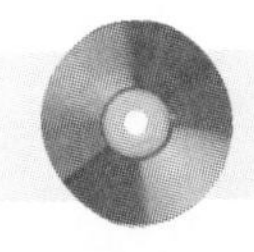

FIGURE 9.15 First Inversion G7 Chord

TRACK 44

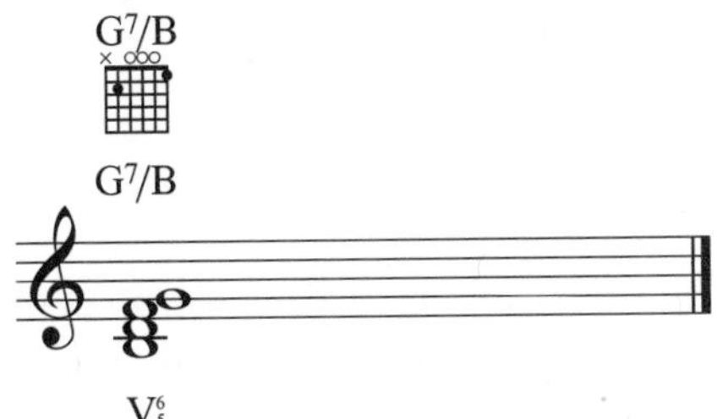

The $^6_5$ may seem confusing, but it's not really; there is a sixth from B to G and a fifth from B to F, so that's where the figuration came from.

The second inversion would put the B up an octave, leaving the D as the note in the bass.

The inversion is specified as a V^4_3 chord.

The fourth is from D to G and the third from D to F.

This chord could also be called G7/D, or G seventh with D in the bass.

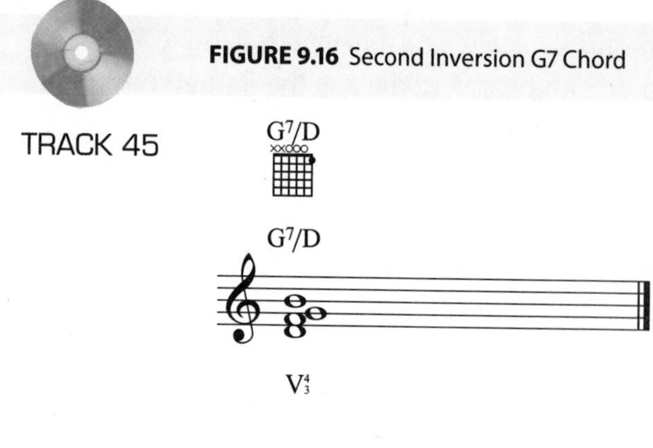

FIGURE 9.16 Second Inversion G7 Chord

The third inversion of a G7 chord places the D up an octave, leaving the seventh of the chord, F, in the bass. The figuration of this chord is called a V_2 chord. The 2 is simply there because the interval from F to G is a second (since everything else in the chord is thirds, you don't need to list them).

This chord could also be called G7/F, or simply G seventh with F in the bass.

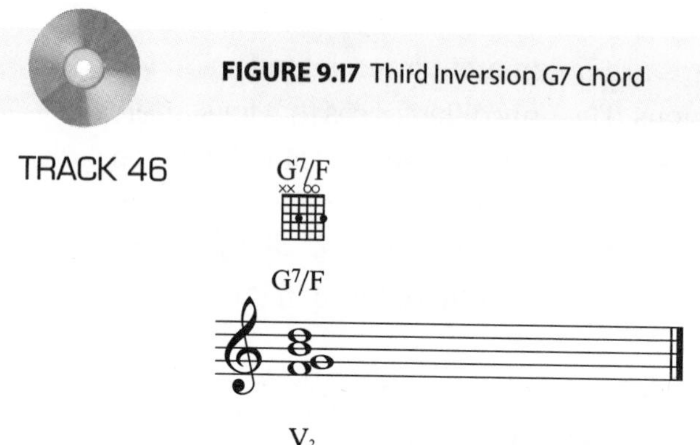

FIGURE 9.17 Third Inversion G7 Chord

Point to Consider

Here's an easy way to remember the inversion figurations of a seventh chord. Start with $^6_5$ for a first inversion, $^4_3$ for a second inversion, and 2 for the third inversion. The numbers simply descend from 6: 65-43-2. That's easy to remember, right?

To recap Seventh Chords:

- If a seventh chord is in root position, no further action is necessary.
- If a seventh chord is in first inversion (the third of the chord is in the bass), it would be called a V^6_5 or G/B (depending on the chord; G is just an example).
- If a seventh chord is in second inversion (the fifth of the chord is in the bass), it would be called a V^4_3 or G/D (if G is used as an example).
- Any seventh chord, regardless of its type—major, minor, augmented, or diminished—can be inverted.

- Every seventh chord in the harmonized scale can be inverted, so every Roman numeral from I to vii can be inverted using the figured bass symbols for first, second, and third inversion.
- If you see a Roman numeral with nothing after it, it is in root position.

See, that wasn't so bad was it? You're essentially through the basic chords now. Now you'll learn a little bit about why composers use inversions, and then you'll take a look at a brief example from J. S. Bach to see how a master uses inversion.

Why Invert?

Why invert chords? Inverted chords make music more interesting to listen to! Using inversion can help chords move from one to another more smoothly; this is called voice leading. Inversion can also help keep bass lines smooth and musical. Root position triads tend to "bounce" around the musical staff in a very jagged fashion. Inversion enables chords to move smoothly from one to another. Take a look at an example from Bach to see inversions in action.

Just a quick note for those of you who aren't studying traditional theory: in the modern music world, especially the guitar-driven rock world, inversion can be a rarity, although you will see inversions come up from time to time. The Beatles' "While My Guitar Gently Weeps" is a great example of inversion in modern music. The first four chords are simply a tonic minor chord with a descending bass note. Each chord is an inversion of the tonic chord in some way. Leave it to the Beatles to keep things interesting. If you look hard enough, you can find many other examples, such as the second chord of Lynyrd Skynyrd's "Freebird." Keep looking at music and see when inversions happen and what the end result is in the music. In modern music, it's almost always to connect chords and their bass notes in a smoother way. On to Bach!

Quick Study: Bach Prelude in C

Bach was the man. Few will dispute his genius and the impact he had on music. Back in the day, more specifically the baroque era, Bach wrote a set of pieces for solo piano called *The Well-Tempered Clavier.* He wrote a prelude and a fugue in every possible key on the piano, just for fun. He started off with a bang! His Prelude in C Major is really something else, and most of you will recognize it. You're going to look at only the first few chords of this piece (even though the rest of the prelude is full of inversions). Even in just the few first measures, you'll see what inversions are all about—especially seventh chord inversions. Take a look at the example and see what's up.

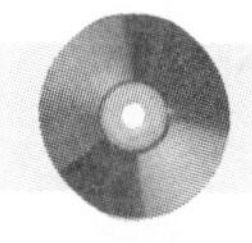

FIGURE 9.18 Prelude in C Excerpt

TRACK 47

Prelude in C

From *The Well Tempered Clavier*

J.S. Bach

Boom! Just in the first few measures, you see a bevy of chords, most of them in inversion! Each measure is simply an arpeggiated chord spread across the piano, so you'll have to take inventory of the notes that happen in each measure to follow along. Look at a blow-by-blow recap of what you see.

Measure One: C major chord (I), root position. No big surprise here.

Measure Two: D minor chord (ii), third inversion! Not a shocking chord, but the inversion allows the C to stay in the bass from the first measure—very smooth.

Measure Three: G7 chord (V) in first inversion. The first inversion allows a B to take the lowest voice. That's only a half step down from the preceding C in the measure before. Again, look how he's connecting these chords.

Measure Four: C major chord (I), root position. The B from the last measure has come back to C. In four measures, with four chords, the bass note has either stayed the same or moved down only one half step.

Measure Five: A minor chord (vi), first inversion. The C stays in the bass because of the inversion!

Measure Six: D7 chord (II—in all fairness, you haven't learned about major II chords, but this one is too good to pass up, major II chords happen from time to time), third inversion. The third inversion keeps the C in the bass yet again!

Measure Seven: G7 chord (V), first inversion. Our C from the preceding three measures has finally moved, but only down to B, one half step!

Measure Eight: C major seventh chord (I), third inversion. The B from the last measure will stay in the bass because of the third inversion of the C major seventh chord. (Give Bach some props here for using a "jazz" chord 200 years before jazz came into existence!)

That's a good place to stop and take inventory. There are a bunch of different chords: C, C Major seventh, D minor seventh, D7th, G7th, and A minor. In eight measures, you went through six different chords, most, if not all, of which were in inversions. What's the result? The result is an abundance of musically interesting chords that move so smoothly from one to another that it almost sounds as if they're molten lava flowing from voice to voice. In those eight measures, our bass note started at C and never went below B! That's only a half step down! Amazing!

You owe it to yourself to check out the rest of the piece. The book stops here because things start to get theoretically complex and Bach introduces chords and concepts you haven't learned yet. By the end of this book, though, you should be able to analyze the rest of the piece with ease. And it's worth looking at—many theorists rely on this piece as a perfect example of common practice harmony in action.

Next up: You get to learn how chords progress from one to another—chord progressions!

Chapter 10

Movements: Chord Progressions

Understanding chords and how they are spelled is only one stage of understanding. Once you can look at a chord and give it a name, you need to look for context. What chord preceded this and what comes after? Are there patterns to look at here? All these questions will be answered in this chapter as you study how chords move from one to another.

What Is a Chord Progression?

Simply put, a chord progression is a movement of chords from one point to another. If you've ever heard a blues song, you've heard a progression of chords! All the pop music from the last 100 years is loaded with chord progressions. If you play guitar or piano, you know all about chord progressions. The trick now is to figure out what they are, why you need to know them, and, more importantly, how this is going to help you.

Chord Stacks

When you studied how to make chords, you looked at the chords a few ways. First, you stacked diatonic notes from the scales and you saw an end result of seven different chords. You also dissected the intervallic properties of every triad and seventh chord in existence. This is one way at looking at chords. But there is another angle to look at. When you talk about chords as being vertical stacks of notes, you essentially are adopting a philosophy that chords are "objects," more specifically, vertical stacks of notes.

The Chicken or the Egg?

When you study a single chord, the concept of vertical stacks works pretty well. As you look back through the development of music, you will see that chords, although they are vertical stacks of notes, are closer to being vertical collisions of voices. What does this mean? Well, imagine that you are not playing guitar or piano and that you are in a choir. There are sopranos, altos, tenors, and bass voices. At the simplest level, there would be one singer per part. Now, if you are in the bass section, singing one note at a time, are you singing chords? No, you're singing a line; a melody, to be more specific. Since one voice can't make a chord, you look at the net result of what all of you are singing. There are four melodies going on at once. Each part is different. Now, if you freeze any single "slice" of vertical time, you could look at all the notes that are sung on the first beat of the first bar and come up with a chord. That would make sense as music should sound rich and consonant, and chords and harmony allow this. Now ask yourself if all the individual lines of music came first, or if the chords were preplanned and the voices simply fleshed out the chords as they went along.

The answer is complicated. It's hard to say for sure because most of the composers are dead, but throughout the development of music, especially classical music, lines ruled and chords were merely afterthoughts.

Put simply: Composers wrote lines of melodies that summed together as chords when you looked up at them (vertical thinking). Since music theory has this wonderful way of looking back on music after it has been composed, it's easy to forget that lines ruled so much of music.

Point to Consider

Chords and melodies are tied together very tightly. When you play a melody, you can almost imagine what harmony is present with that melody. Because of this, it's possible to think melodically and harmonically at the same time. Beyond the theoretical underpinnings of what melody notes fit with which chords, when you listen to a melody, that melody has a way of telling you what chord it wants to have accompany it—all you have to do is listen.

Now?

Is music any different now? Depends who you ask. Do singer/songwriters write in lines? Sure, they sing a melody line, but do the chords they play on their guitar or piano come from that same thinking (linear)? Nowadays, especially in pop music, chords and chord progressions are units that have little to do with the old model. That's not to say that they can't, and that popular music has no voice leading in it, but the largest amount of popular music is simply conceived with chords as blocks of information, and melodies are layered on top of the chords. Now, all of you (the old school and the new school musicians) can learn from each other. Take a look back at history and see what happened.

Progressions in Time

If you use your theory tools, you can look back at any piece of music, new or old, and figure out what chords are used and why. The better question to ask is why. Why did anything happen the way it did? Why did Bach use certain chords and not others? Why did Beethoven and Mozart use similar chords? Were they working from some sort of rule book, so to speak? The answer is no. Harmony developed. Simple as that. Diatonic harmony was a long time in the making. It started with one voice, then a second was added, and so on, and then eventually triads and harmony fell into place. It wasn't until the baroque era that harmony started to solidify into something recognizable. This wasn't because Bach and all of his baroque buddies had a handbook of sorts! The music simply evolved because musicians listened and studied what had come before. They took what they liked and moved forward from there.

Theorists can only look back and try to fit all the music into some set of rules. But this is not always in your best interest. It is worth noting when a certain sequence of chords happens over and over and over again. But trying to figure out why will drive you crazy.

To help you tackle this issue, this book is going to do about 300 years' worth of homework for you, sorting through all the massive amounts of music and coming to some conclusions for you. In the end, you'll see that there are sounds that are associated with feelings, moods, and other things that cannot be quantified with theory. "Amen" can be summarized by playing a IV chord followed by a I chord. Much of music can be summarized this way, but the spark of which chord to use and when is up to you. After you've taken a look at a few examples of some common progressions, the rest of music and composition is up to you to explore. Once you get beyond the basic tools, there are *no* rules. Some of the coolest modern music breaks every rule there is, yet it sounds beautiful. Remember: music first, theory second. In this chapter, you're going to get a bunch of theory; it's up to you in the next chapters to turn the theory into music. It's a good challenge worthy of anyone who loves music enough to study it.

Diatonic Progressions and Solar Harmony

The logical place to begin is with progressions that are purely diatonic (coming from the major or minor scales). Just using the chords from the diatonic major scale can make a lot of music. Take a look at the key of D major and its chords.

FIGURE 10.1 Diatonic Chords in D

If you are in the key of D, any of these chords would be acceptable for use, since they are made up exclusively from notes in the D major scale (just stacked together).

Now, you're looking at seven different chords, some major, some minor, and one diminished. Which ones do you choose and why? Well, first start out with a concept, and then you will explore the chords you see most often.

In any musical key, the tonic, whether it's a note or a chord, carries the most weight and importance. So, you could say that the "one" chord is the center of your universe and you'd be right. In harmony, especially traditional tonal harmony, you pretty much can't escape the fact that the tonic is a point of resolution. Music typically, if not always, comes back to that one chord!

The analogy about the tonic chord being at the center of your universe is going to serve your musical imagination very well. Imagine that the one chord is at the center of the solar system; it's the sun, so to speak. All the other chords rotate around that central chord with different degrees of pull (more on that later). This concept is called "solar" harmony and isn't just something made up for this book; it's actually an accepted way to look at chords. As you will learn, the tonic chord is really important, just like the sun.

Primary Chords

In a major key, there are three "primary" chords, which are the basic chords used to spell out and harmonize the key. The primary chords in any major key are I, IV, and V.

Not coincidentally, all three of the primary chords are major. Now, what can you do with just primary chords? The majority of folk music, sacred music, all of blues, and a good chunk of rock are based on primary chords. Ever heard the phrase "three-chord rock"? Well, those are the three chords. For an illustration, take a look at a song most people are familiar with: "Amazing Grace."

FIGURE 10.2 an example of a lead sheet. For ease of reading, this song was kept in D major. The melody is on top and the chords are listed by symbol only. For the benefit of the guitar players, chord grids were put in. A piano player would have to "realize" the chord voicings on his own, but this does not change the fact that this simple folk melody is properly harmonized with the three primary chords from its home key.

This is the first step to analysis! The key signature tells you D major or B minor, but the existence of D, G, and A chords tells you for sure that you are in the key of D major as those chords—I, IV, and V—are the primary chords for D major.

The primary chords can go a lot further and they are not relegated to pop and folk music. Classical music makes heavy use of primary chords—all tonal music does.

Three chords will get you only so far, so you need to look a bit deeper into the scale to see what you can find to use.

FIGURE 10.2 Primary Chord Study: "Amazing Grace"

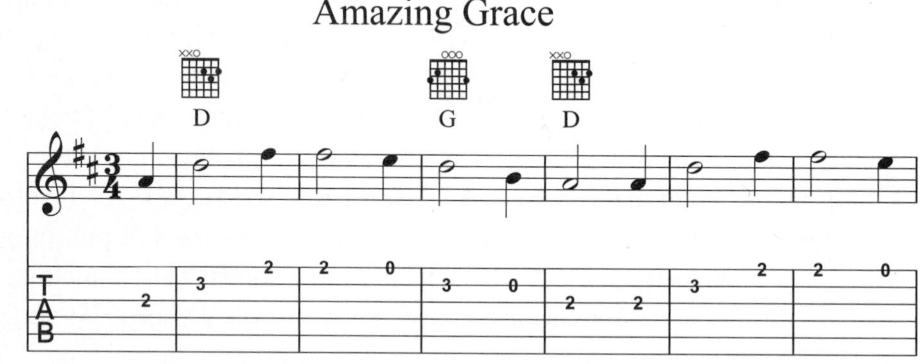

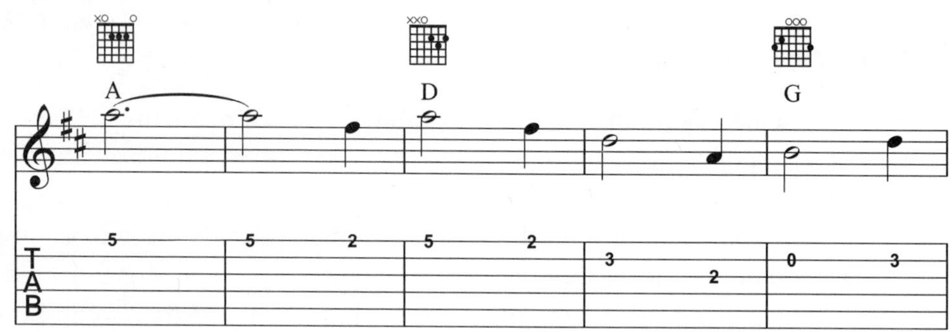

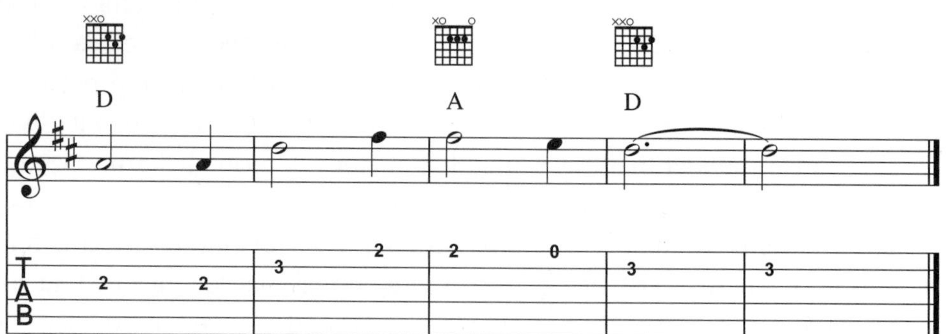

Secondary Chords

The I, IV, and V chords will get you pretty far in music writing and analysis, but you have more options: You have the secondary chords in the key. The secondary chords are the ii, iii, and vi chords in any major key.

As you can see from the lowercase Roman numerals, all three of these chords are minor. Once you know what chords are diatonic to a key just remember that the primary chords are the major ones and the secondary chords are the minor ones!

Point to Consider

But what about the diminished chord? The diminished chord is special and needs to be treated with some care. In general, you find it more in jazz and classical than in pop, although that's not to say it doesn't exist in all styles of music. To learn about the diminished chord, you should look at the solar harmony universe and the chord ladder to see when diminished chords are actually used.

Is music written with only secondary chords? Not often, although if you look for rules, you'll almost always find some rule breakers. What the secondary chords do is embellish the primary chords and give your chord progressions some more variety. Here is an example of a bare chord progression (no melody) with voicings for piano and guitar using both primary and secondary chords in the key of A major.

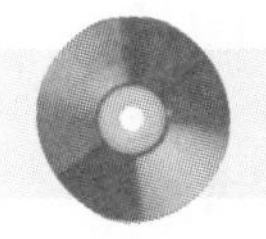

TRACK 48

FIGURE 10.3 Primary and Secondary Chord Progressions

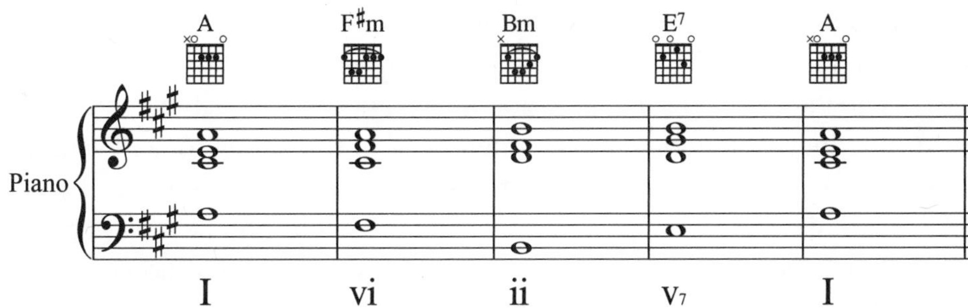

As you can see in the example and hear from the recording, this example flows along well. Only chords that are diatonic to the key of A major are used and while the result may not rock the world of music, it's a nice-sounding chord progression.

The key point here is that chords aren't chosen at random. There are some very nicely established norms when using chords. The first step would be to get a handle on using diatonic chords and writing with them. After you get a handle on diatonic writing, you can explore, through analysis of other music (music you like), exactly how far outside the lines you can color, so to speak.

Now, you're going to learn some typical ways that chords progress from one to another by studying solar harmony and the almighty chord ladder!

Extra Credit

Look at the two examples of chord progressions in this chapter. Notice anything? Well, to start off with, each starts and ends on the tonic chord. The penultimate (second to last) chord was a V chord in each case. Is this merely an accident, or do V chords precede I chords at the end of a progression (also called a cadence)? You'll just have to read on to find out for sure.

Solar Harmony and the Chord Ladder

While there are seven diatonic chords to use, which one to use and why has no steadfast rule to it—no one can tell you how to compose! However, it is possible to look back over the evolution of music and see some trends that are worth studying even if you choose to go off in your own direction and look at chords differently.

Earlier this book touched briefly on solar harmony by stating that the tonic chord is the most important chord in any key and that the other chords circle around it. Now you'll discover what this actually means.

In tonal music, the tonic chord serves two roles: the start and the end. It begins your phrases and ends them. The term *gravity* is hard to explain on paper, but you know it when you drop something on the floor. Musical gravity is such that when you write tonal music, progressions tend to gravitate back to the tonic chord each time. Because phrases tend to want to come to rest and end there, much of music history saw composers work their hardest to prolong the inevitable moment of coming back to the strong tonic. Eventually, tonality in classical music fell out of favor because for too many composers, the strong tonic chord grew increasingly difficult to find new ways to use. Amazingly enough, to this day, tonal music thrives, and harmonic gravity is what gives music its power and beauty.

Here is a really good example of tonal gravity. Make sure to listen or play this example on some instrument right now.

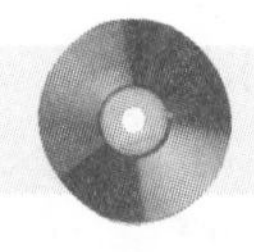

FIGURE 10.4 Musical Torture

TRACK 49

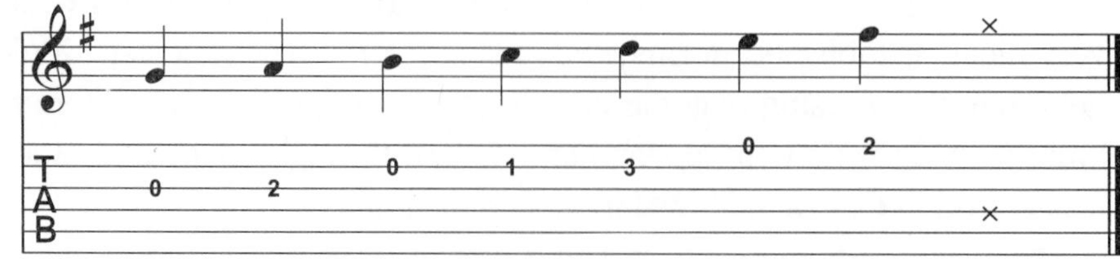

Isn't that brutal? Doesn't that F♯ want to pull up to the G more than you can express? Why does it do that? No one knows for sure, but what you have hit on is exactly what makes melodies and chord progressions move: the inevitable pull back to the tonic note. You saw it with a simple melody; it appears in **FIGURE 10.5** with a single chord voicing:

FIGURE 10.5 More Musical Torture

TRACK 50

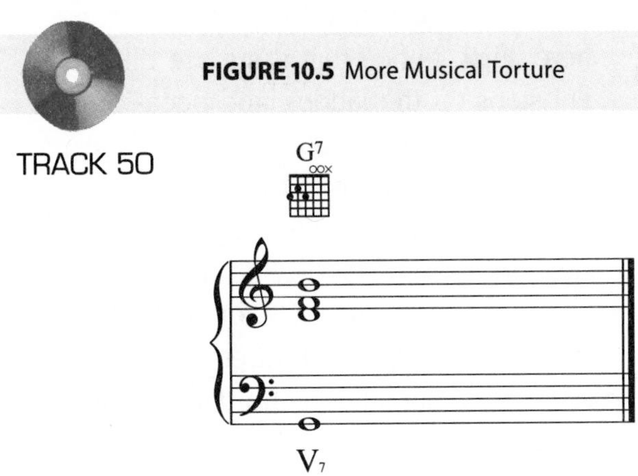

Why is it that this chord refuses to sit still? This chord, a G7 chord, is diatonic to the key of C major. It is the V chord, or dominant chord. In this example, it is a seventh chord. So, why does this chord want to go someplace else? Harmonic gravity. It's not the tonic chord, it's actually one step removed from it; it's the closest chord to tonic (more on that in one second), and it wants to go to tonic. So, here's how it resolves:

FIGURE 10.6 Resolution!

TRACK 51

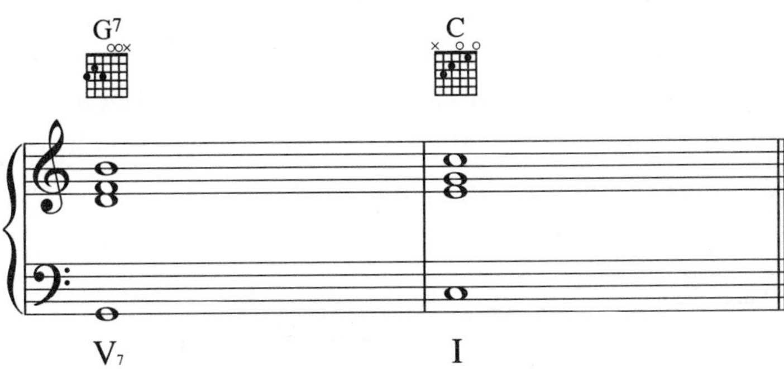

You came back to the tonic, back to the center of the musical system, and finally you have resolution. Tension and release are what make this whole game work.

You've heard about two chords: I and V. Now, look at the rest of the chords and how they align with the tonic chord by looking at the chord ladder.

The Chord Ladder

The chord ladder is a neat little thing that exists to show the relationships among all the diatonic chords in a key. Take a look at the ladder, and then you'll learn more about exactly what it's showing you.

FIGURE 10.7 The Almighty Chord Ladder

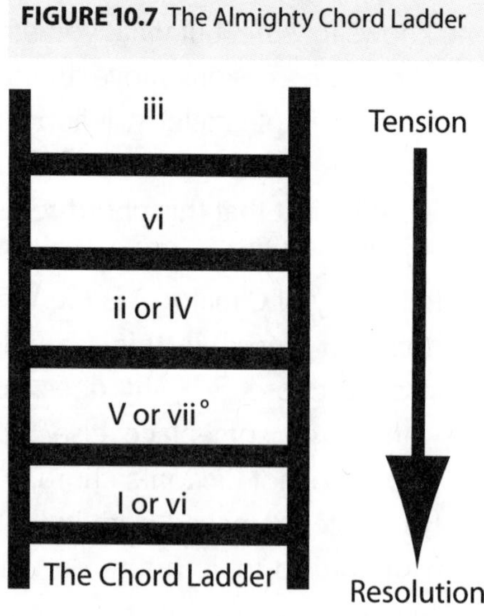

It's a ladder with chords on it! Basically, this ladder is a reference to the "harmonic" gravity mentioned earlier. All the chords in some way fall to the I chord at the end.

There are a few things to look at here. First, notice that there are different steps on the ladder, and occasionally, there is more than one chord on those steps. What does that mean?

When two chords occupy the same step on a chord ladder, it means that the chords can substitute for each other. Before you go any further, you need to know what makes a chord substitute for another chord.

Chord Substitutions

If you look at the first step of the chord ladder, you see the I (tonic) chord and a very small vi chord on the final step. They occupy the same step because both chords can substitute for each other. They can do this because they share common tones; more specifically, they share two-thirds of their tones. In the key of C major, I and vi share the following tones:

FIGURE 10.8 Shared Tones

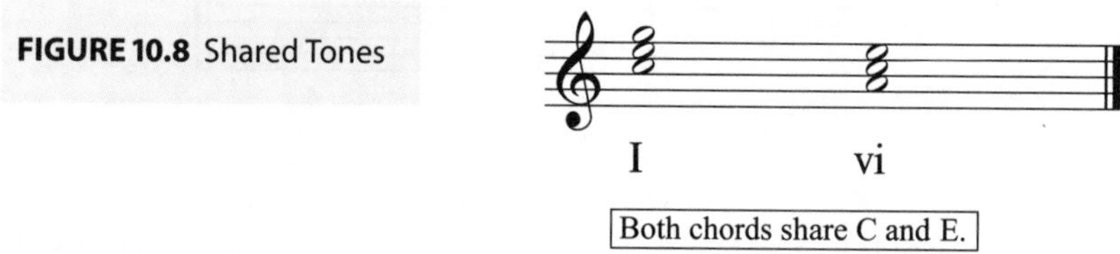

On every step of the ladder, when you find two chords that occupy the same place, it's because they can substitute for each other due to sharing of tones.

Ladder of Fifths

You've seen a circle of fifths, but a ladder of fifths? Many, many chord progressions are based on movements of fifths. So, take a look at the chord ladder without the extra chords and view it as strictly fifth-based movements from the tonic chord up.

FIGURE 10.9 Chord Ladder in Fifths

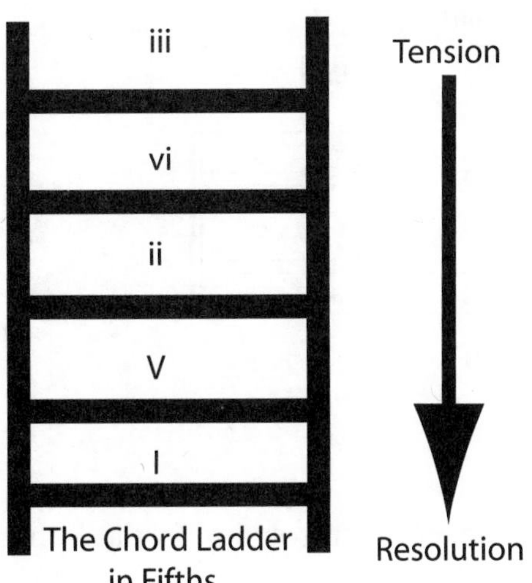

You end up with a progression of iii, vi, ii, V, I. Look at that for piano and guitar in **FIGURE 10.10**:

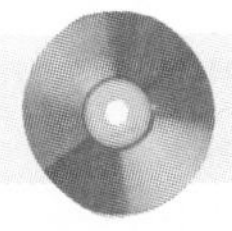

TRACK 52

FIGURE 10.10 Full Fifths Progressions

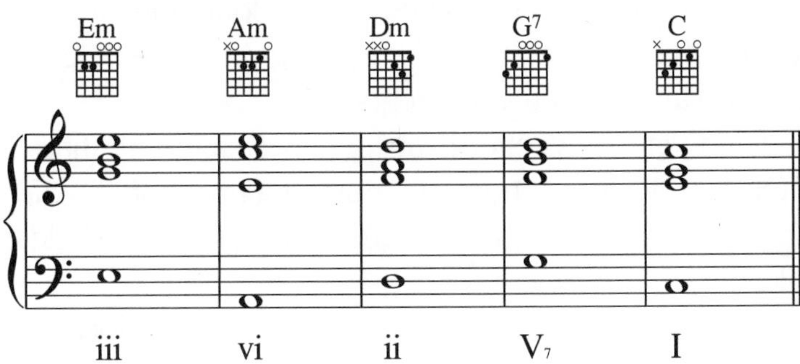

This example sounds fine doesn't it? Sure does!

The next thing to do would be to start to throw in some of the substitute chords. See what replacing the ii with a IV and the V with a vii° chord look and sound like.

You get a nice-sounding progression! Unfortunately, no matter how you slice any of these progressions and no matter how crafty you are, when you get to the V (or its substitute, the vii° chord), you pull back to I. Or do you? Remember the small vi chord next to I on the chord ladder!

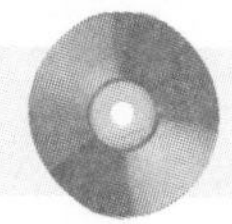

FIGURE 10.11 Use Some Substitute Chords

TRACK 53

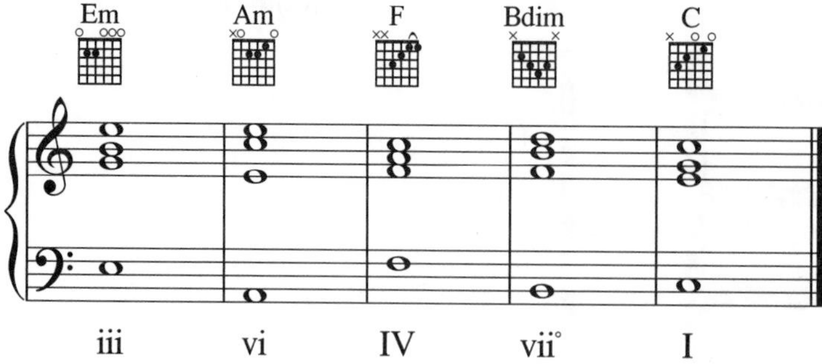

Deceptive Resolutions

The small vi chord is there as a deceptive resolution to the I chord. You essentially break the pattern that V has to resolve to I by allowing V to resolve to vi. It's called a deceptive cadence.

Here's what so neat about the progression: Just when you think you're going to cadence back to I and essentially end the progression, the music pulls a fake out and gives you a vi chord. What this does is it prolongs the progression as it sets you back a bunch of steps on the ladder, giving you more time to keep the musical phrase alive and continue the progression.

If you wondered why the vi chord was in very small print, that's because while it substitutes for the tonic chord, it's more of a transport, magically linking you back to the real vi chord on the chord ladder. Maybe the ladder should have looked like this:

FIGURE 10.12 Chord Ladder Warp!

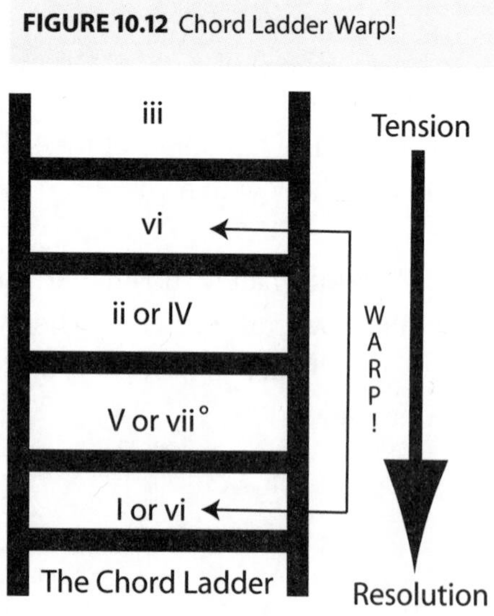

The chord ladder does not dictate what you should or should not use when writing music. It is simply a number of choices that will work well together. You don't have to adhere to it at all. What the ladder shows is a summation of how chords "typically" progress in diatonic situations. Feel free to use it as a starting point and go your own way from there.

Chapter 11

More Chord Progressions

The next thing to do is actually spell out some very common progressions, look at how the minor scale differs from the major scale, and once and for all explain exactly why V pulls to the I chord so heavily each time it comes around. Now you will look at the norms and figure out creative ways to go beyond them. Chord progressions and harmony comprise a vast subject and you have only started to scratch the surface. Other chords and scales exist and yield great possibilities for analysis and composition.

Tonic and Dominant Relationships

Before you get into other chords or any other information, the first thing you want to do to strengthen your understanding of chord progressions is to really understand the relationship between tonic and dominant chords; especially the dominant seventh and the diminished chord that often substitutes for it.

In the last chapter you saw just how strong a pull the leading tone really could have by playing a scale and stopping on the leading tone—leaving the scale yearning to resolve. You also played a single dominant seventh chord and let it hang out to dry, so to speak. Both the dominant seventh chord and the leading tone simply felt unresolved. In the case of the leading tone, you achieved resolution by completing the scale, playing the full scale and concluding on the tonic note. When it came to the chord, you had to play another chord after it to resolve it. The fact that the dominant seventh chord was acting as a V_7 chord was solidified by its resolution to a I, or tonic, chord.

So, here it goes: Harmonically speaking, the existence of a V_7 and a I (or i) chord indicates that you are in the key of the tonic chord. That's all you need when it comes to harmony to define what a key is.

It has always been a challenge to define clearly what a key is, but in tonal music, and especially the common practice period that music theory so often studies, the tonic dominant relationship is what you search for to identify exactly what key you are in.

Now, look at what makes a dominant chord pull so strongly to the tonic chord.

Voices in Motion

If you want to get to the heart of the matter, the relationship between V and I is all about tension and release. You know, yin and yang and all that good balance stuff. V chords, especially when they have sevenths and even more when they are substituted by vii (diminished) chords, are extremely tense. The tension lies in the chord itself.

Look at the V_7 chord and see what you have.

FIGURE 11.1 Dominant Seventh Chord Exposed!

TRACK 54

Stay in the key of C major to keep it simple. The G7 chord shown in **FIGURE 11.1** contains the following tones: G, B, D, and F. Now, go back and remember what you learned about leading tones. Remember how strong those little buggers are? In the key of C, the leading tone is the seventh degree of the scale, which happens to be a B. Guess what? The G7 chord has that note in it. And within the C scale, there exists another leading tone of sorts. Between the fourth and third degree is another half step. When you stop on the fourth degree of the scale (F), it pulls down to E fairly heavily. It's nowhere near as dramatic as the pull from B to C, but it is there. Check it out:

FIGURE 11.2 The Pull from 4 to 3

TRACK 55

In that example, you heard a full scale, which went up to the fourth above the octave (which still counts as the fourth). Again, the note does not want to stay there; it has gravity of its own and pulls back down to the third of the scale. In a V_7 chord, you have the other leading tone (F). So, in one chord, you have the two unstable tones played together at the same time—no wonder it sounds tense! But wait, there's more, You can go one step further into this chord. Since B and F have been identified as your tension notes within the dominant chord, look at the interval that they produce.

FIGURE 11.3 B and F

TRACK 56

By taking these notes out of the chord and playing them together, you get an even better sense of what's going on. The interval from B to F is a tritone, which is the most unstable and dissonant interval you would deal with on most normal days. So, not only does the V_7 chord contain both leading tones (the fourth and seventh of the scale), but the interval created between those tones is a tritone (another unstable sound). This chord is clearly waiting to do something.

The B and the F need to resolve. The B wants to go up to C. The F wants to move down to E. You already have a G, in the G7 chord, so it doesn't need to move. Right there, you spelled the resolution of V_7 to I. The D in the G7 chord can resolve to either C or E in the C chord. Either way you slice it, the third of the G7 chord must go up and the seventh of the G7 chord must go down.

TRACK 57

FIGURE 11.4 A Good Resolution

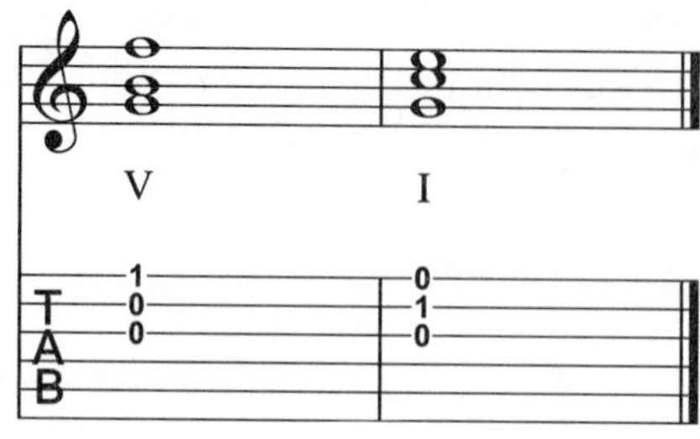

That's it folks, nothing more to see here. If you can grab on to this, you will understand tonality. The relationship between V and I is the cornerstone of tonal harmony. Sure, there is music that doesn't make heavy use of it, but you'll see more dominant to tonic chords than you will know what to do with once you learn to see them.

The diminished chord in the major scale (vii°) often substitutes for V. It has a "dominant function" because it also pulls very strongly to I. The vii° chord contains both the leading tones discussed earlier, and if spelled as a fully diminished seventh, it adds an additional leading tone (the lowered sixth of the scale), which pulls down to a note in the tonic chord. This is why V and vii° can substitute for each other.

Now that you have that figured out, it's time to talk about minor keys and their chord progressions.

Point to Consider

One of the reasons that the relationship between dominant and tonic chords is so important is that if you inventory the tones between both of the chords, you essentially spell the entire scale out (well, almost entirely). The C and G7 chords combine to give us C–D–E–F–G–B–C (a C major scale, excluding A). That's exactly why two chords tell you what key you're in; they spell it out for you with their tones.

Minor Chord Progressions

Minor scales come directly from major scales. With that fact restated, it makes sense that when you create diatonic triads, you'll have the same triads you had with the major scale—the only difference is that the Roman numerals will change position.

Look at a diatonic B minor scale, harmonized into triads.

FIGURE 11.5 Diatonic B Minor Triads

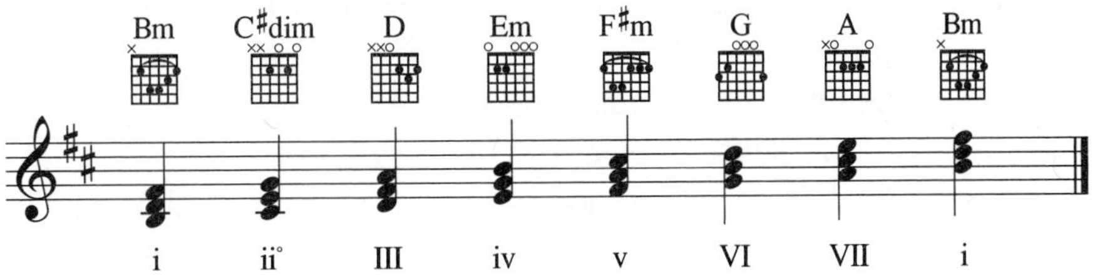

Bm
C♯dim
D
Em
F♯m
G
A
Bm
i
ii°
III
iv
v
VI
VII
i

Now, if you compare this with the related major key of D major, you see the same triads, just in a different order.

FIGURE 11.6 Diatonic D Major Triads

D
Em
F♯m
G
A
Bm
C♯dim
D
I
ii
iii
IV
V
vi
vii°
I

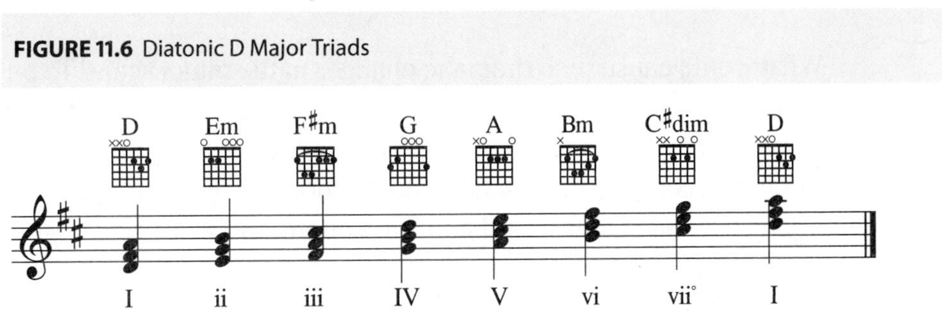

Now, when it comes to the chord ladder, the minor key doesn't look all that different from the major version of the chord ladder.

FIGURE 11.7 Minor Chord Ladder

III
VI
ii° or iv
V or vii°
i or VI
The Chord Ladder (Minor)
Tension
Resolution

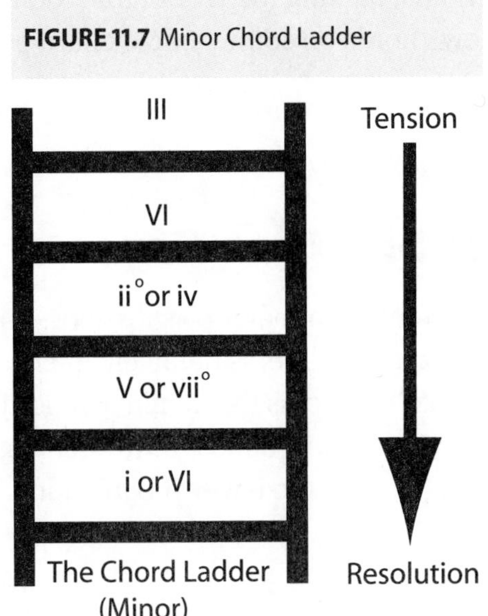

You will notice a few things:

- The ladder progresses in movements of fifths, just like the major chord ladder.
- The substitute chords always share two notes in common with their possible substitutions.
- The V and vii° chords look funny. "The V and vii° chords look funny"? Well, if you compare them to the diatonic triads in **FIGURE 11.5**, you see two main differences:
- The V chord has been changed from a minor triad to a major triad.
- The vii° chord has not only changed from a major triad to a diminished triad, but its root has also moved up one half step.

What would cause such dramatic changes in the minor scale? To put it simply, it's not the same scale (the "natural" minor scale). When you harmonize in minor keys, 99.9 percent of the time, you use the harmonic minor scale as it gives you a major (and dominant seventh) chord on V and a fully diminished chord on vii° (which creates a diminished chord on the leading tone and substitutes for V_7).

We discussed how important the relationship between V and I was at the beginning of this chapter. The relationship is just as important in the minor scale. The natural minor scale does not have the proper V chord (diatonically, it's minor), and the ♭VII chord does not substitute or pull up to the tonic either. So you simply add a raised leading tone to the scale (raised seventh tone), which affects the V and vii° chords, making them both true "dominant" chords. Look at the effect of these new chords on some sample chord progressions in minor keys.

Using Dominant Chords in Minor Keys

Minor key progressions aren't that different from major progressions. You still see lots of movements in fifths and the chord ladder is definitely in effect, but the one thing that you need to really watch out for is the dominant chord functions. As explained above, V and vii° chords are almost always changed in minor keys. Take a look at a simple progression: the i–iv–v progression.

FIGURE 11.8 i–iv–v–i Progression

TRACK 58

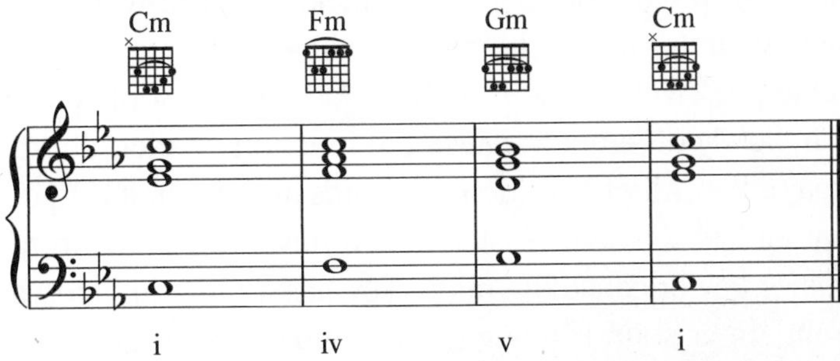

What's wrong here? Well, listen to it. What's missing? You have a common progression, the i–iv–v, and it works on your chord ladder, but something sounds off. The quality of the v chord didn't change. Because it's a minor chord, it simply doesn't have that "gravity" that is expected from the V chord (which should be about as strong a chord as they come). If you simply change the V to a major chord, things get a whole lot better; just listen.

FIGURE 11.9 i–iv–V–i Progression

TRACK 59

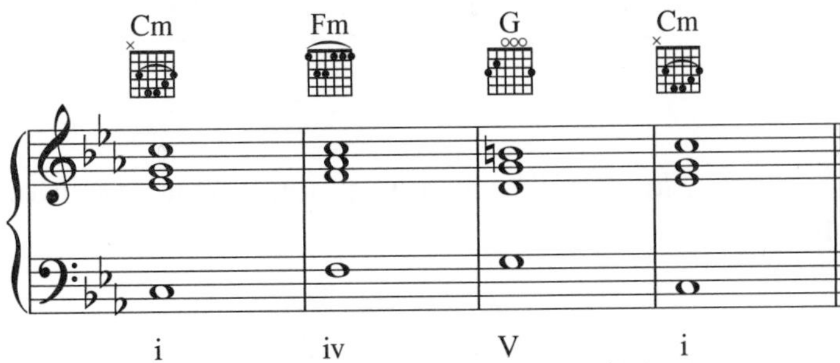

OK, now it sounds better. You always have the option of adding a seventh to the V chord for even more pull, which you can do easily.

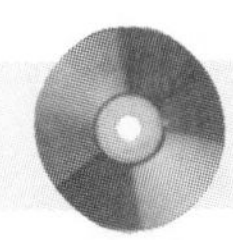

FIGURE 11.10 i–iv–V7–i Progression

TRACK 60

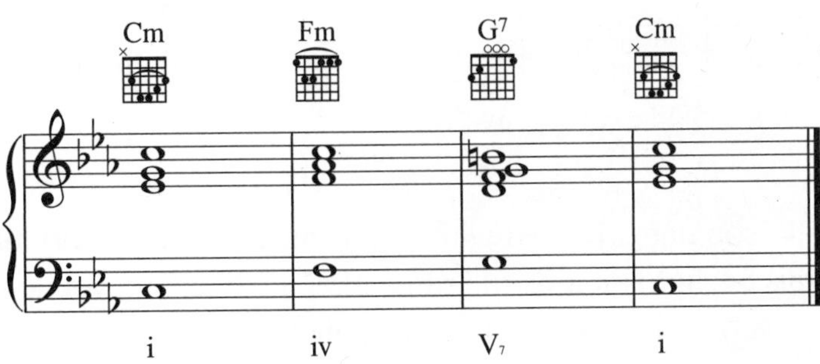

Functionally, both progressions "work," but the added seventh makes things resolve a touch stronger.

Any of the chord progressions from the major key will work well, and as long as you mind your dominant chords, all will be cool!

So, what changes? Well, while the chord ladder may look similar, minor keys sound completely different because the function of each chord is different than in a major key. All of a sudden, iv chords are minor and VI chords are major in the minor key. Also, the distance you travel from note to note is different in the minor key because the minor key has a different interval pattern from the root and, thus, sounds different. Take a parallel progression in major and minor to compare just how different they sound. Look at a I, vi, IV, V progression in C major.

TRACK 61

FIGURE 11.11 Diatonic Major Progression: I, vi, IV, V

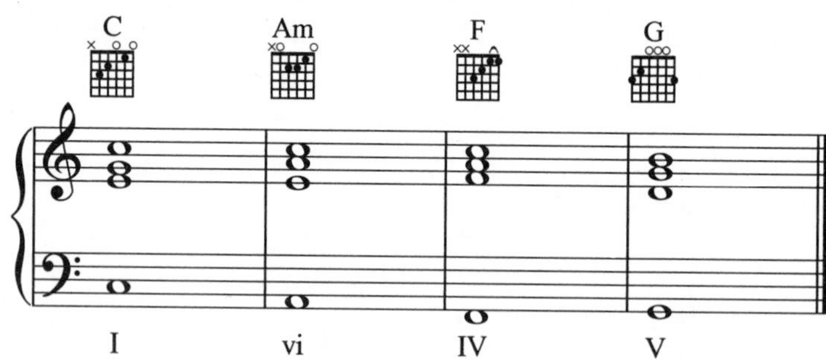

Now, when you transfer this directly to C minor, look at and listen to how much things change!

TRACK 62

FIGURE 11.12 Diatonic Minor Progression: i, ♭VI, iv, V

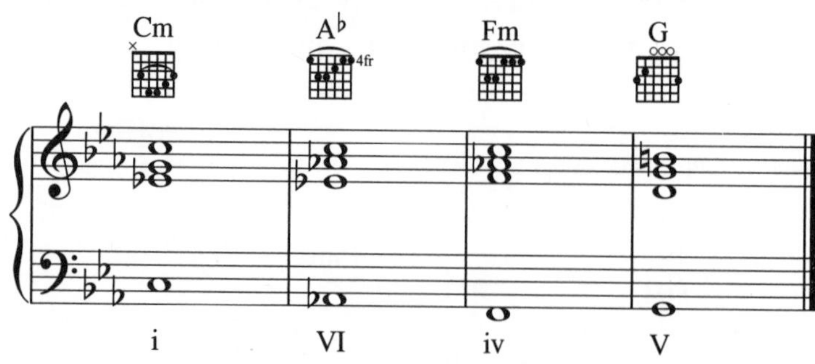

What's the lesson here? To start with, you have to listen to everything. The Roman numerals begin to all look the same after a while, and you can't allow theory to exist solely on paper; it has to come alive.

Now, when it comes to the rest of the progressions, start by mixing and matching chords as you feel appropriate in the keys. Use the accepted ladder of chords as a starting point, but remember that it is by no means a set of rules—far from it! The ladder of chords is a common starting ground. As you start to analyze music on your own, which you will have to as you are not going to get any more examples of chord progressions right now (the music you already have and know holds plenty of information), you will see a great deal of music that uses the chord ladder. Great, you file that music away by how it sounds. Do you like the way it sounds when the scales are used diatonically? It's a very agreeable sound. As you analyze, you will find some music that does not go through the expected set of chords. You may see some huge "rules" broken. You may see chords that simply "don't belong." You can file that away too, because in the end, no one approach will win. The most important thing to ask yourself is, Do I like the sound of what I'm hearing? No matter what your answer is, yes or no, analyze it and figure out what makes it work. If you love it, see if you can adopt some of those movements into your chord progressions. If you hate something, it's also good to see what to avoid in your own writing. Either way you look at it, it's all good, and you will learn the most by looking at as much music as you possibly can. You have a very good set of tools now, and you will continue to strengthen them as you go along, especially in the etude section coming up, where you get not only to analyze but also to create some music of your own based on what you have learned.

Harmonic Rhythm

Another concept that is worth talking about separately is harmonic rhythm. When you study chords and chord progressions as you have to this point, it becomes clear that you are looking at "slices of time" in a very abstract fashion. In certain styles of music, you simply move from chord to chord very quickly, back and forth, repeating as you go. In other styles of music, chords progress very slowly. The pace at which this happens is called harmonic rhythm.

IN TIME

The harmonic rhythm of jazz is typically very fast. Usually, there is at least one chord per measure in most jazz standards. Because chords are improvisational "milestones" for improvisers, they tend to change rapidly. A good counterexample of this is the "modal" jazz of Miles Davis's famous *Kind of Blue* album, which features exactly the opposite: chords that rarely change.

The chord progressions you have studied here thus far have had absolutely no rhythm attached to them because they are examples devoid of music: They are just the raw data. Real music moves in rhythm and so do the chords. So, before you take a simple progression and dismiss it, start playing around with the duration of each chord. Also pay great attention to the music you like and see how often the chords move from one to another. In general, classical music can go either way, either long or drawn out, or very fast. Pop music tends to move at a fairly good clip. It's very hard to generalize; again, you need to look at what you like.

Voice Leading

The term *voice leading* comes up often in discussion of music theory, especially when you talk about chords and chord progressions. Voice leading has two definitions:

1. The art of connecting chord to chord in the smoothest manner possible.
2. A particular practice in music theory that teaches a set of rules for exactly how voices should move from chord to chord; this is almost always taught in four-part writing.

Now, for your purposes, you can concern yourself with the first definition only. Voice leading in the traditional sense is an academic practice that is taught when you study music theory deeply in high school or in college. It's valuable for some things, especially when you consider that all the "rules" are almost exclusively taken from Bach's writing style. Because Bach was such a genius, it's not a bad thing to study. But too many students get very bogged down with all the rules and believe that music has to adhere to them.

Extra Credit

Go back to the last example in Chapter 9 (Bach's Prelude in C) and look at the voice leading from chord to chord, especially the inversions. Better yet, go through the Roman numeral analysis and play them as block chords and listen to how differently they sound. Good voice leading can take a simple chord sequence and transform it into a masterpiece.

The challenge is teaching voice leading in a way that makes sense to everyone. You can allow the academics to teach voice leading their own way; here, you will experience a different approach.

Practical Voice Leading

How can you get practical about this? Well, for starters, chords rarely appear in tightly voiced triads like this:

FIGURE 11.13 A Compact Chord

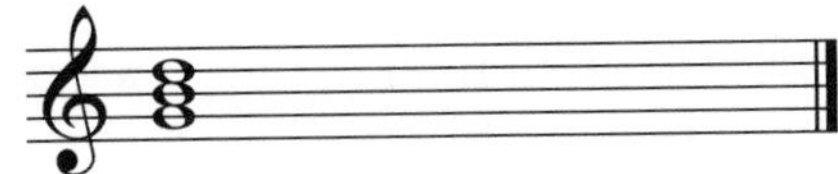

Take this standard guitar chord for example:

FIGURE 11.14 Typical Guitar Voicing

All the voices are fairly spread out. The object of voice leading is to try to smooth the transitions from chord to chord as much as possible.

Here is a simple way of looking at voice leading. In this example, voice leading is intentionally omitted through a ii–V–I progression.

FIGURE 11.15 Bad Voice Leading: Block Chords

TRACK 63

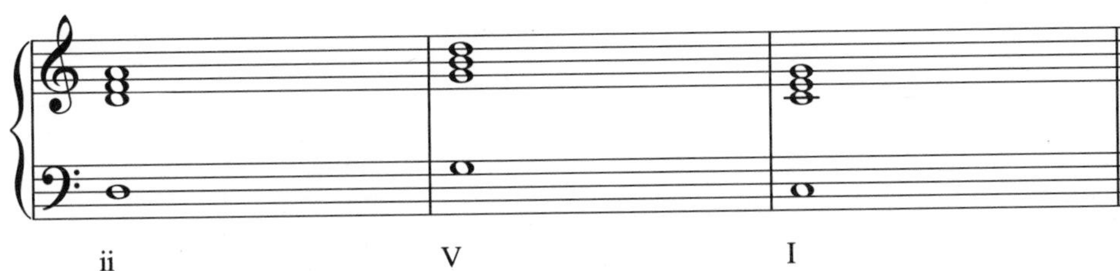

See how all the block chords in the treble staff bounce from one to another? It looks bad and sounds even worse. If you take the following as a mantra, you'll be amazed at the difference in the sound: Wherever you are, get to the closest note in the next chord. Here is the same progression with better voice leading:

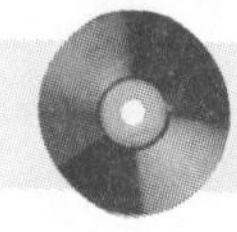

FIGURE 11.16 Better Voice Leading

TRACK 64

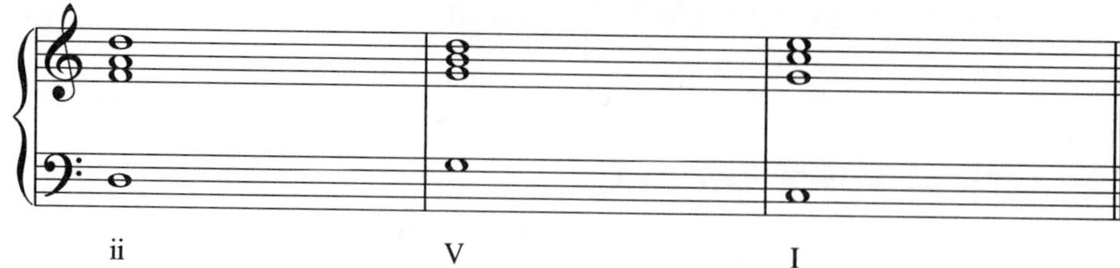

Not only does it look better, it sounds better, too! The chords have more of a flow to them than in the previous example. Always try to connect your chords when you write them. If you remember the premise that chords are not blocks of information but voices that come together, you'll be on the right track. Keep your individual voices moving as smoothly as you can. As you keep learning about how to use chord progressions with inverted chords, your voice leading will only improve.

Chapter 12

Melodic Harmonization

You have read about chords for several chapters, and now it's time to learn about melody. Understanding how chords and melody are related will complete your knowledge of harmony. Chords never exist alone and melodies can't survive without chords to support them. You have learned about scales and how they make melodies. You have learned about chords and their origins. You have studied how chords progress from one to another, but it's time to learn how melody and harmony relate to one another.

What Is Melody?

You have studied so many things in this book so far, yet you have never asked this simple question: What is a melody? Certainly, melody is a very important aspect of music! You have learned about scales, which can lead us to melodies, but never what a melody is.

Well, there is a good reason for not broaching this question—it's really hard to answer. At its simplest, a melody is the "tune" of a song. Just sing "Happy Birthday" to yourself: You just sang the melody. That was easy because that particular song is practically all melody. What is meant by "all melody"? Well, in the case of "Happy Birthday," while you may have some chords behind it, it's not necessary; the tune stands on its own with or without chords. Besides the single line of melody that makes up the tune of "Happy Birthday," there's really nothing else there. Now, for some contrast, listen to a Beethoven symphony and try to sing back what you feel is the melody. You're going to have a harder time doing so because a symphony is not as clear-cut! There are multiple melodies going on at once. You start to see what this section is getting at. So, why go to all this trouble? Well, the relationship between melody and harmony is so crucial to your knowledge that you need to learn to define this as best as you can. No matter how well you understand scales and chords, if you don't understand how they relate to one another, your knowledge will be incomplete.

Supportive Chords

To start to understand the correlation between melody and harmony, use an analogy to view the relationship. Chords are like ladders, supporting melodies. At its simplest, a single melodic tone can be harmonized with a chord as long as the chord has the melodic tone in it.

So, if you are in the key of C major and you have a melody note C and you want to figure out what chord would work with that note, you'd look to the key of C major and its harmonized chords and you'd select a chord that had the note C in it as one of your choices. If you did that, you'd come to these three choices:

FIGURE 12.1 Harmony Choices

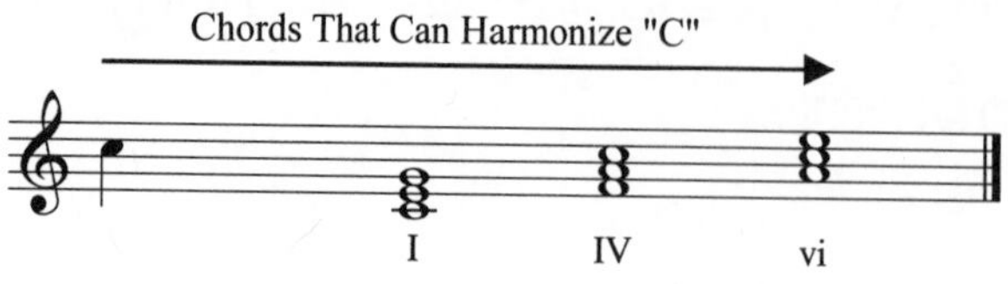

Chords That Can Harmonize "C"

I IV vi

Now, as to which chord you'd choose, that's dependent upon a few things. You could listen to each one and select the one you want. However, you're dealing with one moment frozen in time, and you'd probably want to see the context that this note occurs in throughout the piece, taking into account chords that precede and follow it.

What's important is that you understand that at the most basic level, a single note is supported by a chord that shares the same note. The next chapter will expand on this greatly, but if you ever wondered why "insert any chord here" is being used at any moment in time, look to the melody; it always will be related in some way or another.

When harmonizing single notes, remember that the chord you choose will contain the melody note as either its root, third, or fifth. If you stick with simple triads only, you will always have three choices. Add a seventh chord into the mix and now you have four choices for chords. It's nice to have choices!

Point for Point

As you start this process, you should learn how to harmonize a scale point for point, meaning that each note of the scale would get its own chord. If you realize that each melody note has at least three choices for chords, you come to a staggering number of choices. Rather than list them all, here is an example that works well for your purposes. Instead of choosing random chords, the chord ladder was used as a place to start, and the rest were selected by ear. Here is the result:

FIGURE 12.2 Harmonizing a Scale Point to Point

TRACK 65

Now, that gives you an idea of how to proceed in choosing chords for melodic tones—and dig that groovy flute playing the melody on the CD!

Now, does every melody note get its own chord? Not always. Go back to the example of "Amazing Grace" found earlier in this book and see what's going on.

FIGURE 12.3 "Amazing Grace"

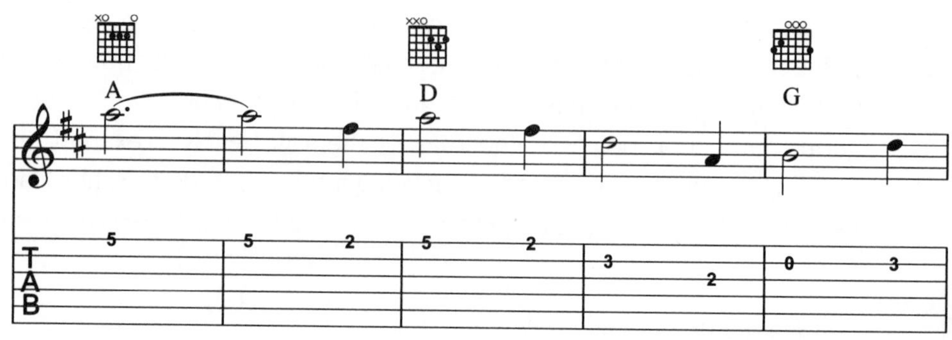

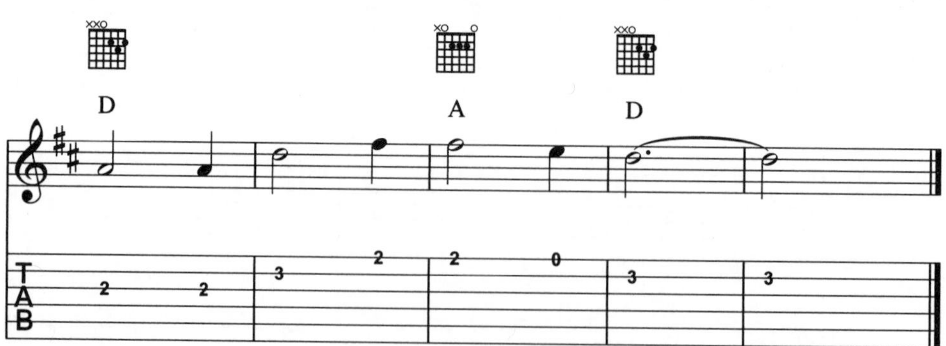

You can see clearly that the harmonic rhythm (the pace at which the chords appear and change) has been slowed down considerably. The truth is that not every note in a melody needs to be harmonized with a chord of its very own. That honestly would be more than overkill!

Extra Credit

Run out to any music store and look at the sheet music to any pop song you like. You will see that 99.9 percent of the time, chords support several melody notes. You'll almost never see a new chord for each melody note unless the melody is very, very slow—at which point the harmony is keeping the song from sounding like a dirge!

Chord Tones and Passing Tones

When you talk about the interaction of chords and melodies, you are talking about one basic point: chord tones or passing (nonharmonic) tones. In **FIGURE 12.2**, you saw each note of the major scale harmonized with its own chord. Since each melody note was found in each chord that supported it, only chord tones were used. In the "Amazing Grace" example, more than just chord tones were used in the harmonization; passing tones were used as well. Now revisit that example and see what's really going on.

FIGURE 12.4 Chord and Nonchord Tones in "Amazing Grace"

The highlights indicate the chord tones; all other notes are passing or nonchord tones.

If you compare the harmony to the melody, you will see many different points of similarity. First off, in general, for a harmony to "work" for any given melody, the majority of the melodic tones should be contained in the chord that supports it. There is no steadfast rule of how many per bar and so on, but for music to sound consonant, the melody needs to line up with the harmony enough times to make you feel like they're in the same key. In the example in **FIGURE 12.4**, you can see chord tones highlighted and the passing/nonchord tones printed normally. A passing tone does not necessarily have to be a tone that moves by step to and from a chord tone, but if you think of the odds, a triad has three notes and a scale has seven, you're most likely using a passing tone as the triad takes three-sevenths of the scale with it and leaves three of the other four tones as passing tones. Only one tone will exist as a true "nonharmonic" tone, but then again, it may sound just fine.

Point to Consider

You're back to thinking vertically again, which is good. It's important to see the effect of harmony against melodies and vice versa. A bit of the chicken-or-the-egg question, which one actually came first. In all your vertical thinking and analysis, don't forget to listen and play each example so that you can hear and not just think about the music. Certain things won't make much sense on paper but will work wonderfully as you listen.

Key Control

One of the nice things about melodic harmonization is your ability to set up the keys you'd like to use. When looking at a single-note melody, it's almost impossible to tell whether you're in a major or a minor key unless you have some harmony to support it. When you start with just a melody, you can control the mood of the piece by choosing either the major or the related minor key. Since any melodic tone can be taken by at least three different chords, you can control your keys very closely.

Here is a very simple example, using a key signature of no sharps and no flats, which could be either C major or A minor. The example uses a whole-note melody over a few bars. Look at the melody by itself:

FIGURE 12.5 Basic Melody

TRACK 66

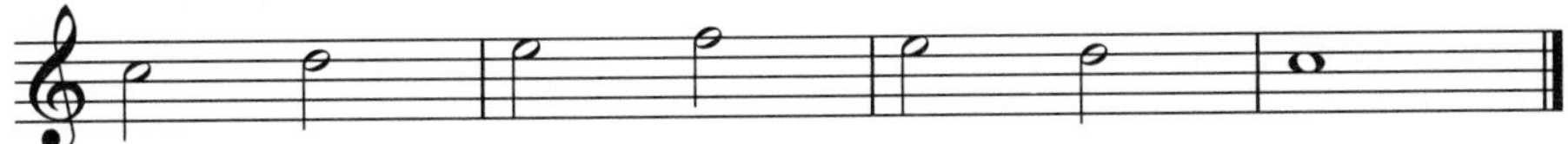

Now, while a melody could go either way keywise, there is one thing that could sway it to the minor key. Remember the leading tone? In the key of A minor, the G♯ is a telltale sign that you are in the key of A minor. The melody carefully stayed away from that—completely on purpose—as that would have locked you into that key.

Getting back to the example, since the G was avoided, look at how this could be made a C major melody:

FIGURE 12.6 Basic Melody Harmonized in C

TRACK 67

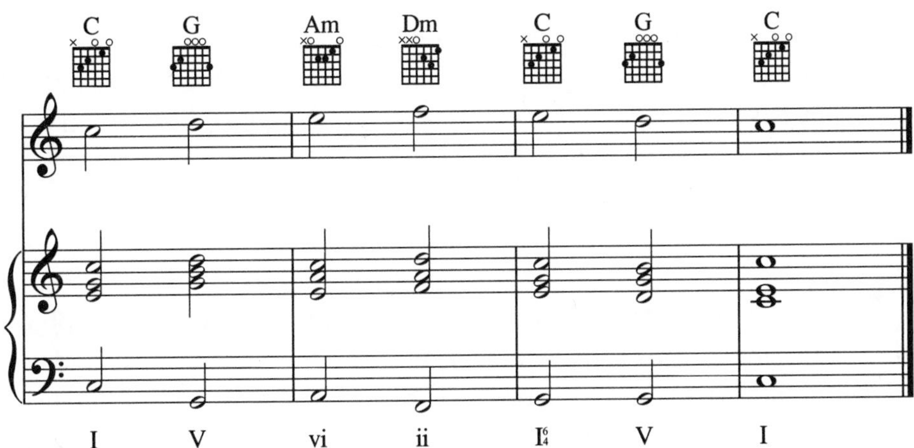

Simply by choosing chords from the key of C, making sure to throw the all-important dominant V chord in, the key of C major is established. There might have been a chord ladder used, but it was more of a process of elimination at a piano or guitar to see what chords fit best with the notes written.

Now, if you want to push this in the direction of A minor, that's easy to do—just use chords from the key of A minor and make sure that it has its own dominant V chord, in this case E7. Here is the result of that:

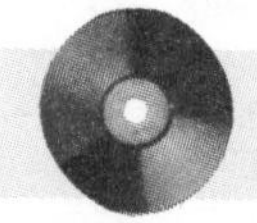

FIGURE 12.7 Same Basic Melody Harmonized in A Minor

TRACK 68

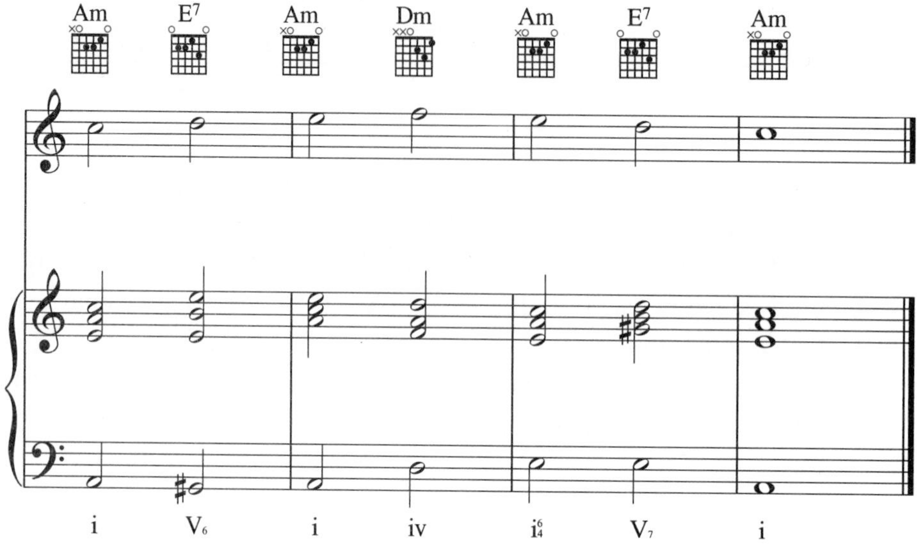

By sticking to A minor chords and typical progressions in that key, it is pretty easy to make this into an A minor melody. Amazing that a simple melody really has to be defined by its chords. This is the general balance that you have to follow: Melodies and harmonies rely on each other. Neither one can exist solely on its own.

Extra Credit

One of the coolest things you can do with harmony is take a phrase of music (like the example above) and harmonize it in one key and then at some other point in the piece, harmonize it in another key. You will take the same melodic material and give it some contrast and another flavor. It will allow you to reuse good material without allowing it to sound stagnant.

True Melodic Harmonization

Move on to another aspect of melodic harmonization, something that doesn't have to do with harmony! Think of a few recent musical acts that use harmony: Simon and Garfunkel, the Indigo Girls, and the Beatles (and others). The harmony referred to here is true melodic harmony: what notes sound consonant with each other. You've no doubt heard some bad attempts at harmony, usually at Christmas parties after a few glasses of eggnog. Someone gets up and tries to sing a second part to "Silent Night" or some other tune. The result is usually less than desirable.

What you'd like to do is have an idea in general of what notes work when harmonizing single line melodies. Historically, this was the evolution of how chords emerged. Gregorian chant started with a single line of music, called monophony. As time went on, a second voice was added. The intervals that were allowed were limited, usually fourths and fifths (hence they are called perfect). Over many hundreds of years, a system of harmony built on thirds, tertian harmony, evolved. Tertian harmony has been the focus of this book as it is the basic formula for harmony. Since *tertian* has as its root "tertiary" or "three," thirds are a great place to start.

One Third Fits All

The first place to look is thirds. Simply put, you can spot harmonize any melody by harmonizing a diatonic third above the original melody.

The "diatonic" part is so key here. You can't just play any third (major or minor) that you feel like, you have to know what key the melody is in and play the right notes that fit with it. Look at a very simple example in D major, consisting of a short melody.

FIGURE 12.8 Melody Waiting to Be Harmonized

To harmonize this melody, you'd simply start a second part, three notes up in the D major scale, and follow the contour of the original melody. The result is shown in **FIGURE 12.9**.

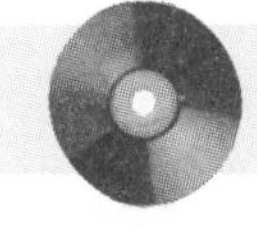

FIGURE 12.9 Melody Harmonized in Thirds

TRACK 69

The second line is harmonized a 3rd above.

Inverse

The inverse of a third is a sixth, and a sixth is another very nice way to harmonize a melody. Typically, you'd harmonize a sixth down, diatonically. What this brings you to is the exact same notes that you had when you went a third up. The difference is that the harmony is now below the original melody note. Both approaches work well. Check out our first example, this time with parallel diatonic sixth harmony.

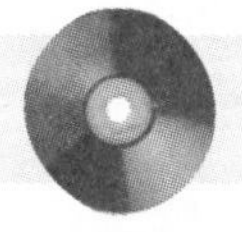

FIGURE 12.10 Same Melody, Harmonized a Sixth Below

TRACK 70

The second line is harmonized a 6th below.

Both sound quite nice.

IN TIME

Historically, when it comes to harmonizing notes and especially the topic of voice leading, moving notes in parallel with each other (where one voice follows the exact shape of the original melody) was something you always had to be careful with. Thankfully, thirds are always nice when used in parallel motion.

Intervals You Can Use

When it comes to harmonizing, there are certain intervals that work almost all the time, and some that are very hard to deal with. Here are intervals by type as a reference for you. Remember that when you are harmonizing melodies in keys, think diatonically for your melody notes!

- **Unison/Octave.** Not really a "harmony" per se, but the effect of "doubling" a melody can be a very nice way to add some textures.
- **Seconds.** Seconds verge on the edge of tension and dissonance and should be handled with care. They can work at certain points in a harmony for some color, but you'll rarely find more than one in a row; you can forget parallelism.
- **Thirds.** You can't go wrong with thirds. They just always sound nice. They work great in parallel, too.
- **Fourths.** Fourths can be nice, but not in parallel. Parallel fourths are one of the major no-no rules of voice leading. However, since there is a fourth interval from the fifth of a triad to the root, a fourth can be just the right interval.
- **Fifths.** Fifths are also consonant intervals that work well. You don't want them in parallels either as they break the other major rule of voice leading. Plus, if you harmonize with straight parallel fifths, it will sound like Gregorian chant.
- **Sixths.** Sixths, the inverse of thirds. These also always sound very good all the time. These work in almost all situations and work especially well in parallel motion.
- **Sevenths.** Another dissonant/tense interval. They may work at certain points, but in general, they won't sound consonant. You're also rarely, if ever, going to see them in succession one after another.

In general, the "tense" intervals, the seconds and sevenths, are not something you should avoid. A bit of tension and release is what music is built on, so using those intervals sparingly may add just the perfect color to your music.

Extra Credit

If you want to study harmony in even more depth, you should check out counterpoint. Counterpoint is best exemplified in the fugues by Bach, Mozart, Beethoven, and Shostakovich. Theorist J. J. Fux's treatise on counterpoint still remains the quintessential work for learning about this subject. A highly recommended read for those of you interested in learning more about how notes interact with one another.

Single Line Harmony

Harmony has been the domain of chordal instruments throughout this book. Sure, a clarinet in an orchestra contributes to a sense of harmony when you look at the whole score, but how can all of the single line instruments (ones that can play only one note at a time) get in on this party? (There are more single line instruments than chordal instruments.)

Remember that thing called an arpeggio? Sure you do—an arpeggio is just a chord played one note at a time. Play enough arpeggios and you end up with chords. They aren't chords in the vertical sense, as single line instruments can't play that way, but they are harmony, more specifically "implied" harmony.

The good news is that if you play a single line instrument, you've probably already played harmony this way—many of you didn't even know you did!

Here is an example:

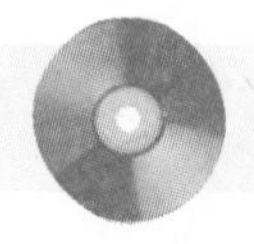

TRACK 71

FIGURE 12.11 Single Line Harmony

Since the arpeggios are labeled and named with Roman numerals, you can clearly see that harmony is definitely going on here. It's simply moving across the page instead of up and down it.

Extra Credit

If you want to see single line harmony, here are a few places to look: the solo cello suites by Bach (and his flute and violin solo works, too) and concertos by Vivaldi, Mozart, and Beethoven. Those are the well-known ones. Every instrument has some principal composers; for example, Kreutzer is known exclusively as a "violin" composer. Regarding your own instrument, you'll easily find etudes and pieces you've played to study.

Single line harmony is an unavoidable part of playing tonal music. Think of it this way: Everything starts as scales. Scales combine to form chords, which, in turn, form harmony. It's almost impossible to write music without being aware of harmony and its implications. Music for those single line instruments would be really boring without some sense of harmonic implications. The music would sort of wander without purpose.

Take a good hard look at the content of any piece of music for a single line instrument and you're going to find a lot more than just notes. The next etude will show you some examples to look at further, but search your own musical archives; you're sure to find more than enough to work with.

Dealing with Accidentals

Here is a short but important question: How do you harmonize a note that is not diatonic to a scale? Say you're in the key of C major and you have a melody note of F♯. That note isn't in any of the diatonic chords, so what do you do? Well, you should go to the next chapter (after the etude) and learn about advanced chord progressions, specifically how to deal with chromatic harmony (harmonizing notes outside the scale).

Chapter 13

Etude Two: Chords and Harmony

Spell the Following Major Triads

Spell the Following Minor Triads

Spell the Following Diminished Triads

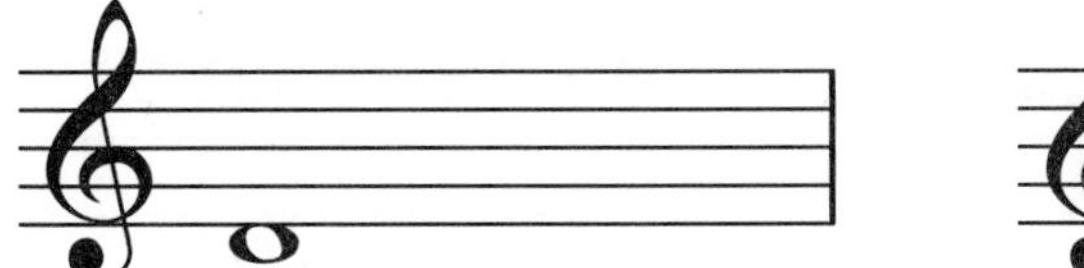
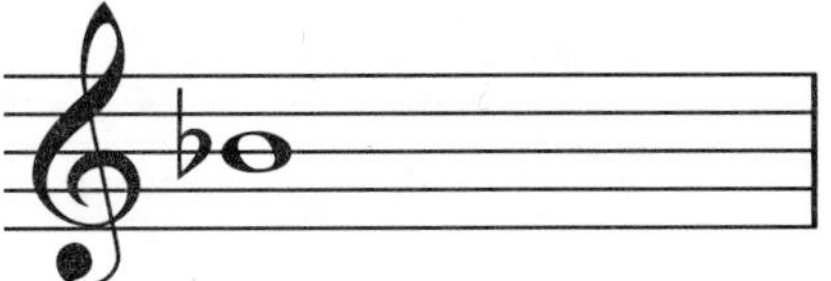

Spell the Following Augmented Triads

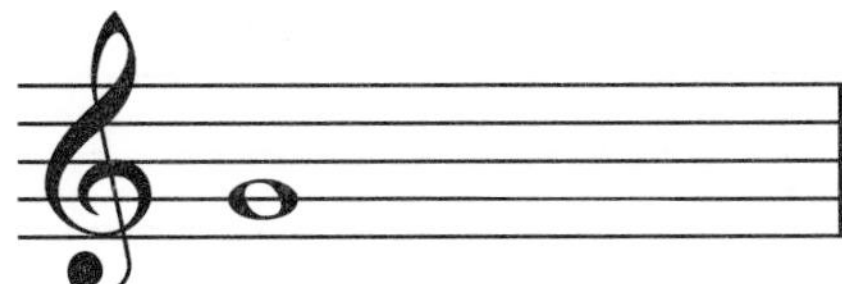
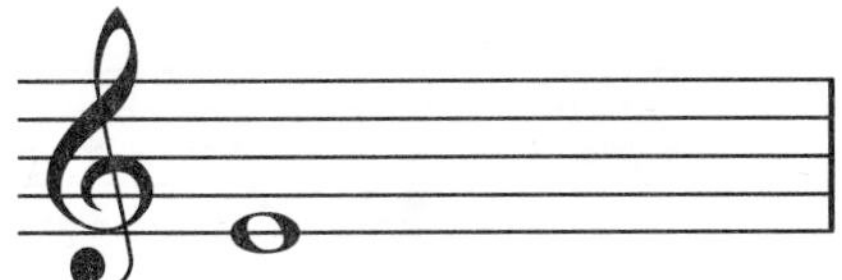
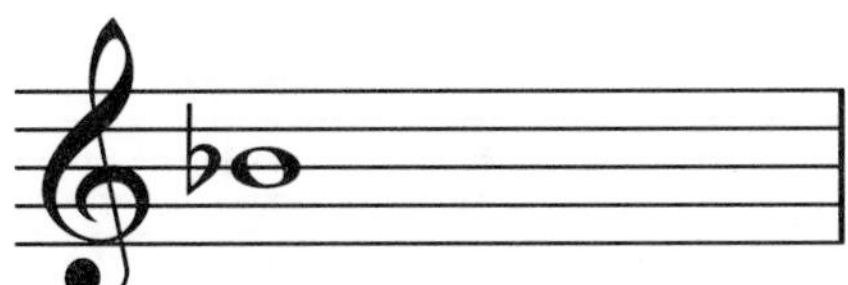
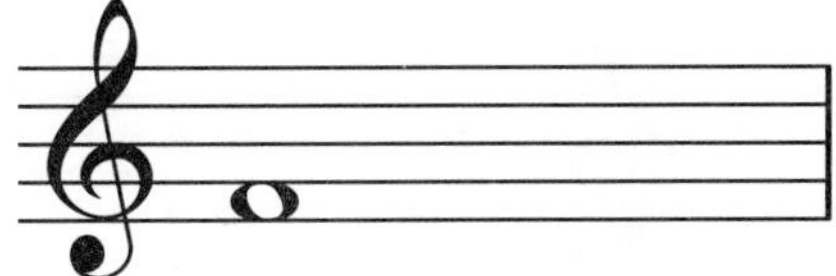

Spell Major Scales, Add Key Signatures, Add Diatonic Triads and Name the Triads

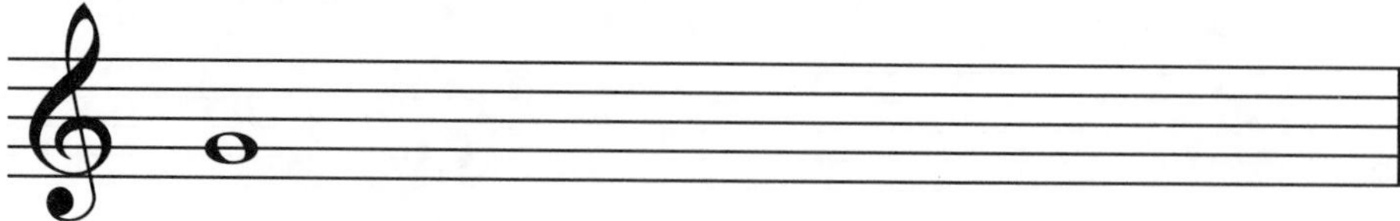

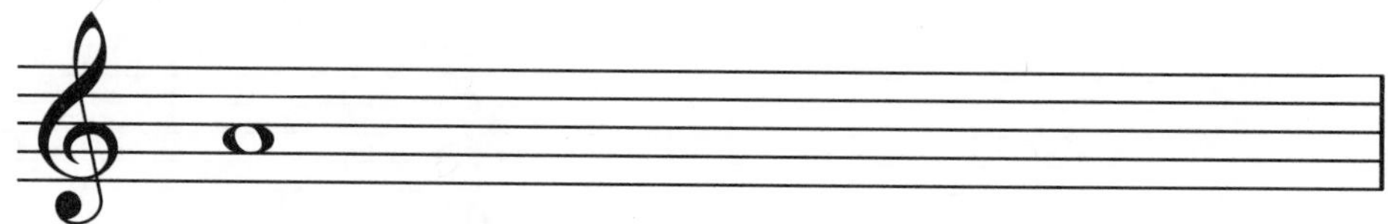

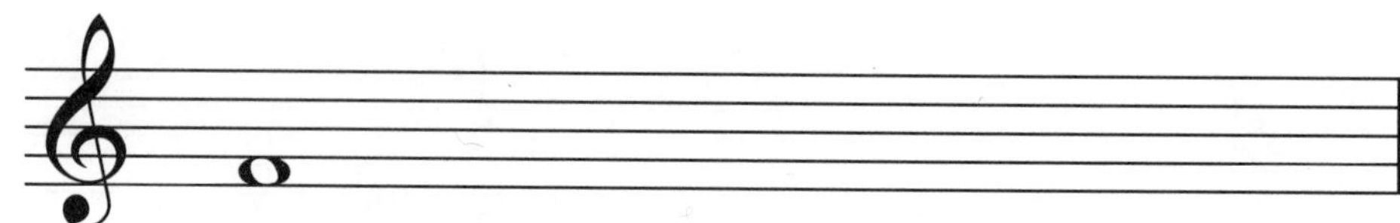

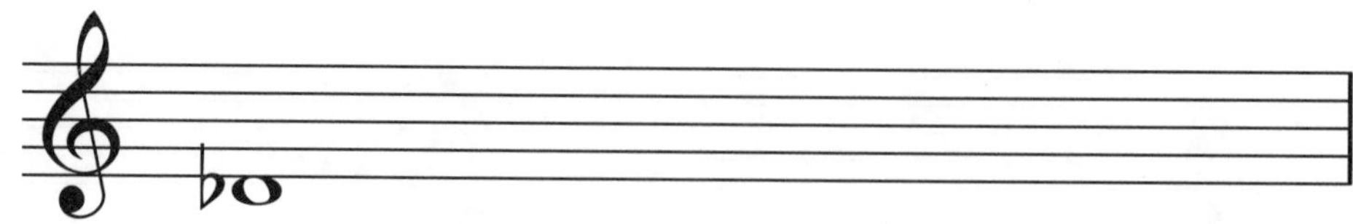

Spell Minor Scales, Add Key Signatures, Add Diatonic Triads and Name the Triads

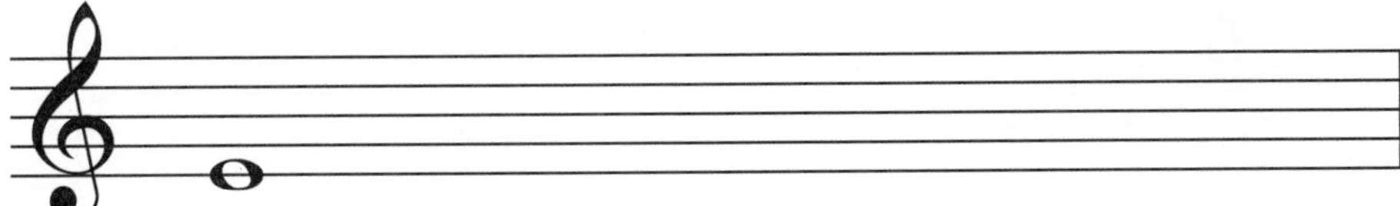

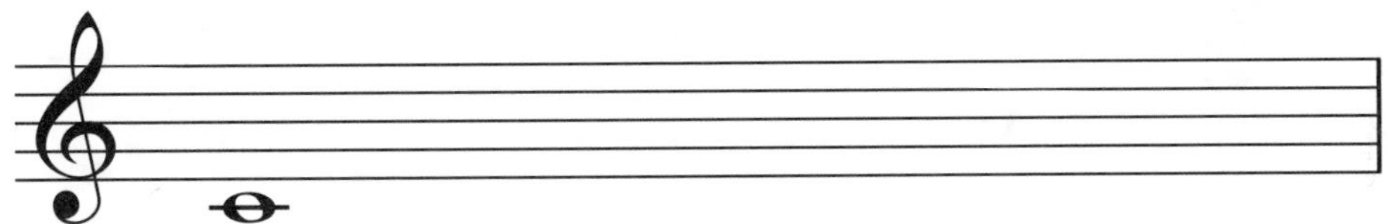

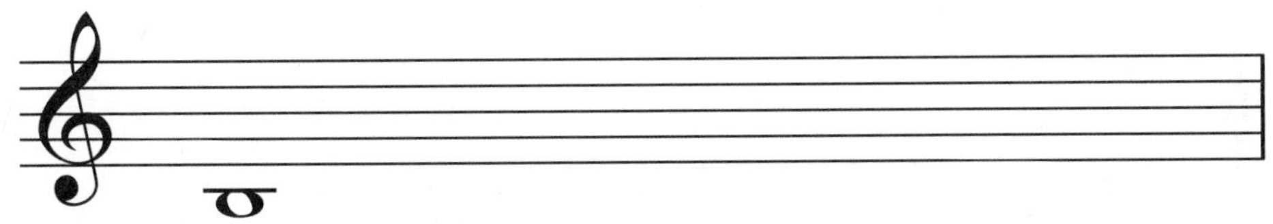

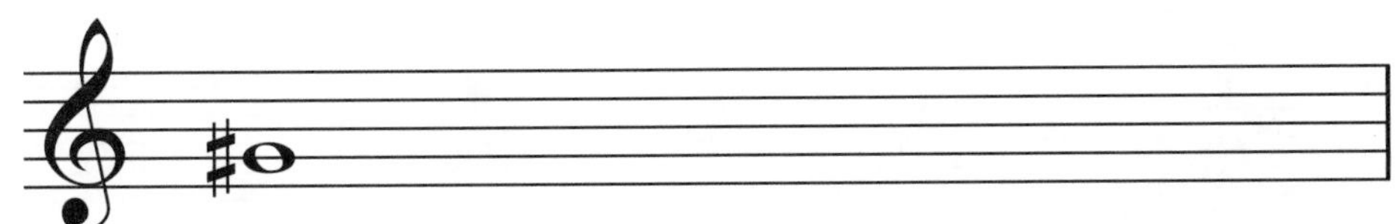

Write The Following Inverted Triads

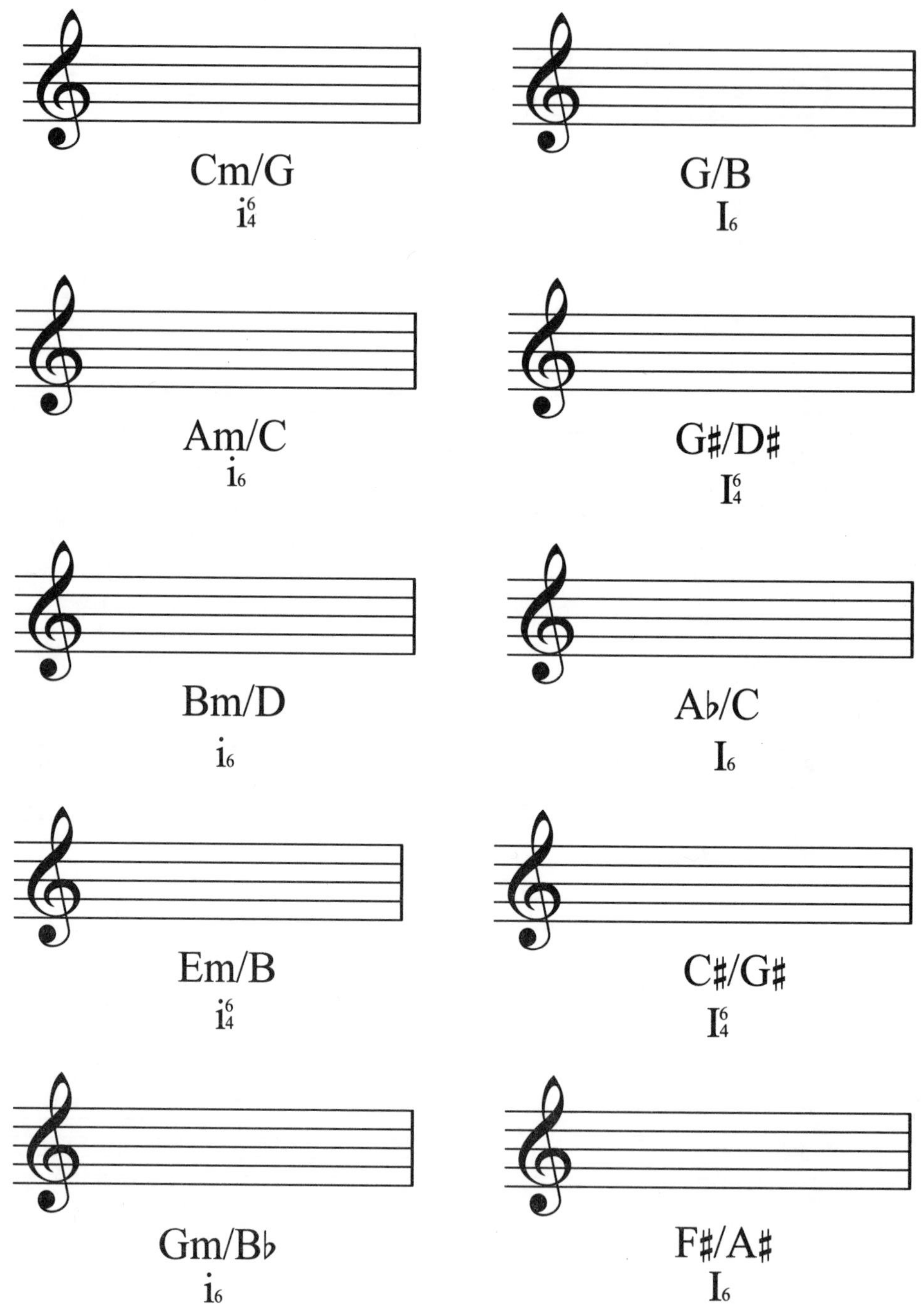

Write The Following Inverted Seventh Chords

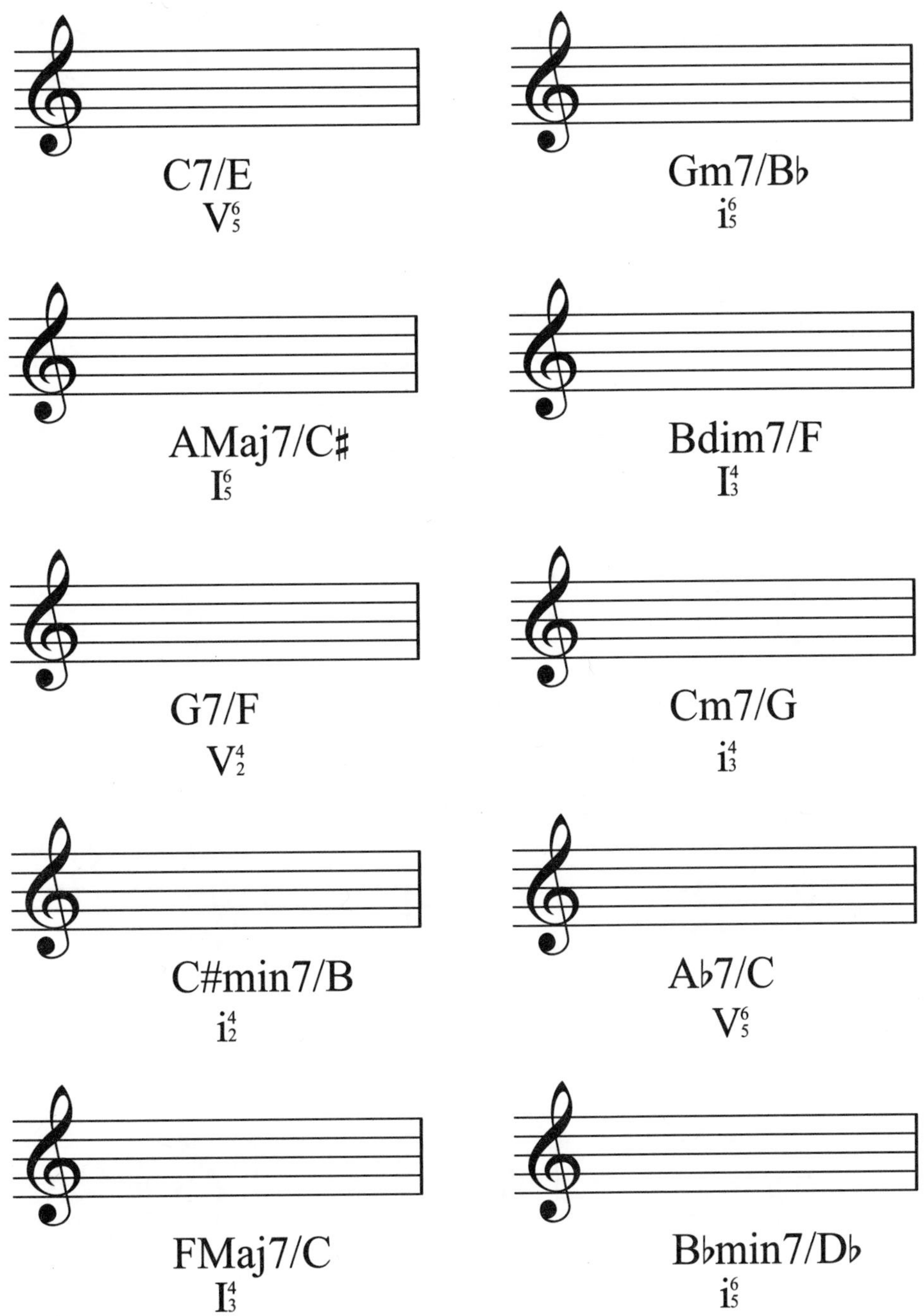

Name The Following Triads, 7th Chords, and Inversions

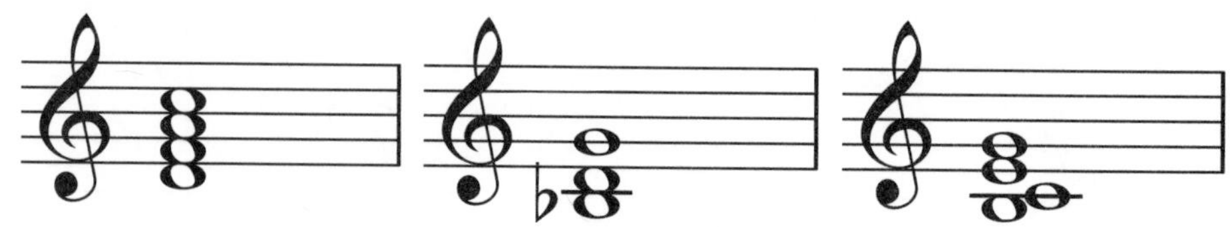

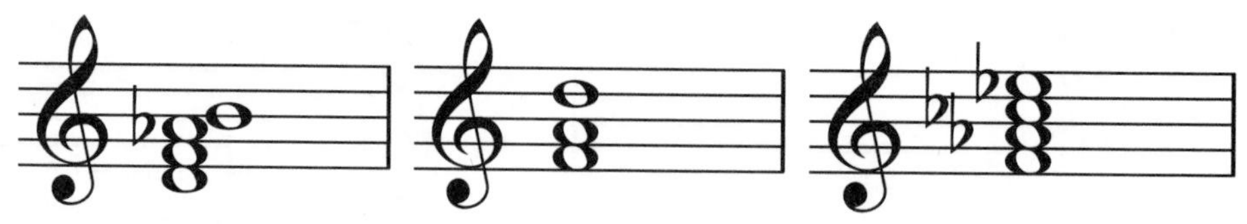

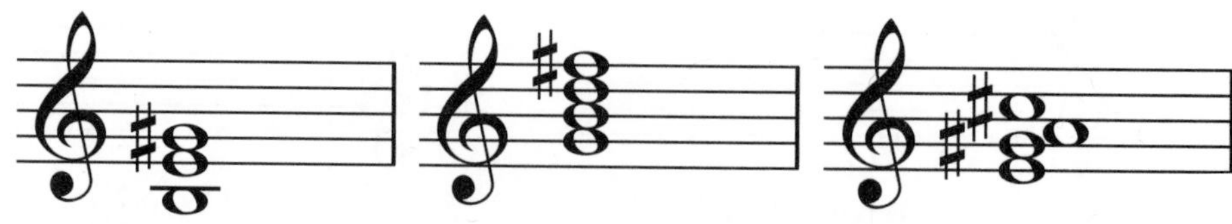

Analyze the Following Major Chord Progressions
Using Roman Numerals and Traditional Chord Names

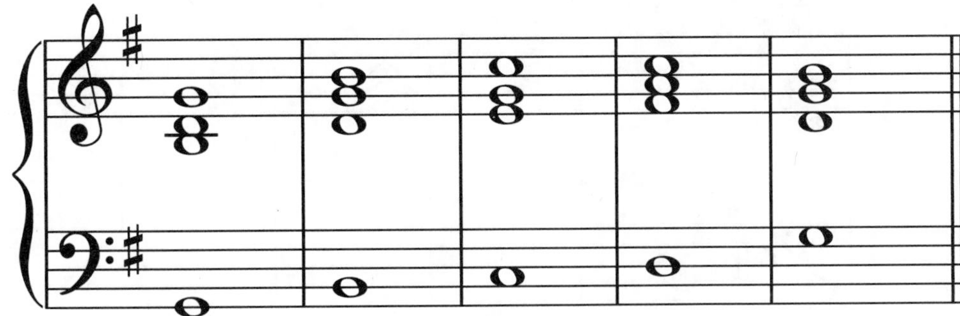

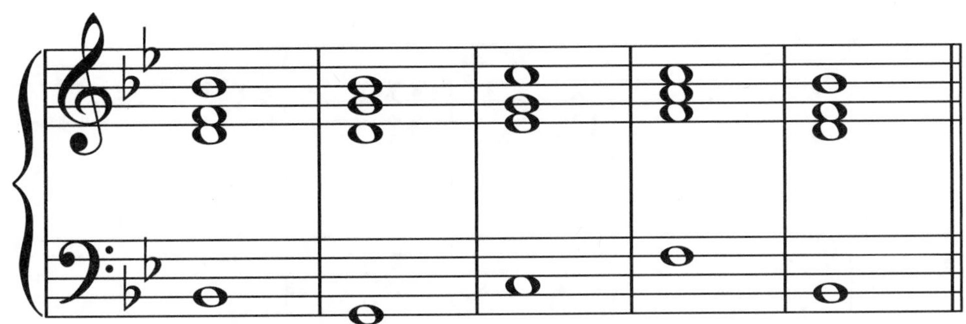

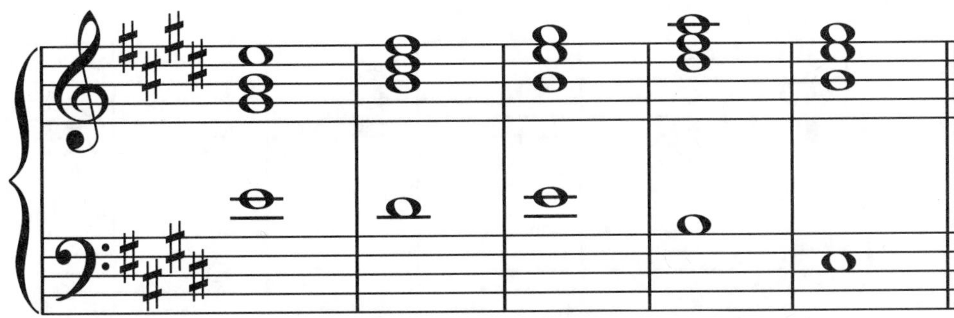

Analyze the Following Minor Chord Progressions
Using Roman Numerals and Traditional Chord Names

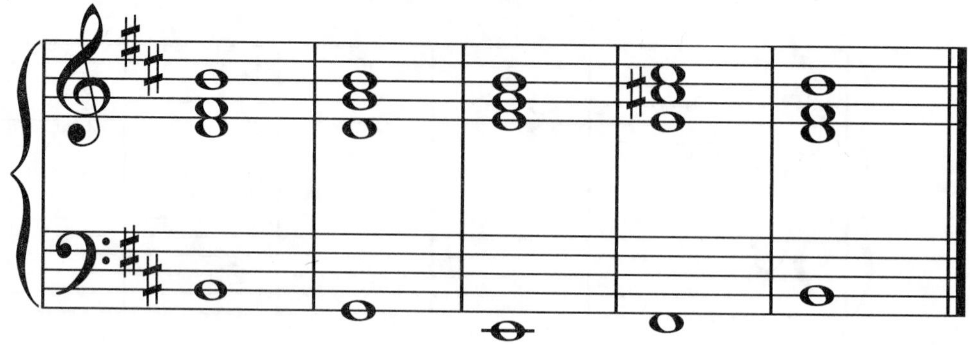

Chapter 14

Advanced Harmony

Diatonic harmony will get you only so far in your understanding of music. As music progressed, the variety and complexity of harmony also evolved. Diatonic chords were augmented with other harmonies to expand the timbre and color of music. In this chapter, you will be introduced to other colors you can explore as a composer and learn more of what you will encounter as you analyze music. You will also cover the important topic of changing keys and modulation.

Beyond Diatonic

As a student of music theory, it's only logical to start learning about diatonic harmony, both major and minor harmonies. Diatonic harmony is a great start, but as with any set of guidelines, composers found ways around these "rules" and started to add other chords into the canon of harmony to give greater variety.

Diatonic harmony supports diatonic melodic writing. How do you deal with melodies that contain notes outside the scales? Also, the chord ladder seems to be something you can't easily get away from. How do you create interesting progressions that don't simply follow the ladder from end to end? You have already learned that the dominant chord is the basic "end" of the progression because when you get there, your options are to either cadence and begin a new phrase or resolve in some sort of deceptive way. Composers over the course of music history sought ways to prolong the amount of time it takes to get to the dominant chord. With diatonic harmony, there is only so much that you can do. By providing some additional chords, composers could "keep the ball in the air" a bit longer, so to speak. This refers to extended harmony, more specifically, secondary chords.

Secondary Chords

A secondary chord is a simple concept: Take any chord in the diatonic scale and precede it with a chord that is related, yet out of the diatonic scale, adding a bit of color and an extra side step in the harmonic picture.

Secondary chords come in two flavors: dominant and diminished chords. Secondary chords can be used with fully diatonic melodies, adding more richness to already functional, melodic writing.

Since dominant and diminished chords are essentially substitutes for each other, you should know why a secondary chord works in any setting.

Secondary Dominant Chords

Here's what you know about dominant chords: They are typically the V chord of a key and they have a very strong tendency to resolve up a perfect fourth or down a perfect fifth (you'll arrive at the same note) to a tonic I chord. You know that they are so strong as to define keys by themselves, so if you moved the V chord temporarily, to precede another chord in the key, would it work?

The answer is yes. A secondary dominant is a simple action that places a temporary dominant chord a fifth away from any chord in the key. Think of this as a harmonic detour.

Now set up an example. Use the IV chord as your target chord. You want to precede the IV chord with a dominant chord. In the key of C major, IV is F major, and F's dominant chord (a perfect fifth away) is C7. The progression would have gone like this:

FIGURE 14.1 I–IV–V–I

TRACK 72

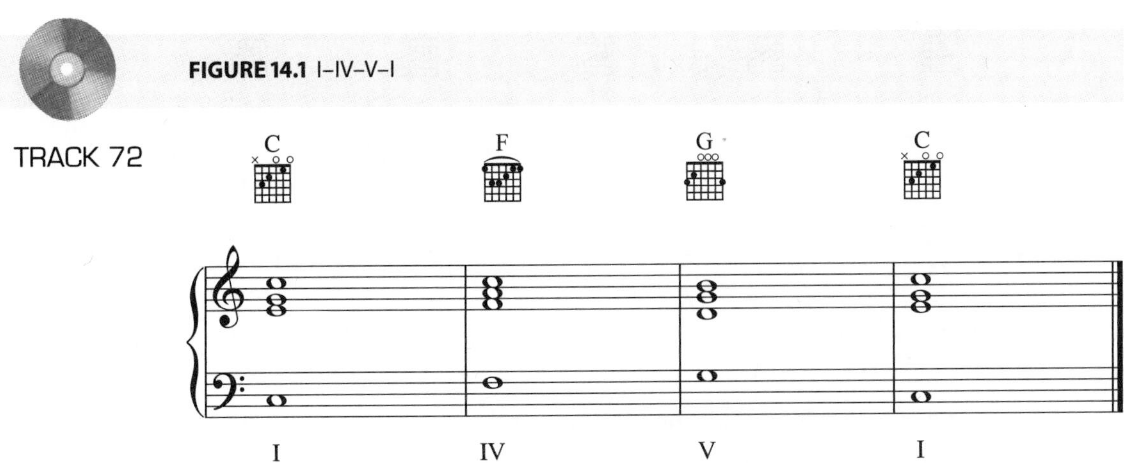

Now, if you add the secondary dominant to IV in the progression, you get this progression:

FIGURE 14.2 I–?–IV–V–I

TRACK 73

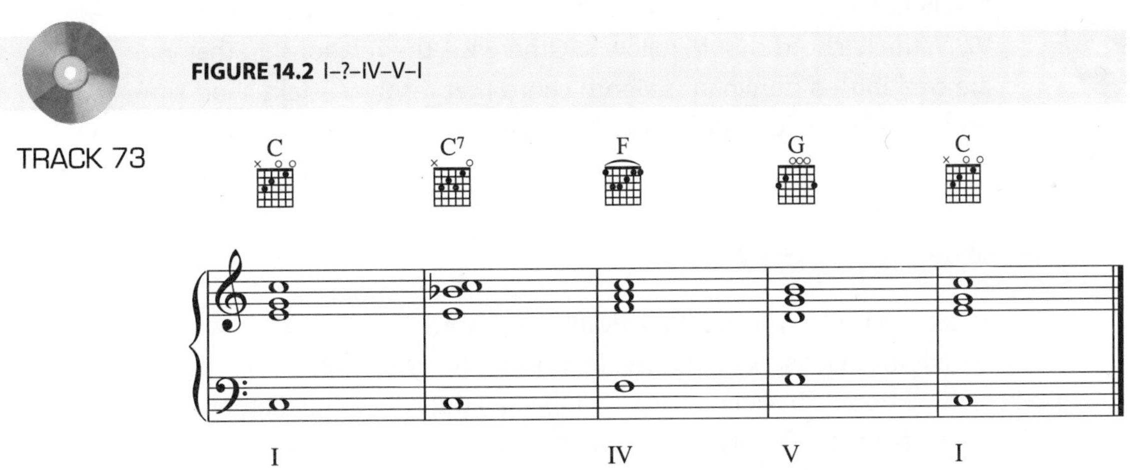

Two things to talk about. First, the additional dominant chord really adds a great flavor to an otherwise "stock" progression. If you think of the other chords that could have preceded IV, few have the flavor of the secondary dominant. Second, what do you call this chord? In the progression, there is a temporary "?" in place. The chord is C7, so you could call it a I_7 chord, but that would miss the relationship between the secondary chord and its destination. Instead, you would call that chord V_7/IV, or "five of four." The word *of* is depicted as a slash and shows clearly that you are adding a chord that is related to the IV chord, instantly resolving to the proper destination: IV.

So, here is the proper naming for the progression using Roman numerals:

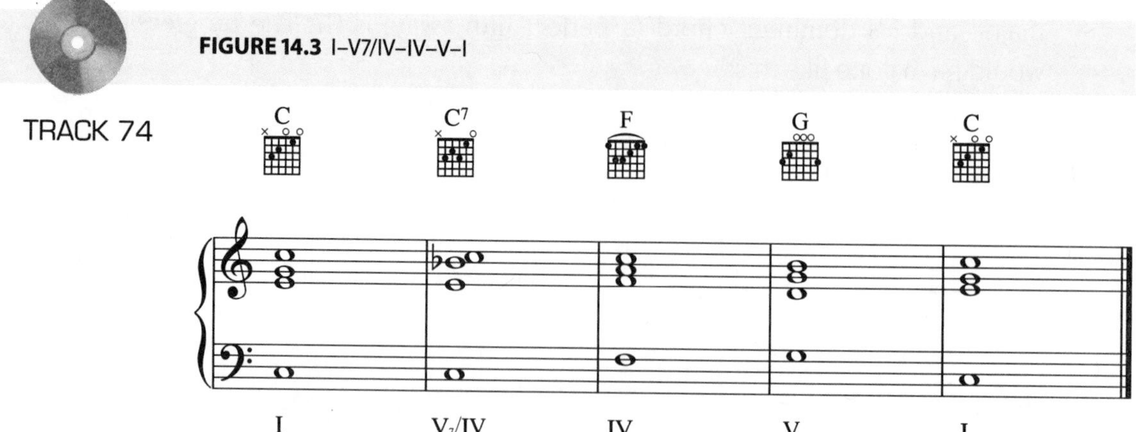

FIGURE 14.3 I–V7/IV–IV–V–I

It is perfectly clear what the function of the nondiatonic C7 chord is in the progression, and you could easily realize this progression (write one yourself) in another key simply using the Roman numerals.

In functional harmony, when you have a secondary dominant chord like V7/IV, the IV chord should follow it. Otherwise, the relationship that you are creating—a dominant seventh chord that resolves—falls short simply because the dominant chord never resolves!

Secondary Chromatic

When you add a secondary dominant chord to a progression, you are always adding at least one "chromatic" note to the progression (V/iii adds two). Since these chords have notes in them that fall outside of the diatonic key, you simply get a greater variety of tones. In the example above, the B♭ would seem to smash our sacred leading tone in the key of C (B), but since it's part of a dominant chord, it sidesteps the key for a second and sets up an expected point of conclusion: IV. Once you resolve, it's business as usual and the actual V chord in the key restores the B♭ to a B natural and the key has function again.

Which Chords?

Which chords can have secondary dominant chords? In a diatonic progression, all chords except the vii° chord can have secondary dominants. In all fairness, you can't count I either, since its dominant is not secondary but diatonic. So, here is a list of chords that can support secondary dominants:

- ii
- iii
- IV
- V
- vi

Just exclude I and the vii° (diminished) chord and you are all set. Now, you can't just throw these chords in whenever you feel like it. Well, you can, if you are writing chord progressions without melodies. But if you are harmonizing melodies, you need to be a bit more careful; certain conditions need to be met! What conditions? You're about to find out.

What Conditions?

Where exactly can you use these chords with a melody that you have already written? Well, a few things have to align for this to work. First, when you are talking about secondary dominant chords, you are actually talking about two chords: the secondary dominant and the chord it resolves to.

Since both of these chords have to have connections to your melody, you need to have a situation where your melody supports both chords in succession.

Here is an example where it works really well:

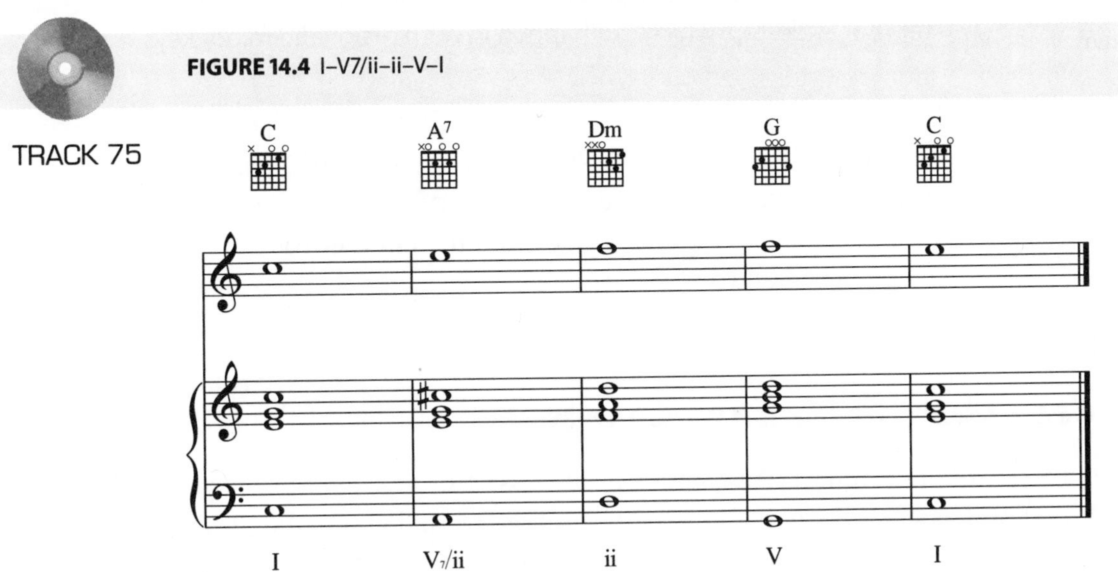

FIGURE 14.4 I–V7/ii–ii–V–I

Using a simple whole note melody, you can see that the second and third chords are your points where the secondary chords come into use. The melody in bars two and three use the notes E and F. Now, you could harmonize E and F lots of different ways. When this progression was being constructed, it was obvious that it would cadence with a ii–V–I; it just sounded right after a few tries at the piano. But what to do with the harmony under the E? There were several choices:

- A I_6 chord (C/E) could have been used to harmonize the E.
- A vi chord could have been used to harmonize the E.
- A iii chord could have been used to harmonize the E.

Theoretically, they all worked on paper. As sounds, there were some issues. The I_6 chord simply sounded funny going to ii; the voice leading of the bass line going from E to D just didn't sit right. The iii chord simply has never sounded that compelling in any diatonic progression (it's too far from I), so that was out. The vi sounded good and would have been a solid choice; however, the V7/ii, which is an A7 chord, was ultimately chosen. The vi chord is an A minor chord; the A7, which was chosen instead, has the same bass note and two-thirds of the chord tones are the same. No wonder it worked so well!

Extra Credit

How do secondary dominant chords apply to minor keys? The exact same way they do in major keys. The key is not the crucial step here, only the chords themselves. A secondary dominant is a dominant chord that resolves to a chord in the key. It is not a key change, rather a temporary sidestep, which can happen in both major and minor keys.

The tricky part is finding spots to use them in your music. Sometimes you use them and don't even know about it! Secondary dominant chords, especially V/V, are quite common in folk, country, and rock music. You may just stumble upon them in a grand, happy accident!

Secondary Diminished Chords

When the function of chords was discussed, especially when it came to the chord ladder, you learned about what chords could commonly substitute for each other. The V (dominant) chord can be substituted by the vii^{o} chord. Both chords function as "dominant" chords in that they resolve back to tonic with strength and great pull. So, in the spirit of secondary dominant chords, what about secondary diminished chords? Yes, those exist too. If the chords basically function the same way, you can use them the same way.

Secondary diminished chords have their own set of rules. Think about regular diminished chords. Typically, you see these chords as vii° chords, so you can infer some rules about their actions.

A secondary diminished chord will:

- Be either a diminished triad or a fully diminished seventh chord.
- Be built a half step lower than the chord it is resolving to.
- Always resolve up by a half step.

As for their written symbols, instead of calling them V/something, call them vii°/something.

You see secondary diminished chords in classical and jazz much more than you do in pop music because the diminished sound is not as accepted and common as other chords.

Regardless, they are very nice chords because they have a very slippery sound to them. What does "slippery" have to do with music? It's all about the voice leading! Here's a demonstration in the same example you had before:

TRACK 76

FIGURE 14.5 I–vii°/ii–ii–V–I

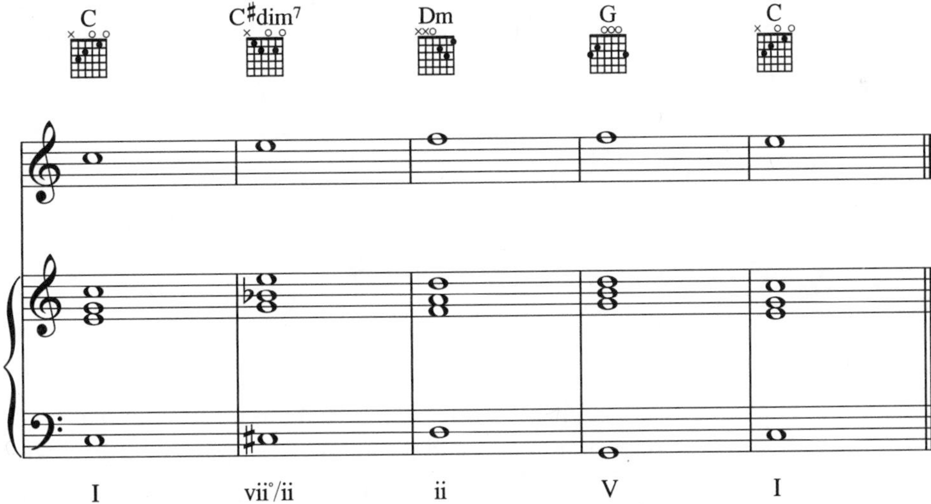

Here is the same melody as in **FIGURE 14.4**. The note that had to be harmonized was an E. Everything else was more or less set. In **FIGURE 14.4**, V/ii, an A7 chord, was chosen. In this example, vii°/ii, a C♯ diminished chord, was selected. Since the chord was only a half step below the ii chord, the secondary diminished chord slid into the ii chord. Even the bass line from the beginning of the progression—C–C♯–D—was a very smooth and slippery movement of bass notes and harmonies.

Both A7 and C♯ diminished support the E as a melody note as they both have E in their chords, but more than that, if you were to step outside the key of C for a second and think about A7 as a dominant chord, you would have to imagine the key of D for a second (the key where A7 is V). The substitute dominant chord in the key of D is C♯ diminished! If you compare **FIGURE 14.4** and **FIGURE 14.5**, you'll see that all that happened was that a secondary chord was chosen for the ii chord, but each example simply substituted a "dominant" chord of some sort (either dominant or diminished) that resolved normally to the ii chord.

A "temporary" V I (dominant tonic) relationship, on another chord besides the "real" tonic chord, has been provided. That's why these chords work—they provide the pull, the tension and release that you need, but they do so at other points in the harmony. I know this may seem a bit hypothetical, but just put it to use and you will hear it for yourself.

Chromatic Harmony

The secondary chords come under the umbrella of chromatic harmony, meaning that they provide notes outside the key or they help to harmonize melodies that use notes outside the key. Here is a simple example of a chromatic melody that is basically in C major but adds a chromatic note that is needed to harmonize:

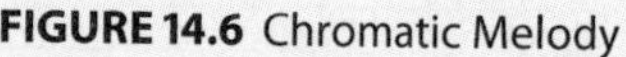

FIGURE 14.6 Chromatic Melody

The melody is largely in C, but the F♯s that are added need to be dealt with. You have no chords that deal with F♯ that are diatonic to C major. But you may have some secondary dominants or diminished chords that do so. Try your best to harmonize the rest of the chords and exclude the F♯ (or at least the measure that it's in).

FIGURE 14.7 Chromatic Melody with Partial Chords

You are left with a fairly benign I–vi–?–V7–I progression.

To deal with the chord in "?" you need to look to the chord after it, a V chord, G7 in this key.

What's the secondary dominant of that chord? V/V is D7, spelled D–F♯–A–C, so it works! Plug it in and see how it sounds:

TRACK 77

FIGURE 14.8 Chromatic Melody, Full Harmonization

Look, it works! Not only did you take care of the chromatic note in the melody, but you also generated a pretty interesting chord progression, one that any theory teacher would be proud to see!

Note: You could have also used vii°/V (F♯ diminished) as a good substitute chord for the D7 as both D7 and F♯ diminished; in this case, since there was a D in the melody and the diminished chord has an E♭ it's best to stick with D7. Functionally, it would have been okay, but to the ear it's not pretty.

Chromatic harmony is a very interesting topic. Take note of how composers deal with chromatic notes in their melodies and which chromatic chords they use.

IN TIME

There are two other chromatic chords that are often studied in high-level theory. One is called the Neapolitan sixth chord, and then there are what are called augmented sixth chords. Both are important chords in the development of harmony but are a bit beyond the scope of this text. If you further your study, you will no doubt encounter these chords from time to time.

Modal Mixture

What is a modal mixture? It's very common when you are in a major key to basically borrow aspects from other keys as you go along. The most common way to do this is to borrow chords from the minor key with the same name (C major/C minor). These are called borrow chords, and they are a pretty neat way to spice up your harmony. Because the major and minor key are so close in some respects, you can interchange these chords for some really cool sounds. Look at some examples and see what chords you can borrow!

Borrowed Chords from Major

Here, you are in a minor key (any one you choose) and you are going to borrow some chords from the major key. Look at the diatonic major and minor keys together to see what their harmonic differences are.

If you look at the chords, number by number, you, of course, see differences; they are, in fact, different keys! Now, think about this: You typically talk about minor keys, and you also talk about the addition of dominant chords on V and diminished chords on vii to make the keys function better. This is also analogous to the discussion of the harmonic minor scale and its chords. In a sense, you have already "borrowed" the V and vii chords from the major key. The other most common chord to borrow is the IV chord from the major key.

FIGURE 14.9 Parallel Major and Minor Harmony

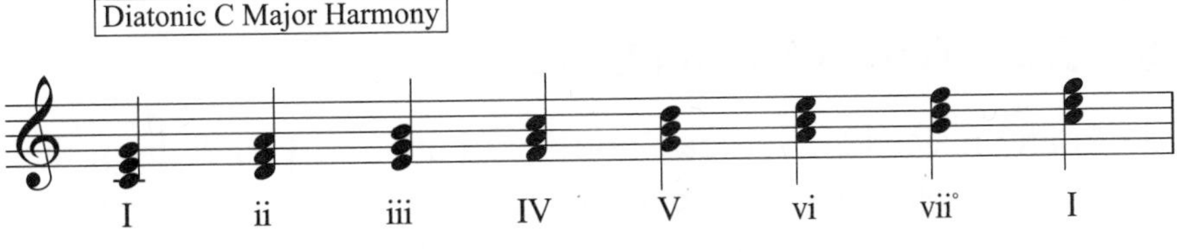

Here is an example, using a major IV chord in a minor key.

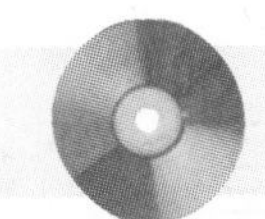

FIGURE 14.10 Borrowed IV Chord in Minor

TRACK 78

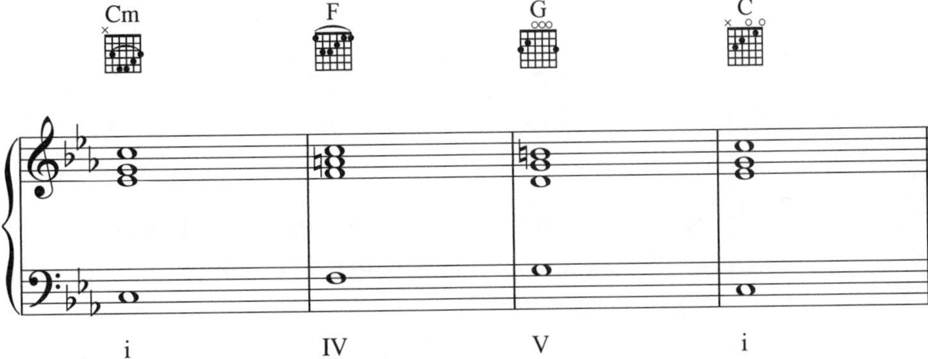

You could certainly take any chord from the major key, but if you count IV, V, and vii°, that's three typical chords that you see often in minor keys. Add to that secondary dominant and diminished chords, and you have a pretty nice lineup of harmonic choices.

You could even think of a Picardy third (a raised third that forms a major triad in the final chord of a composition in a minor key) as a borrowed I chord, but since it happens only at the end of pieces, it's not a true borrowed chord.

When you start looking at borrowing from the minor key, into major, you see a lot more choices!

Borrowed Chords from Minor

In any major key, you can borrow a bunch of chords from the parallel minor key. Looking back at **FIGURE 14.9**, you can see the differences. The typical chords that are borrowed are: iv, ♭VI, and ♭VII. In the jazz chapter (coming up next), you will hear about one other chord that is used in modern music, the ii°. For now, you should know about the iv, ♭VI, and ♭VII. Start with iv. The iv chord is very commonly used in major keys and it's all over music of all genres and age! You find it in Mozart and the Beatles. Here is a nice example using a iv chord in a major key context.

FIGURE 14.11 Minor iv in Major

TRACK 79

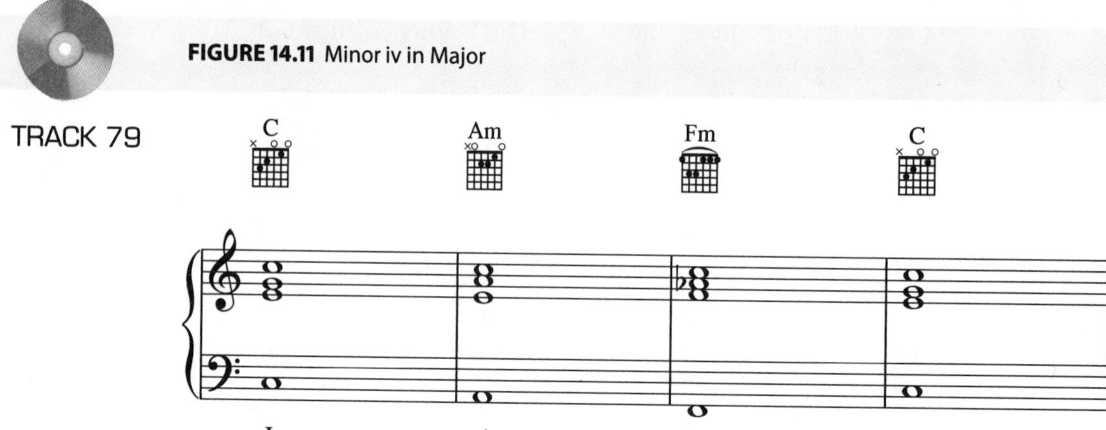

You don't even have to look that hard to find this borrow chord. It's actually more common in folk and pop music than in common practice styles. It's all over the Beatles' music!

The next two chords are the ♭VI and ♭VII.

In **FIGURE 14.12**, you see these particular chords, ♭VI and ♭VII, commonly ascending toward the I chord, typically coming between V and I as the example illustrates. There are other ways to use them, but this is by far the most common.

The reason to talk about borrow chords at all (it's considered a fairly high-level subject) is because you see them so much in all different styles of music, across genres and time periods. Most importantly, you see them in pop music as well, so this may eliminate some of the chords you've been trying to analyze that simply didn't seem to fit into the key.

FIGURE 14.12 Excuse Me, Can I Borrow That ♭VI and ♭VII Chord, Please?

TRACK 80

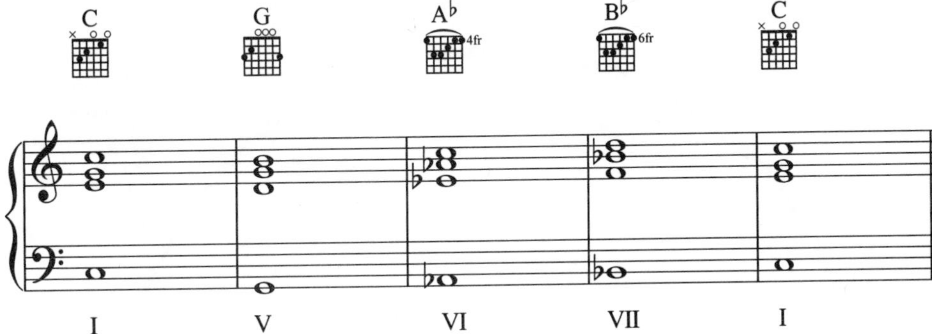

Modulation

Here's a huge topic: How do you change keys? This topic is large enough for its own book, but the title *The Everything® Harmonic Modulation Book* just didn't seem to flow, so it will get a section here. Modulation is simply the art of shifting the tonal center to another key and staying there. What do you know about tonal centers? Well, you know that basically, they involve chords and melodies that define certain keys. Most importantly, dominant V chords and tonic I chords are the basic ingredients.

You have learned about secondary chords; they provide a temporary tonal shift. This shift is only for a moment. But if you took the idea of secondary chords and simply held on to them for a long enough time, then you could shift the tonal center to another key. You could finally modulate!

What keys can you modulate to? The simplest way to change keys is to go to a key that is spelled very closely to the key you are in. The rule of thumb is simple: The fewer notes you have to shift, the easier your job is. Start to look at the "related" keys.

Related Keys

Related keys are keys that share notes in common with one another. The more notes they share, the more closely related they are. Go back to the key circle for a second.

FIGURE 14.13 The Circle of Keys

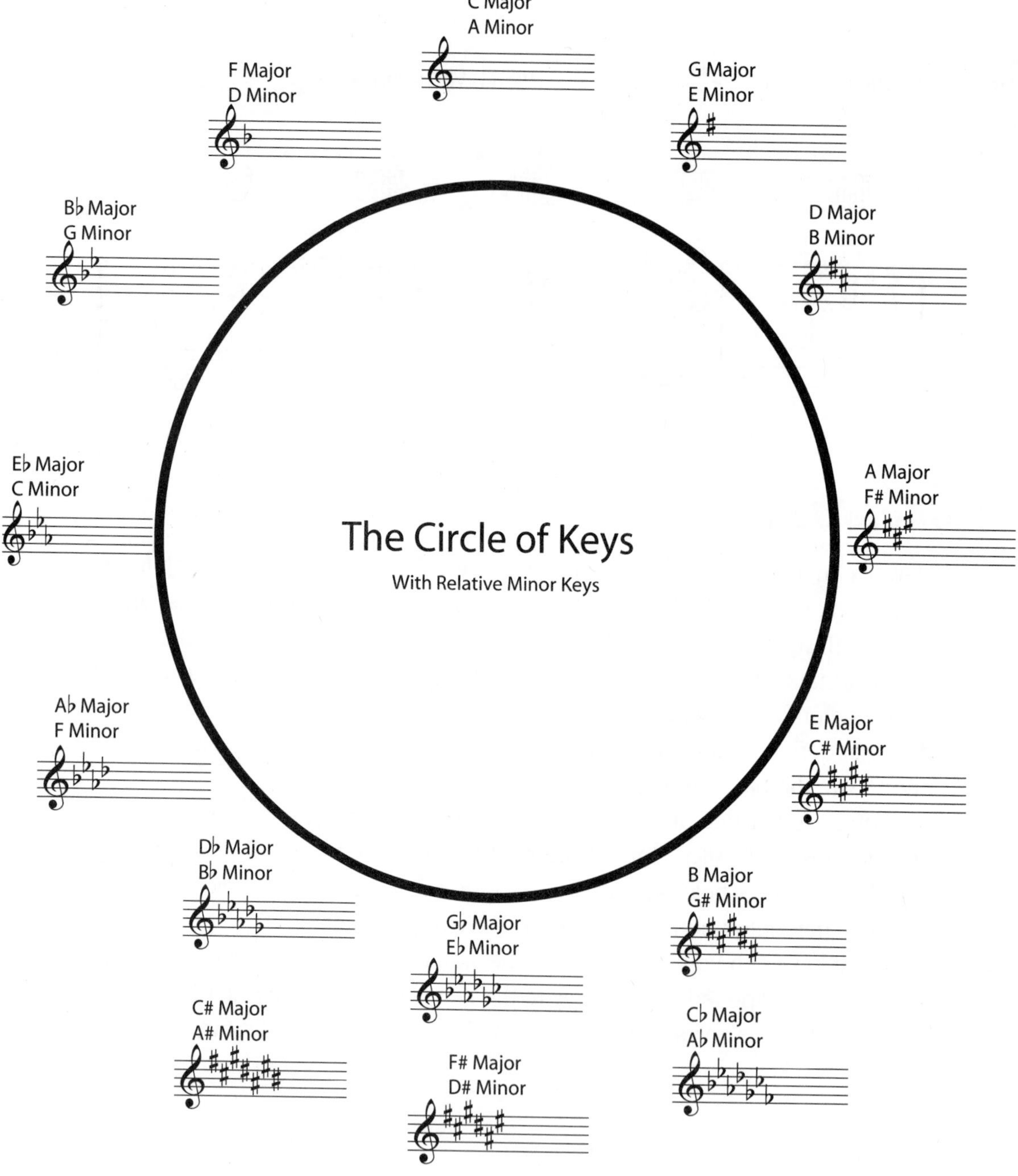

Say you are in C (an old favorite). The closest related key would be one key to the right or one key to the left, so G and F are keys that you can move into easily. As you start to lose notes in common, it becomes more difficult to slip into a new key. Nothing's impossible, but typically, you see movements by fifth, either up to G or down to F, if you start in C.

New Dominants

When you throw a secondary dominant in, you alter a key's landscape by adding a chromatic tone. In these situations, that chromatic tone always goes away. Well, what if you stuck with it? What if you had a section of music that you kept analyzing V/V, V and it never really came back to I? Well, you may have just stumbled onto a modulation.

Here's an example. Start out in C and end up in G. This will be a fairly long progression because you want to set up the idea of the key change and establish the new tonic/dominant relationship so that it sticks.

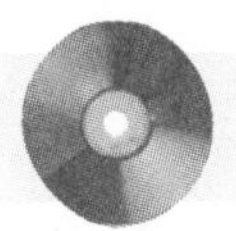

FIGURE 14.14 Simple Harmonic Modulation

TRACK 81

As you can see and hear, you started in one key and ended up in another. You achieved this with two devices. The first is a secondary dominant to the new key. Your goal was to move to the key of V (G major), so to do so, you'd need V in the new key (V of G is D7), so you made sure to do that. The minute the V/V showed up, you had an F♯ in the key. The trick is not letting it go back to F♮, so you did the progression again to really solidify the sound of the new key. The other way that this is accomplished is with common chords. For example, to change keys, you need to think in the new key for a second. A I–IV–V progression in any key is pretty strong. You can pull off that progression by using common chords. I–IV–V in the key of G is G–C–D. In the key of C, you have C and G chords already! The only addition is the D, which you get via the secondary dominant chord (V/V). The real trick is not making the G chord a G7. G7 would pull back to C; in the example, it's kept simply a triad. Common chords can go further in helping you establish a new key. I–IV–V is not the only progression, as you already know. Look at other common chords. (Notice how you can analyze **FIGURE 14.14** in both keys? The analysis is provided for you in C and G. It makes much more sense to look at the second line in G.)

Common Chords

Whenever you are thinking about modulating to a new key, it's nice to know what chords the two keys share; these chords are easy to use effectively. Use the key of C and F this time and look at how you might modulate. The V/V is never a common chord; you always have to change the key for that one, but you have a bunch of other chords that do work. Here are the diatonic triads of C and F major.

FIGURE 14.15 Chords in C and F

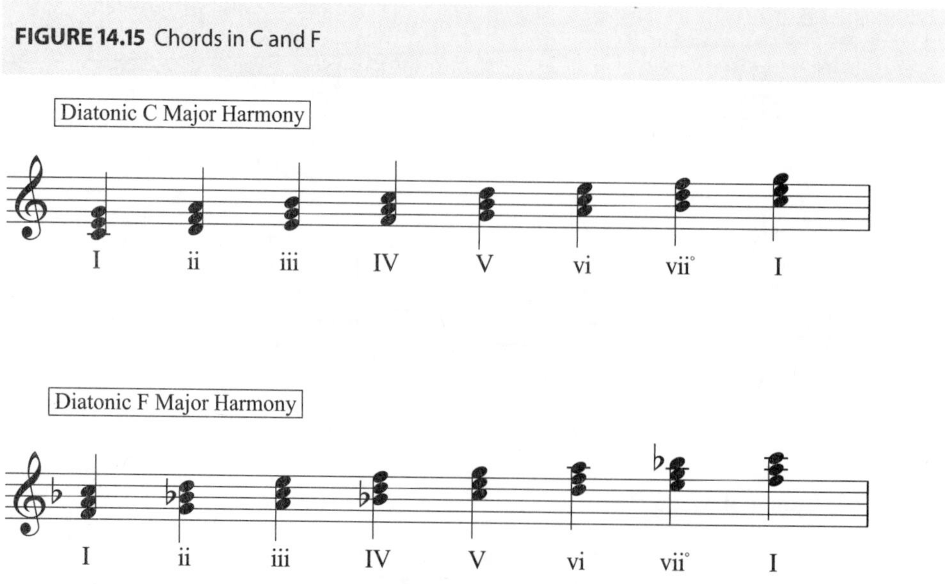

You see a bunch of chords in both keys—C, Dm, F, and Am. In the key of F, those chords are V, vi, I, and iii respectively. So, you actually do have a V/V chord in this case—it's just not a C7 chord—which you need to fix with a chromatic note. In the key of F, the vi chord is important. What you are missing is a pre-dominant chord, either ii or IV. Both of those chords are not common, but no worries, once you've done the whole secondary dominant (or diminished) thing, the next progression after the cadence can continue on as if it's in the new key. The G minor chord you're going to add won't sound odd, because you've already introduced the chromatic tone (B♭) to the key; it will actually sound like it belongs to the key of F!

FIGURE 14.16 Common Chord Modulation

TRACK 82

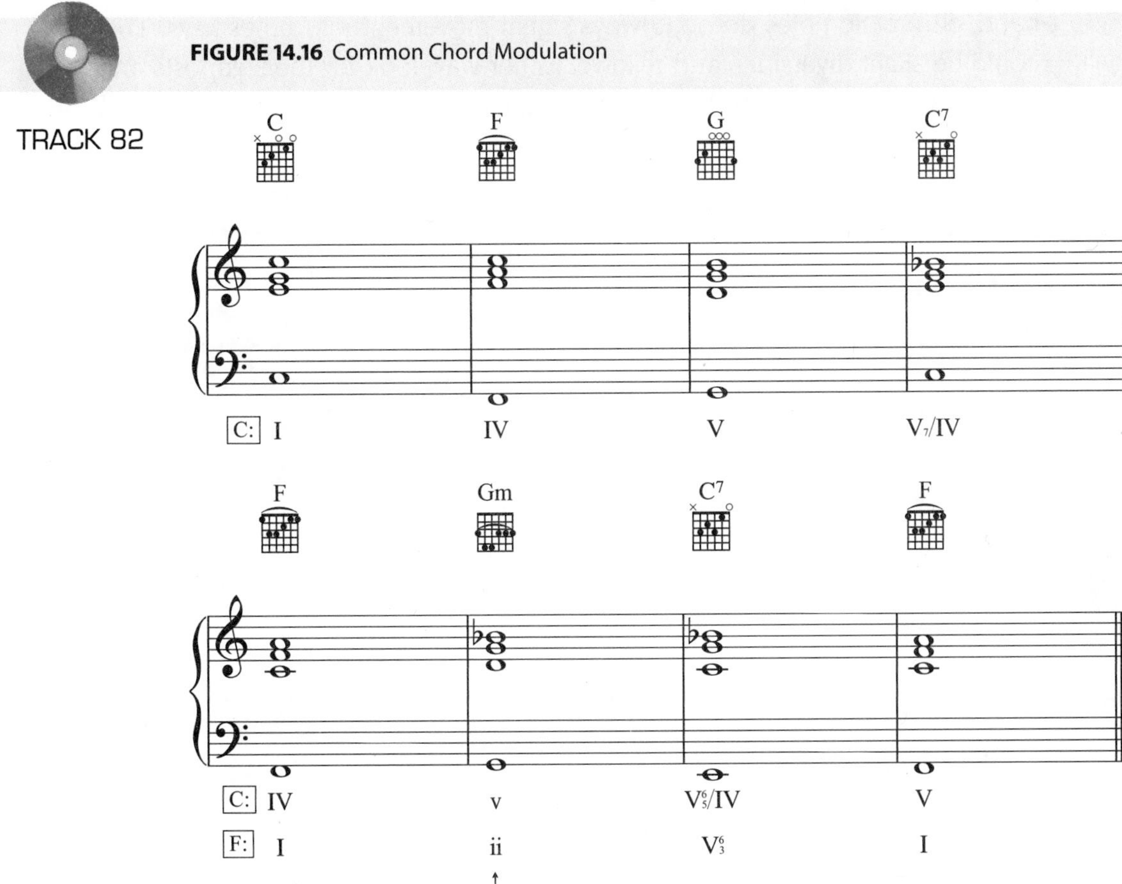

The way to make a secondary dominant not feel "secondary" is to simply not turn back to the old key at all—you simply keep going in the key of F and use typical, diatonic progressions for that key. As you keep writing in the new key, the listener will forget about the key of C since you have "tonic-sized" the F chord so many times it sounds like you have modulated, and you have.

Modulation is a big topic with some very simple rules. You know how harmony works and you know that to move you have to shift the harmony to the new key. The trick is to do some analysis of music, especially classical music (because of the common modulations), to get used to seeing exactly how it's done.

Just a word of warning: Sometimes the hardest part about modulation is simply knowing a modulation when you see it. As soon as you see chords that don't make sense in your original key, take that as a clear sign that you may not be in that key anymore! Look for patterns in other keys. If you can fit the mystery progression into another key, then chances are that's exactly where you are. One last thing: You can't modulate without a chromatic note. On the other hand, chromatic notes do not always signal movement into other keys. They could be slight diversions and resolve. Either way, look for the signposts and, most of all, listen. If a chord sounds like a I, it probably is!

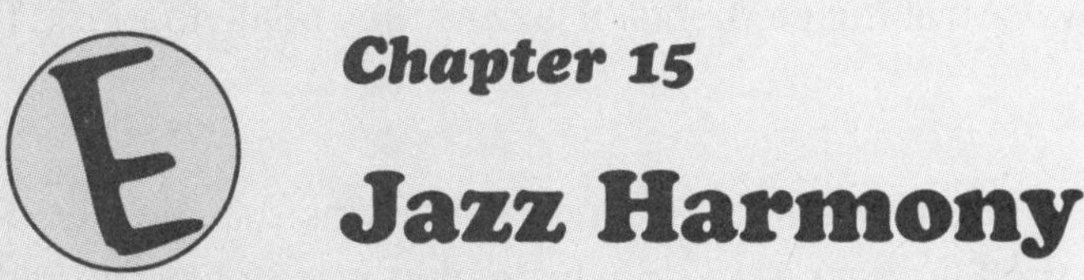

Chapter 15

Jazz Harmony

You have already dealt with harmony on many different levels in this book. Yet, in modern times, harmony has diverged into a very unique art form that is truly American: jazz. Although jazz harmony reminds us of traditional tonal harmony, it looks and feels quite a bit different. Now it's time to look at what makes jazz harmony unique, as it's a crucial part of the history of music.

What Is Jazz?

Jazz is a very young genre of music that continues to evolve and reshape itself at a breathtaking pace. Every ten years or so, jazz seems to reinvent itself; the rate of change in jazz is quite astounding. Jazz is categorized by several important characteristics. One is instrumentation: bass, piano, drums, saxophone, and trumpet come to mind when one thinks of jazz. The other main part of jazz is improvisation. It's actually the strongest component of playing jazz: improvising melodic solos over chord changes. It's one of the things that truly sets jazz on its own! Now, look at the elements of jazz as they relate to music theory.

E IN TIME

Jazz is one of the few purely American art forms that do not directly come from the European tradition. Instead, it was slowly formed from its origins in gospel music and the blues music of the Deep South. It quickly grew into art music through the great jazz innovators such as Louis Armstrong, Miles Davis, Charlie Parker, and John Coltrane, just to name a few.

How is jazz different from other styles of music? Primarily improvisation and instrumentation; those are aspects that are unique to jazz. Consider jazz in relation to other styles of music. Does jazz use scales, diatonic chords, triads? How does its harmony work? What are the essential ingredients of jazz? The rest of this chapter is devoted to breaking jazz into its small parts.

Jazz Harmony

Jazz harmony is unmistakably rooted in the tradition of music theory that you have studied thus far. It relies on melodies that are harmonized with chords. The principal difference between jazz harmony and other harmony is its use of chords that are taller than triads. "Taller" as in vertically, on the page, like this G13 chord.

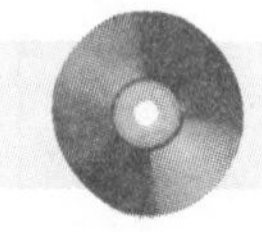

TRACK 83

FIGURE 15.1 G13 Chord

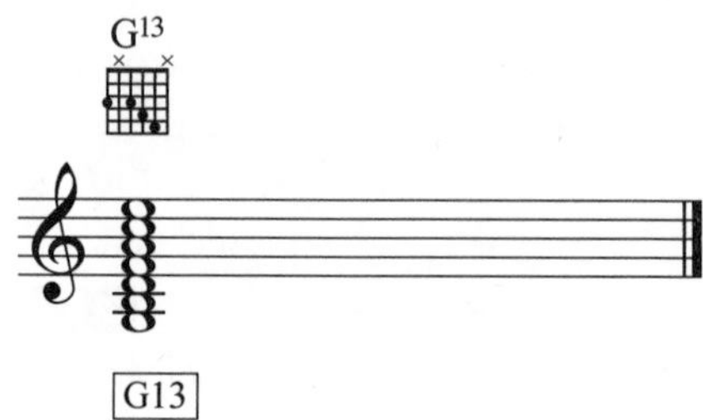

The G13 chord is considered a "tall chord," as it's tall on the page. It fits into a class of chords called extended chords. To understand extended chords, you need to understand extended intervals. This book's earlier discussion of intervals didn't say much about extended intervals, but jazz harmony requires it. You need to know what a 13th really is and what extended intervals are.

Extended Intervals

By now, intervals should be a common part of your music theory experience. Funny how there's more to learn about them now! Intervals have shown you the exact distance between any two notes. Up until now, you have not distinguished intervals larger than an octave. You heard about them, but you never saw them put into practice.

Do a quick review: After you pass the octave (which is also called an 8th), you distinguish these larger intervals with, you guessed it, larger numbers. Any interval larger than an octave is considered an extended interval. However, there are some intervals that are never extended.

Music theory does not distinguish the distance of a third or a fifth differently, no matter what octave it is in. Much of this has to do with historical practice, but the real reason lies in triadic harmony.

Point to Consider

Since the majority of jazz chords include extended intervals, you just need to remember your rule of nine in order to decipher what a ninth from C is, for example. In jazz, the seventh chord is the smallest unit you will see, and typically, taller chords are more common than seventh chords, so you'll need to know your extensions in order to succeed.

If you start stacking thirds on top of one another, you get this order: C–E–G–B–D–F–A–C.

Or as intervals: root, third, fifth, seventh, ninth, eleventh, thirteenth, and root.

Using the rule of nine you learned in the interval chapter, you know that the extended intervals (ninth, eleventh, and thirteenth) spell the same as a second, fourth, and a sixth; they are just an octave away. The reason you don't see tenths and seconds (thirds and fifths) is that when you stack thirds, those intervals simply don't come up. Once you get to thirteen, the next third brings you back to the octave.

The other reason that thirds and fifths are not counted as extended intervals becomes clear when you hear them compared to other intervals (such as seconds versus ninths). To most ears, thirds and fifths sound the same no matter what octave they occur in. This is not to say that they sound identical, but the difference is so minute that you don't need another name for them based on whether they are more than an octave apart. A second sounds very different than a ninth. Try this out on your instrument and hear for yourself!

Extended Chords

Now that you know about extended intervals, you need to look at extended chords. You learned about four families of chords: major, minor, diminished, and augmented. When sevenths are added into the equation, you get a fifth chord family: dominant chords (major triads with minor sevenths). These basic five chords and their extensions make up the majority of jazz harmony. To get by in jazz, you need to understand major, minor, and dominant extensions first. You will deal with diminished (which is typically note extended) and augmented chords later.

Extended Major

The basic jazz major chord is the major seventh chord. As you recall, a major seventh chord is a major triad with a major seventh interval added to it. In addition to the seventh, you see major chord extensions. Major chords can be written the following ways and all still fall under the umbrella of "major" and, thus, substitute for each other:

- C Major 7th
- C Major 9th
- C Major 11th
- C Major 13th

The formula for these chords is pretty simple to spot: root (major) "extension." Any chord that follows that formula is in the major seventh family. For example: F Major 9th is a major seventh chord, but F9th is something else because it lacks the necessary "major" component in its name. Knowing these basic rules will make life much less confusing as jazz deals with chord symbols more often than actual written voicings. That's right, in jazz, you turn symbols into sounds.

In jazz, all major chord extensions take their notes from the major scale built off the root. A D Major 13th chord will take all of its notes from the D major scale. This is important because the spelling of the individual notes has to follow the home scale or the chord won't sound right.

Extended Minor

The basic jazz minor chord is the minor seventh chord. As you recall, a minor seventh chord is a minor triad with a minor seventh interval added to it. In addition to the seventh, you see minor chord extensions. Minor chords can be written the following ways and all still fall under the umbrella of "minor" and, thus, substitute for each other:

- C minor 7th
- C minor 9th
- C minor 11th
- C minor 13th

The formula for these chords is pretty simple to spot: root (minor) "extension." Any chord that follows that formula is in the minor seventh family. For example: F minor 11th is a minor seventh–type chord, simply extended.

In jazz, all minor chord extensions take their notes from the Dorian scale built off the root. A D minor 13th chord will take all its notes from the D Dorian scale. This is important because the spelling of the individual notes has to follow the home scale or the chord won't sound right. In jazz, the home scale for minor chords is the Dorian mode, not the "expected" natural minor scale. This is one of the places where jazz starts to pull away from traditional harmony—its use of modes for harmonic and melodic purposes.

Extended Dominant

The basic jazz dominant chord is the dominant seventh chord. As you recall, a dominant seventh chord is a major triad with a minor seventh interval added to it. In addition to the seventh, you see dominant chord extensions. When used in practice, many jazz players will simply call these chords "seventh" chords and leave off the moniker "dominant" as it's implied. Dominant chords can be written the following ways and all still fall under the umbrella of "dominant" and, thus, substitute for each other:

- C7th
- C9th
- C11th
- C13th

The formula for these chords is pretty simple to spot: root "extension." Any chord that follows that formula is in the dominant seventh family. For example: F11th is a dominant seventh–type chord, simply extended to the eleventh.

Typically, with dominant chords comes chordal alterations. An alteration is some sort of change to the fifth or ninth of the chord. An altered dominant chord may read like this:

- C7♭9♯5

Even though that chord looks kind of scary, it's still very plainly dominant because at its core, it's a C7 with other stuff added to the end of it. You will look at this in more depth in the section entitled Substitutions and Enhancements.

In jazz, all dominant chord extensions take their notes from the Mixolydian scale built off the root. An E13th chord will take all its notes from the E Mixolydian scale. This is important because the spelling of the individual notes has to follow the home scale or the chord won't sound right. In jazz, the home scale for dominant chords is the Mixolydian mode, not the major scale (that's reserved for major seventh chords). This is another example of modal use in jazz.

Other Chords?

What about diminished and augmented? Well, in jazz, the diminished seventh chord is very common, and it is written exactly how you'd expect to see it: C°7. The other type of diminished chord, the half diminished chord, is found in jazz very often, but it rarely goes by its classical symbol of Cø7. The symbols for full and half diminished simply look too close to each other. To rectify this, half diminished chords are written as "Minor 7♭5" chords, which gets you to the same chord and completely avoids confusion with the other diminished chord. Almost 99.9 percent of the time, if you see a diminished chord, assume that it's a fully diminished seventh chord.

As for augmented chords, they appear as you'd expect them to, in the two varieties you studied in the seventh chord chapter: Cmaj7+ (C–E–G♯–B) and C7+ (C–E–G♯–B♭). You can extend an augmented chord, but it's pretty rare. For most things, if you can decipher the major, minor, dominant, diminished, and augmented chord symbols, you're mostly there.

Jazz Progressions

If you want to study the harmony of jazz, you're going to have to head to Tin Pan Alley. Jazz players took songs from the Great American Songbook and used them as vehicles for jazz improvisation. They would play the melodies instrumentally (or sing them if a vocalist was involved) at the start of the tune; this is called playing the head of the tune. Once that was done, the chords that formed the harmony of the song remained while the soloist improvised a new melody; this is called blowing on the changes. At the end, they'd play the melody one last time and that was it.

IN TIME

Tin Pan Alley was the gathering place of a group of composers who wrote in the late nineteenth and early twentieth centuries and created the Great American Songbook, which is simply a collection of Broadway songs and other tunes that defined American music during this period. Stephen Foster, Cole Porter, and Jimmy Van Heusen are all contributors to this genre.

Because jazz players favored these songs so much, their melodies and harmonies became the foundation for what is known as jazz harmony. These songs became the songs that all jazz players know and play today; they are aptly referred to as "standards." The harmonies of these songs have some regular patterns that appear over and over again, and thankfully these can be studied! Start with the diatonic progressions.

The Diatonic Progressions

In jazz, if you simply take the diatonic major scale and harmonize each chord up to the seventh, you can learn a lot about how jazz harmony functions. Here is the A♭ major scale harmonized in seventh chords.

FIGURE 15.2 Harmonized Scale in 7ths

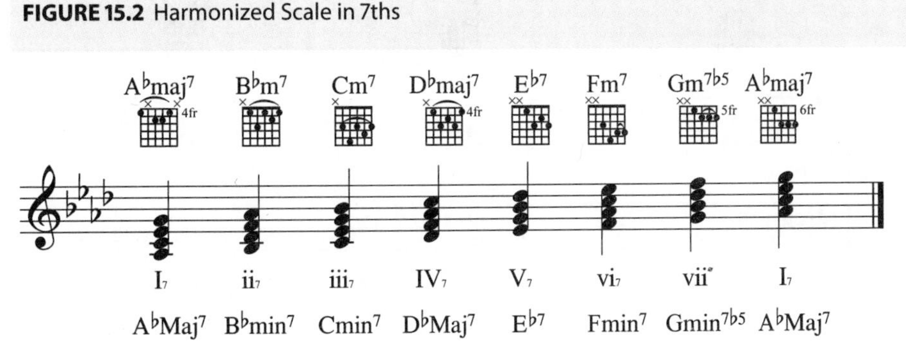

You'll be happy to learn that the basic jazz progressions are diatonic and still follow the chord ladder. Start with the mighty jazz progression of the ii–V–I.

ii–V–I

In jazz, nothing is more common than the ii–V–I progression. Take a look:

TRACK 84

FIGURE 15.3 The ii–V–I

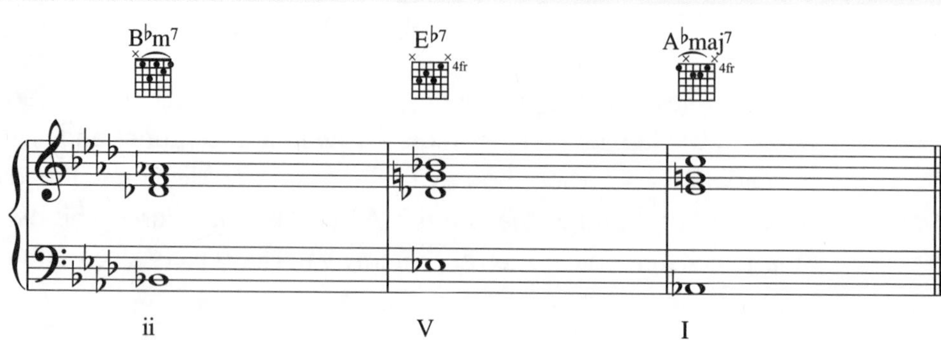

If jazz harmony were distilled down to one central point, it would be the ii–V–I progression. It's simply all over jazz music. Sure, jazz gets more complicated, but the ii–V–I is the basic harmonic unit that all jazz players use.

What's interesting is that essentially, a ii–V–I is a substituted IV–V–I (as ii and IV substitute for each other), which is just a I–IV–V (remember those simple primary chords?) reordered. Why change the IV to ii? By doing so, you create three different chords: a minor seventh chord, a dominant seventh chord, and a major seventh chord. That sound became the sound that made jazz sound different than other styles of music.

Add some extended chords and you get a very distinctive jazzy vibe out of this progression.

TRACK 85

FIGURE 15.4 Jazzed Up ii–V–I

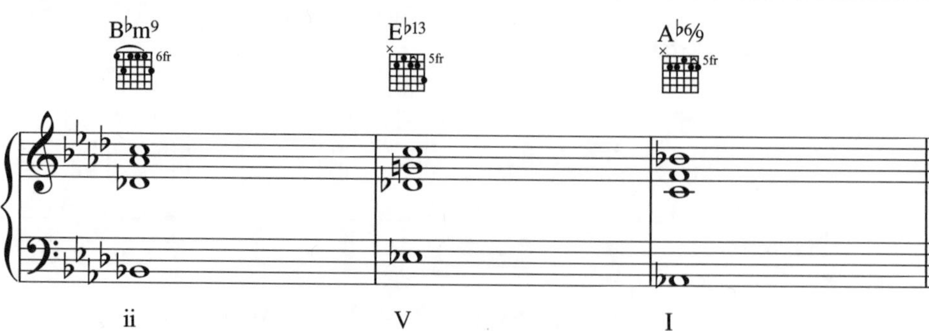

Add a few more chords before the ii and you reach the other common jazz progression, the iii–vi–ii–V–I:

FIGURE 15.5 Longer Jazz Progression

TRACK 86

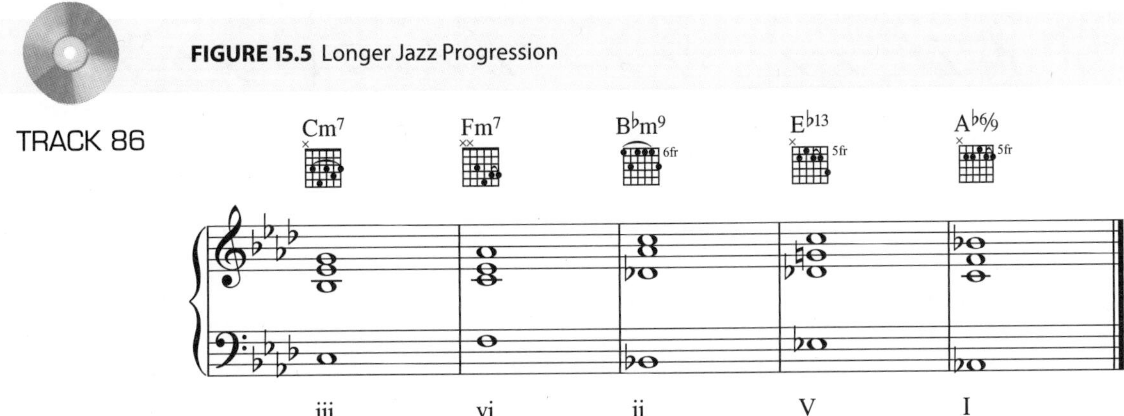

Minor Progressions

There is a minor key equivalent to the ii–V–I progression in major. It's still a "two five one," but the qualities of the chords change. Instead of it being Dm7–G7–Cmaj7 (in the key of C major), the progression becomes Dm7♭5–G7–Cm7.

FIGURE 15.6 ii–V–i in a Minor Key

TRACK 87

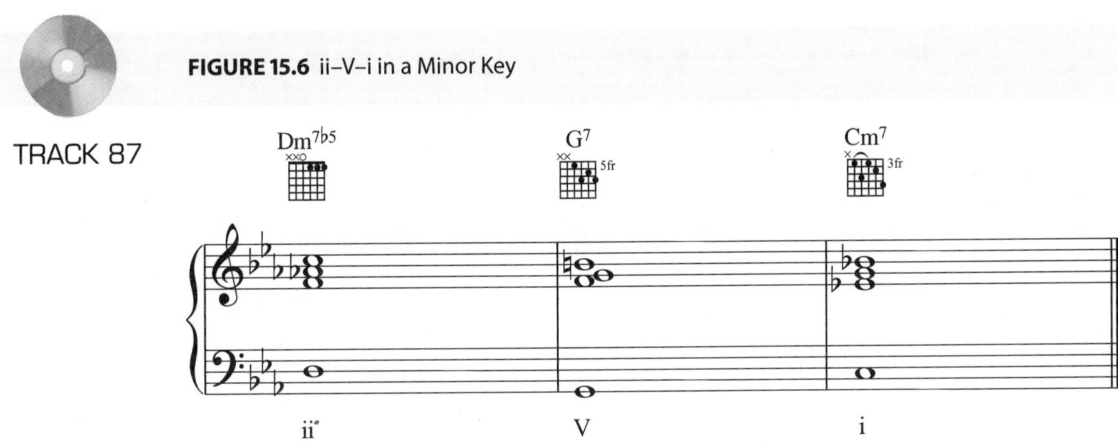

This progression is easy to spot because you also have three distinct chords, with a dominant chord in the middle. Look for the min7♭5, that's usually the signpost that screams "Hey, minor two five coming" and look to see if the chords that follow it line up.

Now, look at how a real jazz tune is put together. Here is a very common standard, without the melody, just the changes (jazzspeak for the chords).

FIGURE 15.7 A "Real" Tune

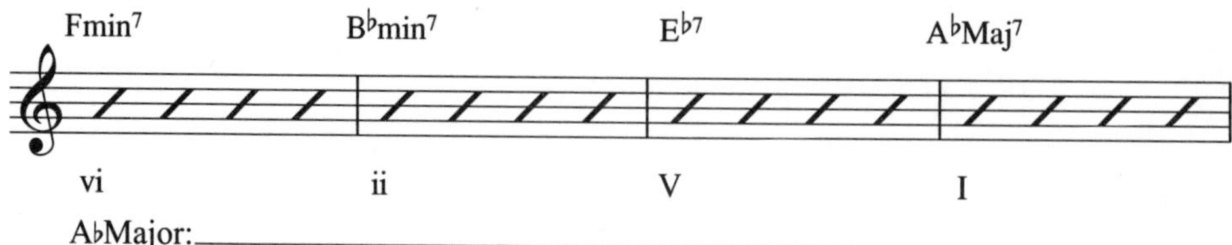

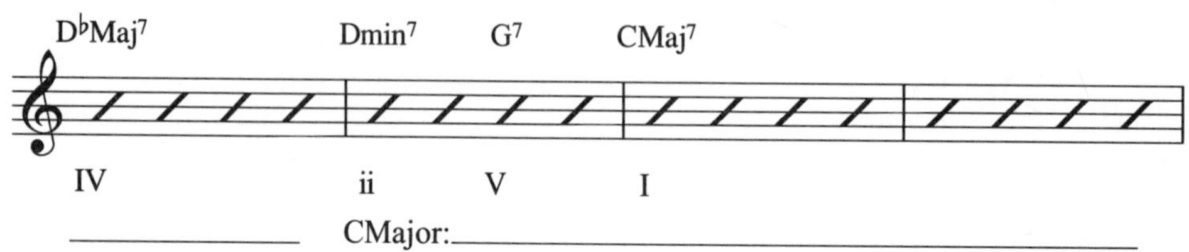

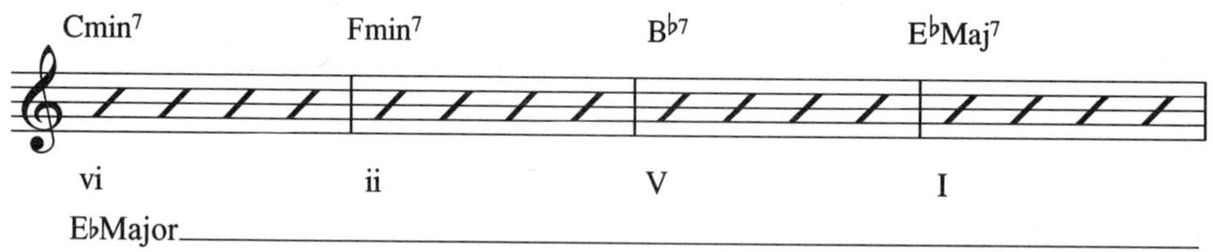

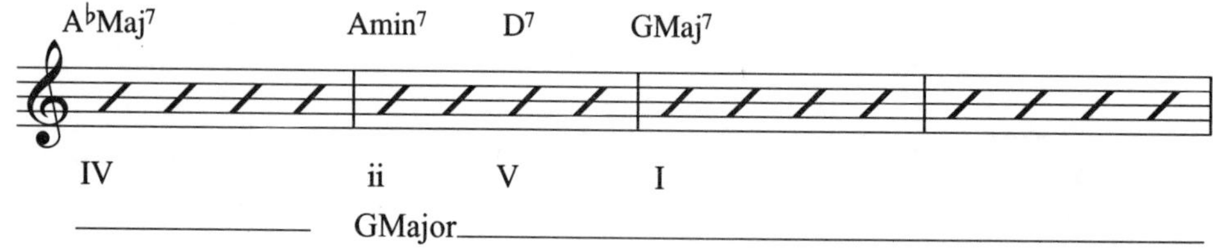

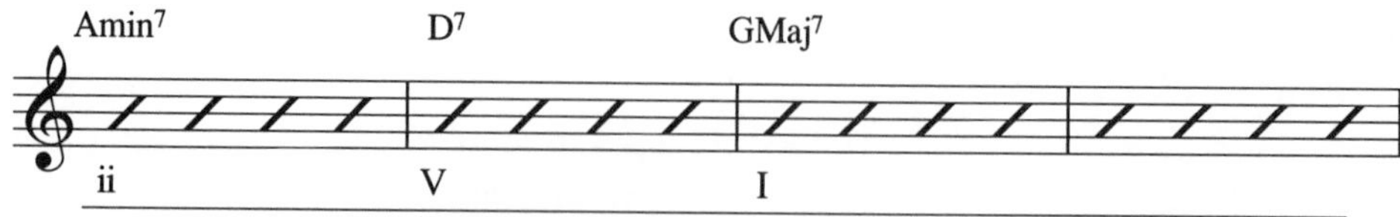

FIGURE 15.7A A "Real" Tune

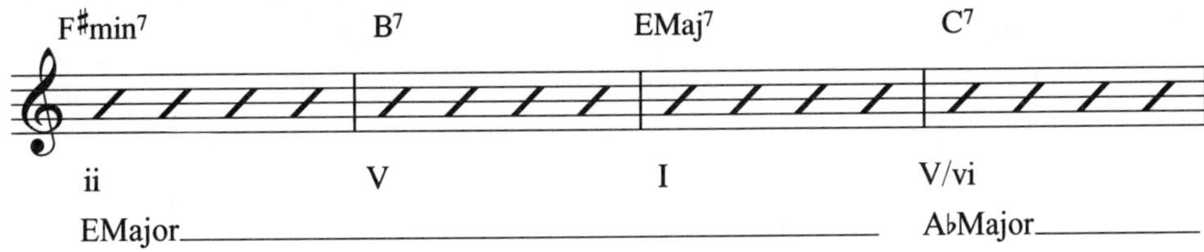

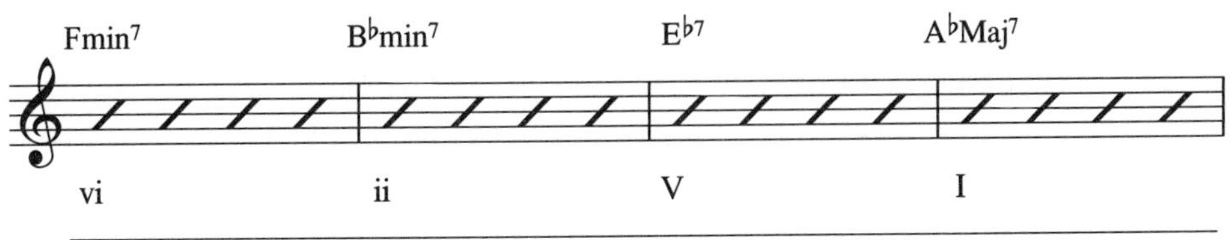

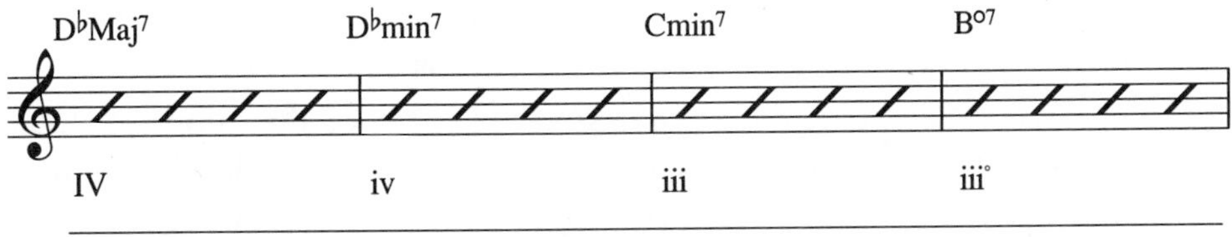

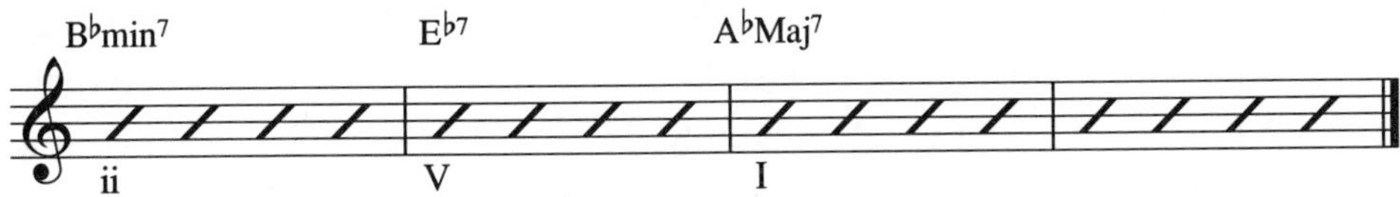

Notice the analysis under the chords. You see loads of ii–V–I progressions, in many keys, both major and minor. This is very standard practice for jazz (changing keys often), but beyond that, the progressions are fairly simple; it's just modulating often.

IN TIME

FIGURE 15.7 is essentially a lead sheet. This skeletal form of music tells you what chords to play on what beats, and if a melody is present, the melodic line. If **FIGURE 15.7** had a melody, it would be enough for an entire band to play with. The chords would be "created" from the symbols, the bass player would "walk" a bass line that made sense with the chords, and the melodic players would improvise on the chord changes.

Substitutions and Enhancements

One of the cornerstones of jazz is the ability to change aspects of the harmony as you see fit. Listen to ten different versions of the stalwart standard "Autumn Leaves," and you will hear strikingly different approaches to a tune that is known by practically every jazzer in the known world. The reason that you can change things up so much lies in the essence of jazz substitution.

As you saw in **FIGURE 15.7**, jazz harmony is expressed as written chord symbols. The player has to "realize" these chord voicings and play them in his or her own way. There is no set way to voice C Major 7 on the piano or guitar; there are literally hundreds of different ways to play the same chord (see the *Everything® Guitar Chords* book as an example). You rarely get the written voicings; it's always up to you to voice the chords as you see fit.

When you voice the chords, you can enhance the chords; actually, you're expected to. Think of it as "supersizing." You see a C Major 7th chord, but that's really just a suggestion. It's telling you that you need to play a chord in the family of C Major 7th, but you are free to extend it as you see fit. C Major 7th could just as easily be C Major 9th, it's up to you. This is one of the nice freedoms afforded to you as a jazz musician.

It's also true in reverse; if you see a very tall chord, you have the chance to reduce it to its smallest part. If you see an F13th chord, you can say to yourself, "OK, it's just an extended dominant 7th chord, I can reduce that chord to F7." Doing so isn't wrong; actually, it's pretty common. The only thing to ponder is why you would see such a tall chord. Sometimes composers put them in there for a very good reason. Often a chord exists because it supports a particular melody note (the melody is the 13th). You should try to learn to play every chord you see, but that's another story. Reducing is fine, with one notable exception: alterations.

Chord Alterations

A chord alteration, as discussed earlier, is tampering with the fifth or ninth of the chord in some way. You typically see this is on a dominant chord, although you could see it anywhere. Chord alterations are not something that you can typically ignore. They are always there for a good reason. Usually it's to support a melody note of some sort.

Here are some conditions to keep in mind when dealing with altered chords.

- When in doubt, play them as written!
- Alterations to the fifth must be played as they affect the core triad.
- Alterations to the ninth don't have to be played as long as you reduce to a 7th chord and leave the ninths out altogether.
- It's probably not a good idea to extend an altered chord any higher than written. Altered chords can have funny extensions that are not clear and expected. When in doubt, play what you have.
- Always look at the melody that goes with the altered chord. Is the melody note the reason for the alteration? If not, why alter the chord at all? Maybe it's altered for harmonic color and beauty and not necessarily function.

These tips will assist you in your understanding of why you see altered chords, when to use them, and how to play them.

Lots of dominant chords are altered because as dominant chords, they typically function as V chords in jazz, so they will resolve to I. Because they are V chords and they resolve to I strongly anyway (because of the pull between the 3rd and the 7th) composers and players like to alter them as the alterations have little effect on the V chord's proclivity to resolve! You simply end up with a more colorful chord, which is a very jazzy thing.

Blues Forms

Now that you have heard about chords and harmony, it's time to cover the blues, a basic ingredient in jazz. Jazz grew from the blues and still relies on the blues as a standard form and song style. The blues is just plain cool. Everybody's got the blues at one point or another! Jazz folks have the blues pretty often. In addition to the standard American Songbook tunes that everyone knows and loves, the blues remains a very important form for jazz players. Every self-respecting jazz composer has written a blues tune or two or three or four. The blues exists in two varieties: minor blues and major blues. Each blues song is exactly twelve bars (or measures) long. Blues songs follow a strict repeating harmonic formula, so it's easy to transpose them into any key, and in general, they are easy to learn to play.

12-Bar Major Blues

The 12-bar blues is taken from the "traditional" blues you might hear in the blues clubs or by someone like B. B. King, but the jazz players have adapted the harmony just a little bit. Take a look at what a traditional 12-bar blues piece looks like:

FIGURE 15.8 Traditional 12-Bar Blues

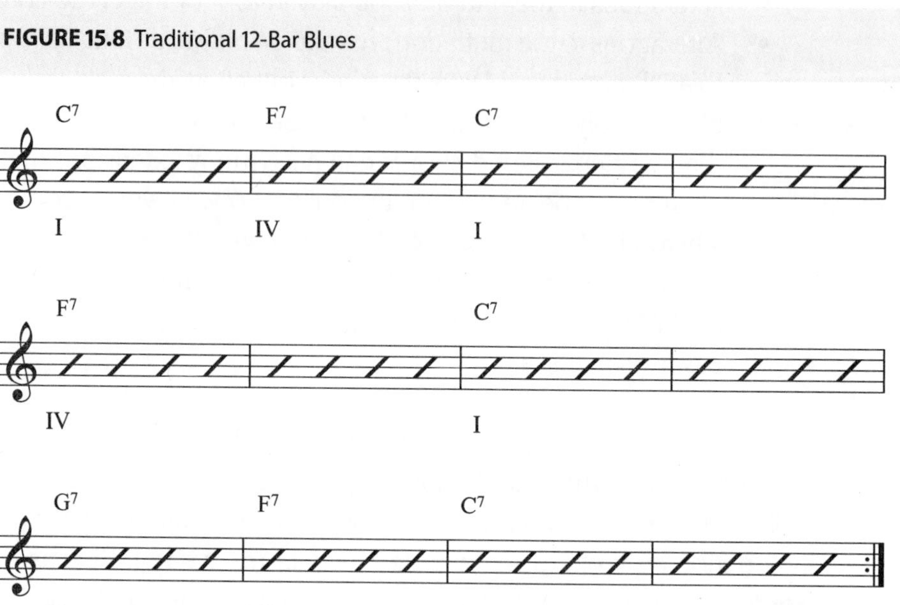

Now, contrast that with the blues that most jazz players play.

FIGURE 15.9 Jazz Blues

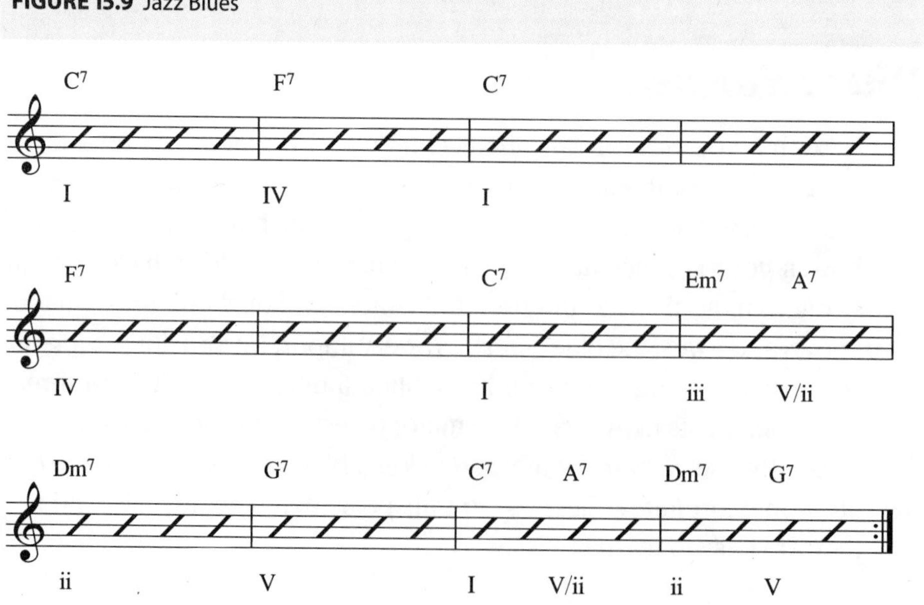

The last five measures are where you see a change. Instead of the traditional blues V–VI–I ending, the standard jazz ii–V–I progression is thrown in. Preceding that ii chord, a V/ii is thrown in to set up the progression and make life a bit more interesting for the improviser.

Notice how the Roman numeral harmony, chord symbols, and guitar chords are given for each example. This way, you can transpose the chords into any key you need to. The B♭ blues is definitely one of the most used, standard jazz/blues keys, so it's a very good one to start with.

Here's a list of jazz tunes that are based on the 12-bar major blues:

- "Now's the Time" (Charlie Parker)
- "Blue Monk" (Thelonious Monk)
- "Straight, No Chaser" (Thelonious Monk)
- "Billie's Bounce" (Charlie Parker)
- "Tenor Madness" (Sonny Rollins)

There are a million more, but this will get you started. Make sure to transpose them into different keys! If you don't play harmonies, learn some melodies (all the jazz blues have "heads," so learn those).

12-Bar Minor Blues

The final variant of jazz blues is called the minor blues, and you guessed it, it's in a minor key!

Take a look at the minor blues.

FIGURE 15.10 Minor Blues

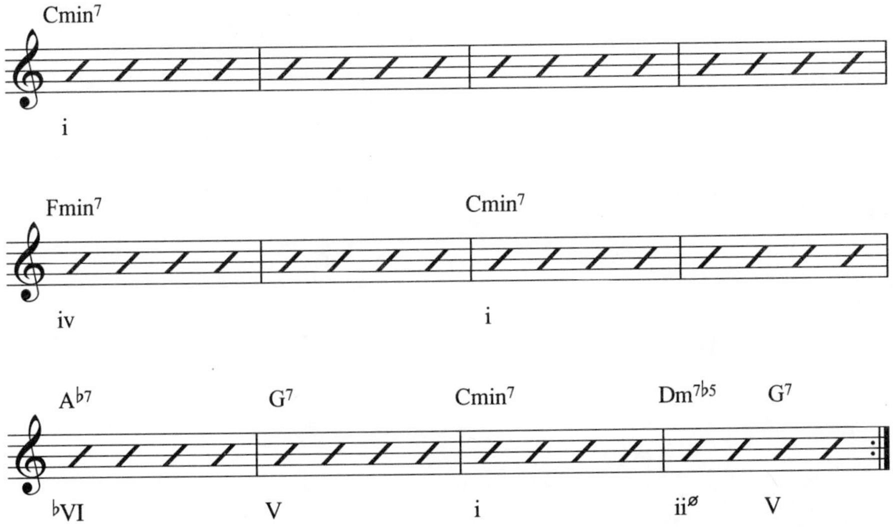

Cmin^7

i

Fmin^7 Cmin^7

iv i

A$^{\flat 7}$ G^7 Cmin^7 Dm$^{7\flat 5}$ G^7

$\flat$VI V i ii^{ø} V

You see some basic harmony, such as your i and iv chords, the expected dominant V chord that you need for minor keys. The chord that is slightly off is the ♭VI chord that precedes the V chord in bar nine. That's simply what makes a minor blues work the way it does; a definite difference between the major and the minor.

Extra Credit

If you're looking for jazz tunes to play, check out a "real book," which is a takeoff on the "fake books" that include melodies, basic chords, and lyrics so musicians can improvise with any song. There are tons of real books available on the market, and each is a repository of hundreds of jazz lead sheets with melodies, words, and chord changes. It's a great place to study and learn some great music while you're at it.

Also, you'll notice a turnaround in the last bar of a Dmin7♭5, G7. This turnaround sets the i chord up in bar one so the tune can loop around. The progression is the "minor" version of a ii–V–i progression, as you learned earlier in the chapter.

That wraps up your general overview of jazz harmony. Sure, there's more to look at, but this will get you more than started. If you have a real interest in jazz, that are some great books that deal with jazz harmony to read and study; either that or consult a good jazz teacher! Either way you look at it, nothing beats listening to as much music as humanly possible.

Chapter 16

Transposition and Instrumentation

One of the most confusing and maligned aspects of music theory is the nature of transposing instruments. Few topics frustrate students more than this. Transposing isn't difficult, only misunderstood. When you learn about the instruments and their transpositions, you also can learn about their musical range, how to write for them, and how to analyze music that contains mixtures of transposing versus nontransposing instruments. To truly study music, you have to know that what you see isn't always what you hear.

What Is Transposing?

Suppose Josh plays the alto saxophone and Bill plays the clarinet. They get together and jam one day. Josh writes a short melody on the sax, notates it, and hands it to Bill to play along with. To their shock and amazement, the resulting sound is terrible. What was supposed to be two instruments playing the same melody in concert ended up as a cacophony! Confused, they set out to understand why alto sax and clarinet can't read the same melody. What they discover is that transposing and the natural keys of instruments has caused this musical calamity. All their lives, Josh and Bill were taught that C is C and D is D and so on. Unfortunately, this is not always true; it depends which instrument you are looking at.

Concert Pitch

The pitch of any note is a mathematical event. Notes exist as vibrations of air. The speed at which they vibrate can be measured and is expressed in hertz (Hz). This is the only true measure of a note, its frequency in hertz. A large group of instruments exist that play in "concert pitch," meaning that when they play or read a note on the musical staff, they are getting the "mathematically correct" answer. When a piano plays a middle C, it's playing a note with a frequency of 261 Hz—it's an exact thing; the piano is playing concert pitch. There are a large number of instruments that play concert pitch. Here is a list of popular instruments that play concert pitch. These are also called C instruments.

- Violin, viola, cello, bass
- Piano
- Harp
- Guitar/bass
- Flute/piccolo
- Oboe
- Bassoon
- Trombone
- Euphonium
- Tuba
- Pitched percussion (except glockenspiel)

The entire list above plays in concert pitch. There are some exceptions: Guitar and bass transpose an octave down in order to keep their music in the staff, but they are still considered concert. The piccolo and glockenspiel read an octave lower than they actually play. This is also meant to keep these very high-pitched instruments within the range of the staff for reading comfort.

What Does Transposing Mean?

Here is a list of the common instruments that transpose:

- Clarinet
- Soprano, alto, tenor, and baritone saxophone
- French horn
- Trumpet, baritone horn
- English horn

There are other transposing instruments out there, but these are the ones you will see most often.

A great example of a concert pitch is an orchestral tuning note. When a symphony orchestra tunes up, the oboe player plays a concert A note. The rest of the orchestra tunes up to this concert A note. Most metronomes that provide a tuning pitch also provide the same concert A (A = 440 Hz).

A transposing instrument reads the exact same music as everyone else. The only difference is that when a tenor sax plays a written C, the note that comes out of the tenor sax would not register as a C on a tuner or match a C on a piano. An entirely different note comes out! A concert B♭ is heard when a trumpet plays a written C. This is what is meant by *transposition*. Look at an example. If you play a short melody for the tenor sax on the top staff, what you actually hear is the bottom staff!

FIGURE 16.1 Transposing Melody

Now you start to see the possibility for confusion. If you didn't know about this, you might be very confused. Just think about poor Josh and Bill. Amazingly, this isn't always taught in the study of an instrument. Most students just learn to read the notes in front of them. But you are here for more than just playing! You want to understand what you are looking at, and if a score has multiple instruments on it, you can't trust your eyes! You have to know what you're really looking at.

Why Does This Happen?

Good question. Why can't we all just get along—er, play in the same key? There are two possible reasons that certain instruments transpose and others don't. The first is history. Brass instruments rely heavily on the overtone series to make their notes happen. Brass instruments used to add "crooks," which were additional pipes, to their instruments in order to play in different keys. The French horn was a good example of this. In time, as the instruments evolved and valves were added to the brass instruments, the additional crooks were no longer necessary. Certain instruments evolved into certain keys and stayed there. It's now been so long and there has been so much music written that it would be very painful to change.

IN TIME

Think you're immune to this? Play in a rock band? Imagine this: You play in a blues band and you bring in a sax or trumpet player to expand your sound. When it comes time to teach the melodies, what are you going to tell the musician to play? If he or she wants to solo on the E blues your guitar player is so fond of, exactly what will you say? You need to know how transposition works.

The second reason is best shown in the sax family. There are four saxophones in common use today: soprano, alto, tenor, and baritone. Each of the four saxophones transposes differently. The reason that it's done this way has less to do with history and more to do with the ease of the player. Each of the four saxophones, while physically differing in size, has the exact same system of keys that Adolphe Sax invented in the 1800s. The sax transposes four different ways so that any sax player trained on any one of the instruments could play any of the saxophones without having to relearn anything. Each saxophone reads the same treble clef melody and the composer makes sure that each part is transposed correctly on paper for the proper sonic result. Some other instruments also do this.

Transposing Chant

For too many years, students have been baffled, perplexed, and generally confused as to how to transpose correctly for instruments. But you can learn a chant that will help you make sense of it. The answer lies in knowing two things: You have to know the full name of the instrument and you need to know the chant.

Each instrument has a key name. But a trumpet isn't usually called a B♭ trumpet, is it? *Trumpet* usually suffices. Knowing the full name of each instrument is one key to understanding how it transposes. The other key is the chant, which goes like this: The instrument's key name is the note that you hear in concert pitch when that instrument reads its written C. (Thank you, Scott Lavine.) Now put that to use, using the B♭ trumpet again, which has a key name of "B♭." To understand how the chant helps, add this information into your chant: The instrument key name (in this case B♭) is the note you hear in concert pitch when that instrument (trumpet) reads its written C. Simply, when a trumpet plays a written C, you hear a B♭.

FIGURE 16.2 Trumpet Transpose

This means that whatever note or notes are written for trumpet will come out exactly one whole step below what is written. So what can composers do to fix this? Simply write the trumpet part up a whole step, in a written D. The trumpet player will read and play the D, yet a perfect C will come out in concert key.

Sound down, write up. For most transposing instruments this is the case. There are a couple of zany exceptions, but you don't need to worry about them right now. For the most part, you write parts up and they sound down. Just remember the chant.

B♭ Instruments

There are a few common instruments that exist in the key of B♭ together and thus transpose the exact same way. The B♭ instruments include the B♭ trumpet, B♭ clarinet, and B♭ soprano saxophone. Each of these instruments follows the same rule: Whatever they read comes out a whole step down.

FIGURE 16.3 B♭ Transpose

There is another instrument that is called a B♭ instrument: the B♭ tenor sax. It's a little bit different than the others—it transposes an octave and a whole step down. When a tenor sax plays a C, you indeed hear a B♭, but it's a full octave lower than the other B♭ instruments. To write parts that sound correct, you have to write the part up a whole step in the case of clarinet, trumpet, and soprano sax. In the case of tenor sax, write it up an octave and a whole step (or a major 9th). The other instrument that follows this same transposition is the B♭ bass clarinet.

FIGURE 16.4 Tenor Sax Transpose

E♭ Instruments

There are two common instruments that are in the key of E♭. The first is the E♭ alto saxophone, and the other is the E♭ baritone saxophone. Being in the key of E♭ means that when these instruments read a written C, an E♭ concert pitch is heard. The E♭ alto saxophone transposes a major sixth away from where it's written. This means that a melody written in concert pitch would have to be transposed up a major 6th in order to sound correct on the alto saxophone.

FIGURE 16.5 Alto Sax Transpose

The baritone saxophone is also in the key of E♭; the only difference is that the baritone is a full octave below the alto sax, so it transposes at the intervals of a major sixth and an octave (or a major 13th). In order for a melody written in concert key to sound correctly on a baritone sax, it must be written a major 13th up! Remember, it sounds down, but it must be written up.

FIGURE 16.6 Baritone Sax Transpose

F Instruments

Two instruments transpose in the key of F: the French horn and the English horn. Both the French horn and the English horn (which is a tenor oboe) transpose in the same way, exactly a 5th away. If a composer writes a melody in concert key and wants the French horn and English horn to play them correctly, he must write the melody up a perfect 5th in order for it to sound correct.

FIGURE 16.7 French/English Horn Transpose

Octave Transposes

The guitar and bass are unique transposing instruments. Both the guitar and the bass play in concert key. That is, when guitar and bass play the note C, an electronic tuner would register the note C. But the guitar and bass "octave transpose"; that is, the pitch they read is an octave higher than the sound that comes out of their instruments. This is a slightly unusual practice. The reason for this makes perfect sense! If guitar and bass did not transpose like this, their music would be extremely low on the staff—most of the notes they played would be many ledger lines below the staff. And you know how annoying it is to read that way. Guitar and bass raise their notes an octave higher to keep the majority of the notes on the staff for ease of reading.

You could go your whole life never knowing this and you may never even notice! If you ever have to write a unison line for guitar or bass, you'll know exactly what to do.

There are other instrument transpositions that you haven't learned about here. There are clarinets in A and trumpets in D, and French horns can be in almost any key possible. As long as you realize that the name of the instrument is the note you hear (in concert pitch) when it plays a written C, you will know how to read and understand that instrument.

FIGURE 16.8 Guitar Transpose

Analyzing Scores

At this point, you've gotten pretty far into chords and theory and can make your way through myriad musical situations with confidence. You've analyzed your favorite pop songs and more with ease and now you've decided to step up. You've decided to go to the library and check out the score of a symphony orchestra. You went German! You checked out one of Beethoven's nine symphonies. Now, you'd like to know what's going on in Beethoven's head; he is a genius after all. So you crack open the score for the Ninth Symphony and see that there are a lot of instruments in it. Here's what you see in the score listing of required instruments:

- Piccolo
- Flute
- Oboe
- Clarinet (in B♭, C, and A)
- Bassoon
- Contrabassoon
- French horns (in D, E♭, B♭, and bass B♭)
- Trumpet (in B♭ and D)
- Trombones
- Percussion, including pitched percussion (timpani)

- Violin
- Viola
- Cello
- Bass
- Four-part choir

Well, that's quite a list. What's even worse is that there are instruments there that you have not even dealt with. What's an A clarinet? Horns in D, E♭, B♭, and bass B♭? You wonder what is going on.

Welcome to a full symphony score of the nineteenth century! A conductor/composer would only view scores like this: transposing scores. You see exactly what the players read on their music stands. If you want to figure out what is going on, you'll have to transpose the parts into concert pitch to figure out what's there, and you'll have to do it basically at "first sight."

Begin by picking a few single chords to analyze in the fourth movement. (The fourth movement contains the famous "Ode to Joy" part everyone knows and loves.) Now, the Ninth Symphony is very long, so we're just going to analyze two measures of it. (This part is in the key of D minor.)

You have the full listing of instruments above, but Beethoven does not use them all at the same time. The section you are looking at features only flute, oboe, clarinet, bassoon, contrabassoon, horn in D, horn in B, trumpet in D, timpani, violin, viola, cello, and bass. Take a look at the excerpt. (On the CD, the voices are played with a synthetic symphony orchestra. Listening to a "real" recording of this monumental piece will do you some good.)

Pretty impressive-looking, right? The chords in question are highlighted on the staff. In order to start, you need to figure out which instruments are in concert key and which ones need to be transposed. This is actually easier than you think. Remember the listing of instruments (which is also on the score excerpt)? If the instrument isn't concert pitch (that is, it transposes), it will tell you in its name, such as B♭ clarinet and so on.

TRACK 88

FIGURE 16.9 Beethoven's Ninth Symphony Excerpt

Flute
Oboe
larinet in B♭
Bassoon
ontrabassoon
Horn in D
Horn in B
rumpet in D
Trombone
Violin 1
Violin 2
Viola
Violoncello
Double Bass

So, look at the transposing instruments alone and figure out what they are really playing.

FIGURE 16.10 Transposing Instruments

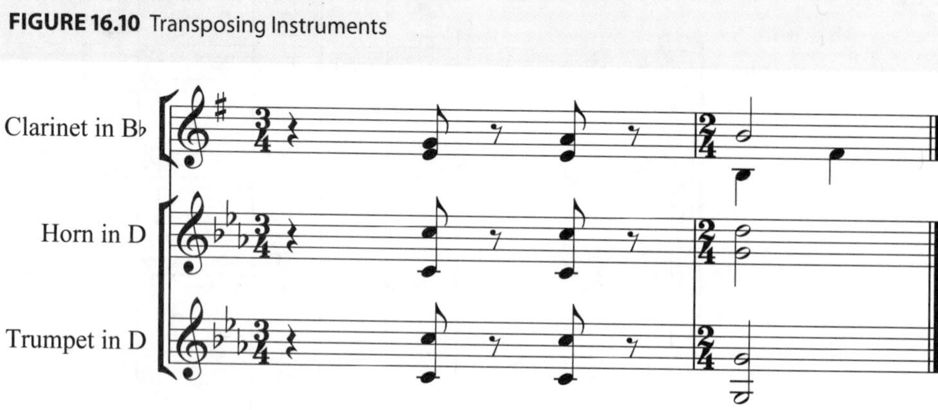

We segregated the clarinet, French horns, and the trumpet. Now go over their transpositions one by one so you know what to do to each instrument to bring it to concert key.

- Clarinet in B♭. Everything is written a whole step higher than concert pitch. Transpose the notes down a whole step.
- Horn in D (the horn in B isn't used in this example). Everything is written a whole step down. To read it in concert pitch, transpose the notes up a whole step.
- Trumpet in D. This is the same as the French horn in D; transpose it up a whole step to get to concert pitch.

Now you need to adjust those notes so that they read in concert pitch. Here is what they look like in concert pitch:

FIGURE 16.11 Transposing Instruments in Concert Pitch

Now throw them back in the score in concert pitch and you can get to work analyzing. Here is the full score in concert pitch:

FIGURE 16.12 Full Score in Concert Pitch

Now all you have to do is start reading from the bottom up and putting some chords together. Remember that the bass and the contrabassoon are the lowest-sounding pitches, so you can get your roots from there. Amazingly enough, when you analyze the piece, you come to these three chords:

FIGURE 16.13 Chord Analysis

B♭, G minor, and A triads! Triads! What, were you expecting more? Sure, you have so many instruments in an orchestra, you'd figure that there would be many different notes, right? Wrong. The basic foundations of harmony don't change. Beethoven was a tonal composer, and in those times, tonal meant triadic and seventh chords. So, all in all, it's just a matter of taking a three-note chord and voicing it throughout a huge orchestra, doubling notes in different instruments to create the sound. When you analyze this music, you can still break it down to the small parts and thankfully figure out what's going on—as long as you know what notes the instruments are actually playing!

Realizing that a full orchestra is playing only fairly simple triads and seventh chords is a bit of a revelation. For some, it can make the act of symphonic composing less impressive. Have no fear; the real genius in writing for large groups is not what chords are present, as chords are just the culmination of melodies that intersect vertically. The brilliance is in writing for the different groups of instruments and making them sound cohesive.

Instrument Ranges

As long as you're studying these instruments so deeply, you might as well learn the ranges of the instrument families. You might be looking to theory for help in your compositions, and there is nothing more useful than understanding what you can and can't write for certain instruments.

The following charts show the ranges for just about every instrument you should have a handle on. You can see their ranges from the extreme top to the extreme bottom. Realize that no chart will ever truly take the place of studying scores and reading some great orchestration books, but it will save you from making some silly mistakes (like writing in the wrong key or writing completely out of an instrument's range).

Here are the charts for your reference.

FIGURE 16.14 Vocal Ranges

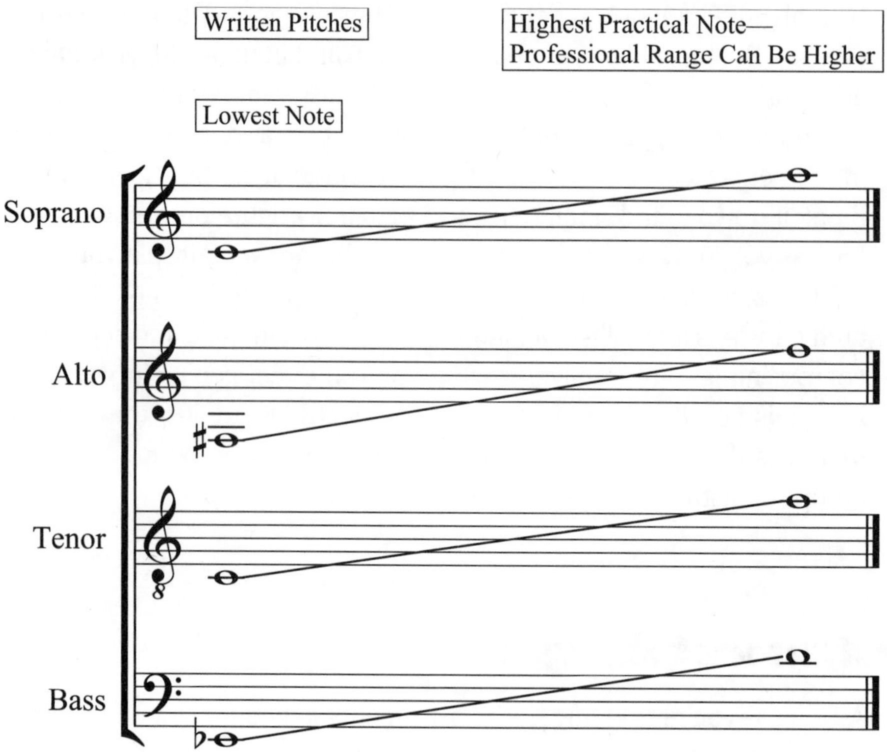

FIGURE 16.15 String Ranges

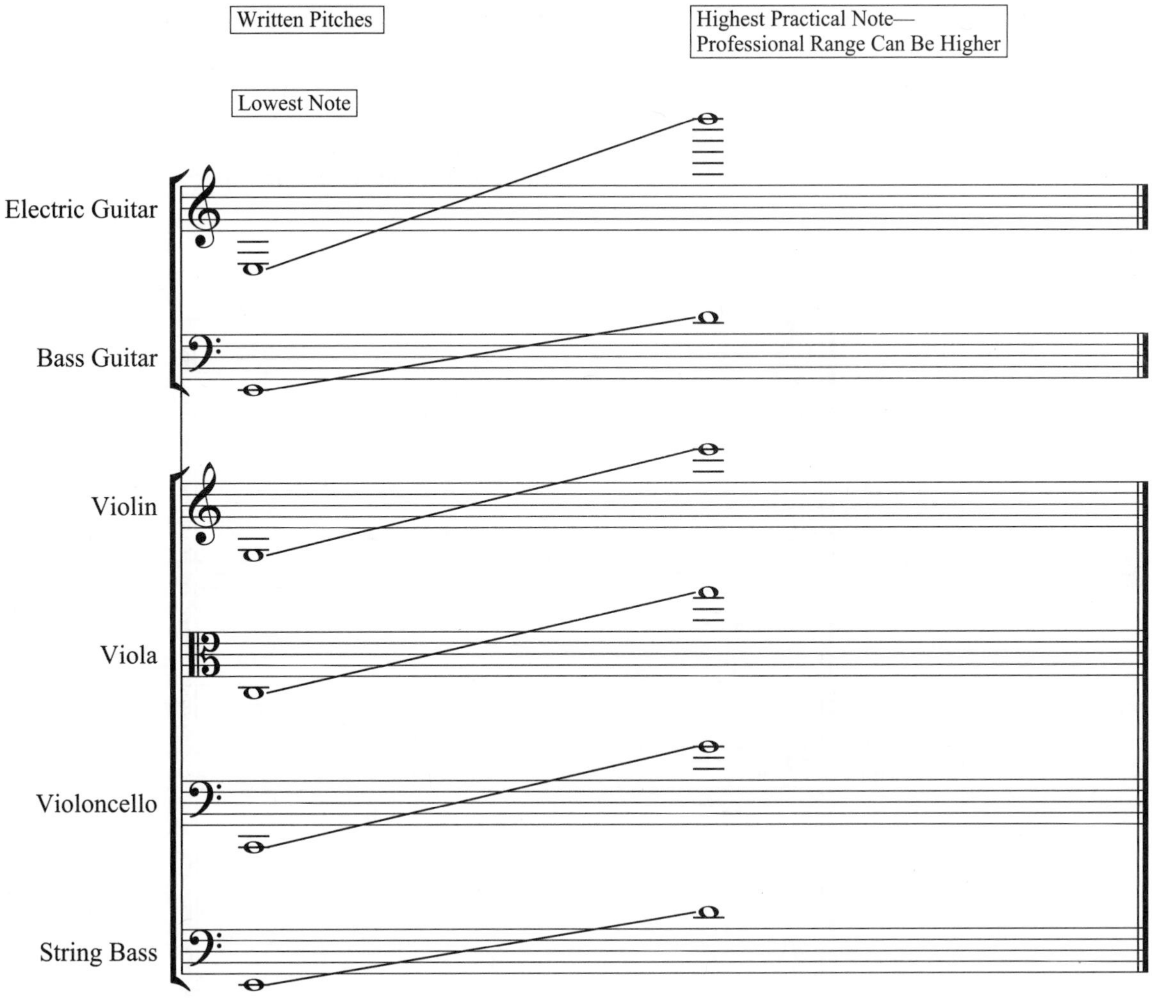

FIGURE 16.16 Brass Ranges

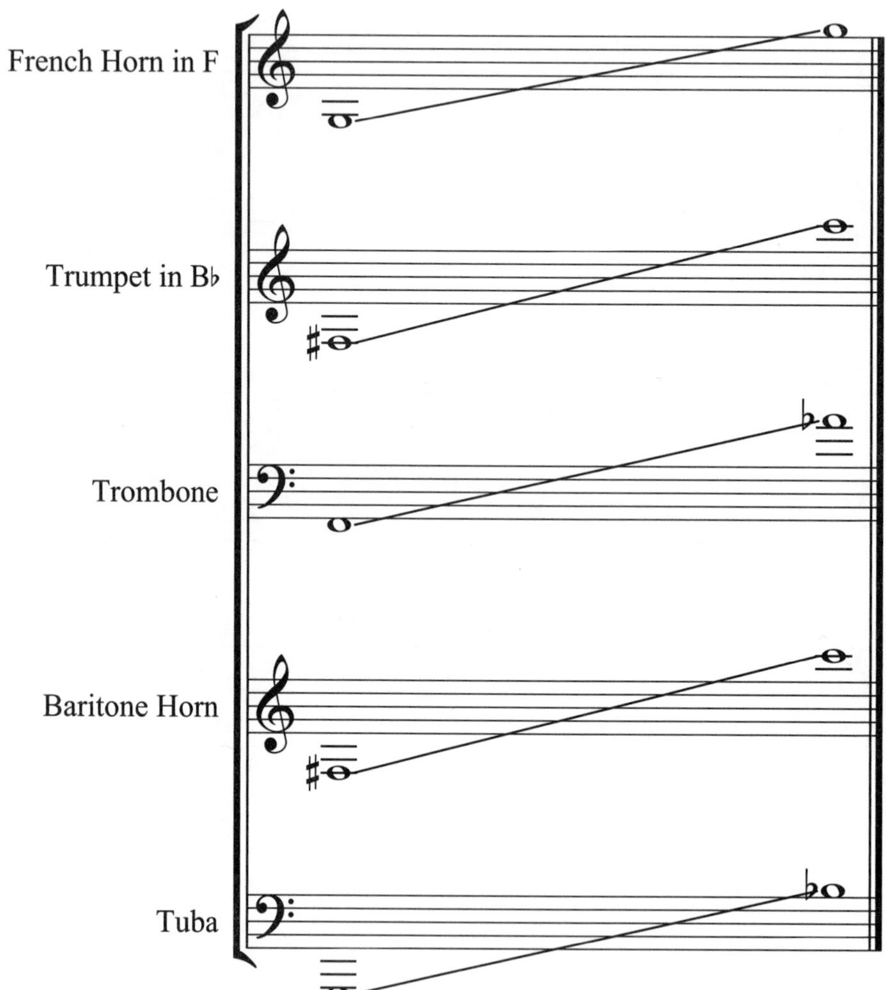

FIGURE 16.17 Woodwind Ranges

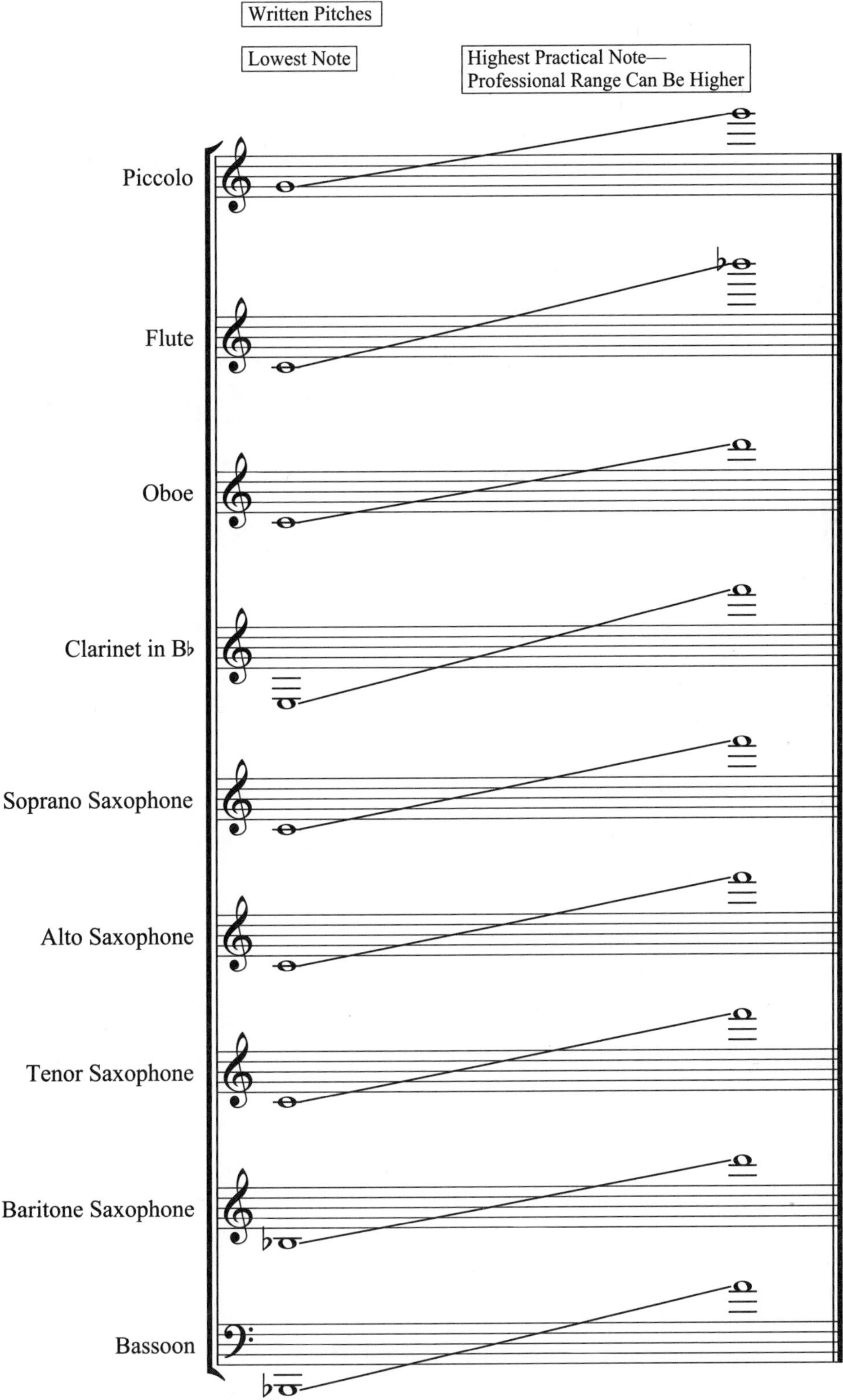

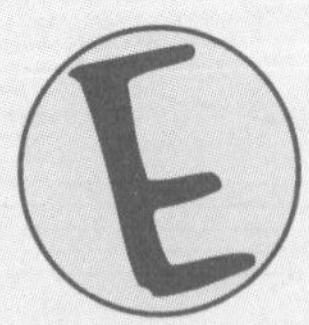

Chapter 17

Etude Three: Advanced Harmony, Jazz Harmony, and Transposition

Spell the Following Chords

Spell a V/ii in D Major

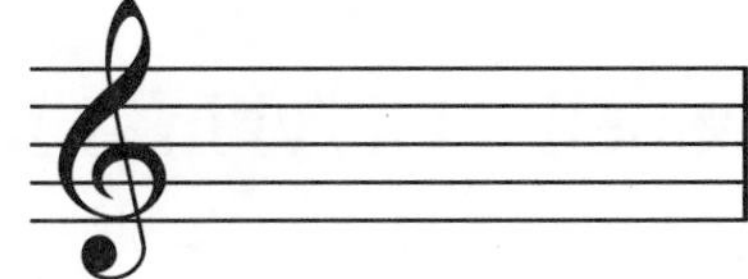

Spell a V/iv in C Minor

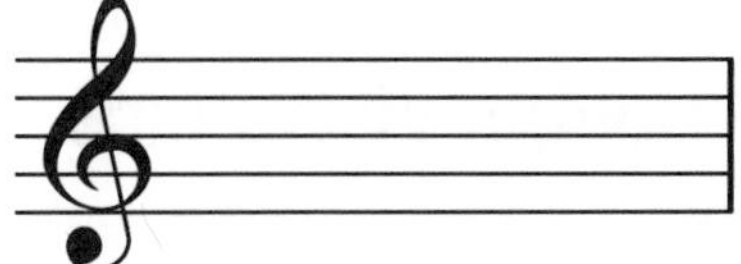

Spell a V/vi in A♭ Major

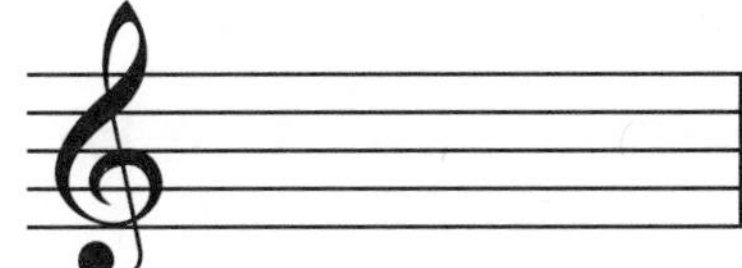

Spell a V/iii in B Major

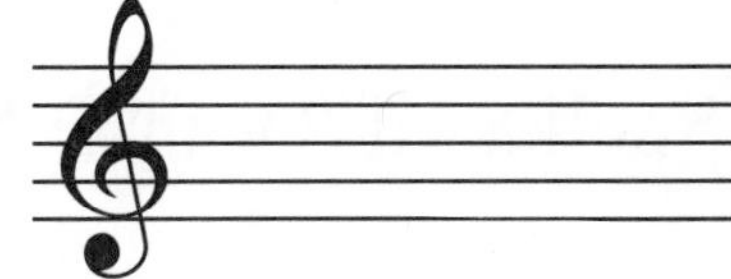

Spell a V/V in F♯ Minor

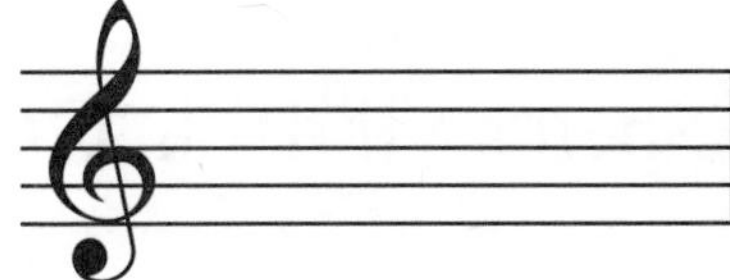

Spell the Following Chords

Spell a vii°/vi in A Major

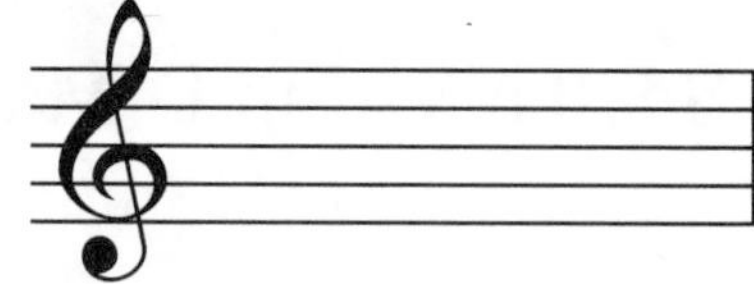

Spell a vii°/iv in B Minor

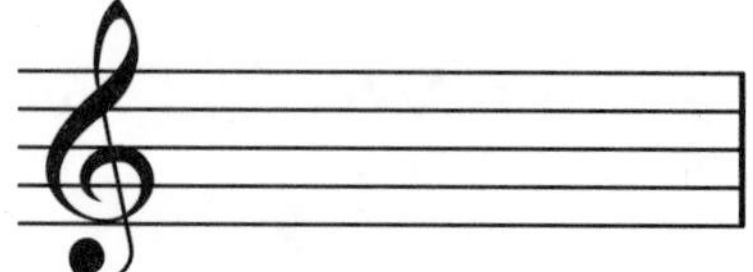

Spell a vii° /ii in B♭ Major

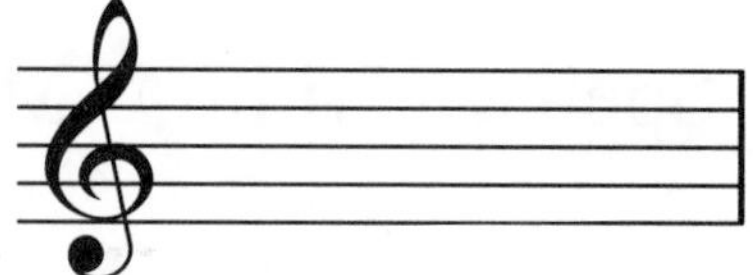

Spell a vii°/IV in E♭Major

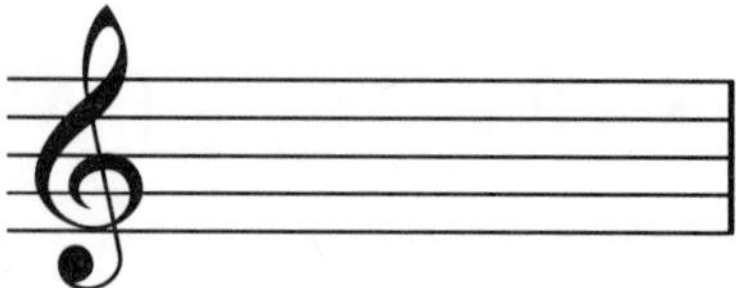

Spell a vii°/III in G# Minor

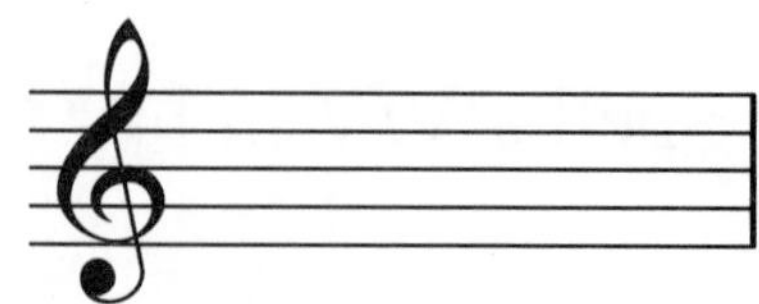

Spell the Following Borrowed Chords

Spell a iv in C Major

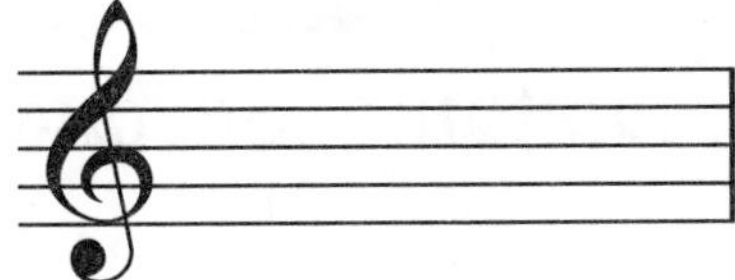

Spell a IV in E Minor

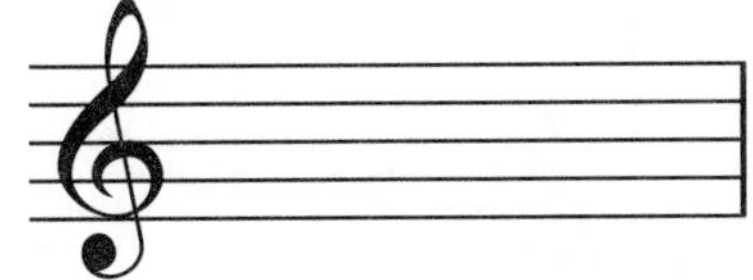

Spell a ♭VI in D Major

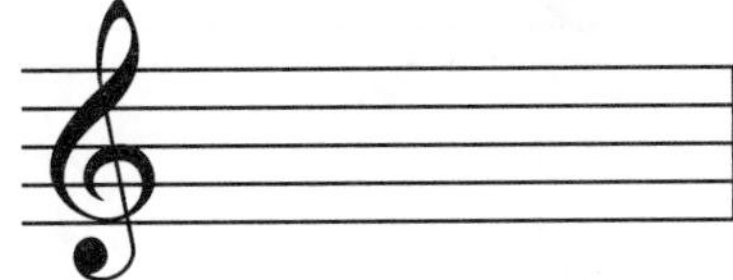

Spell a ♭VII in A♭ Major

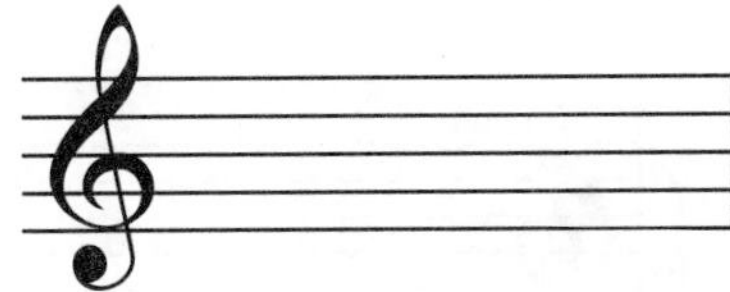

Spell a vii° in F♯ Minor

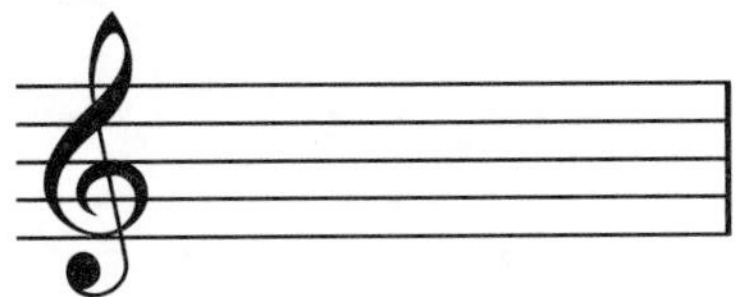

Using the Space Provided, Write a Melody and Harmonize It Using Any Combination Of: Diatonic, Secondary, and Borrowed Chords

Spell the Following Jazz Chords

C# minor 7

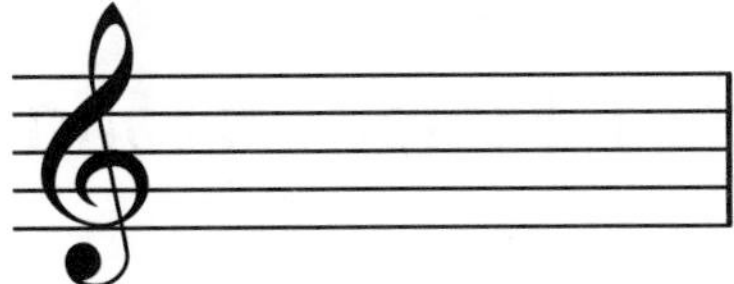

F13

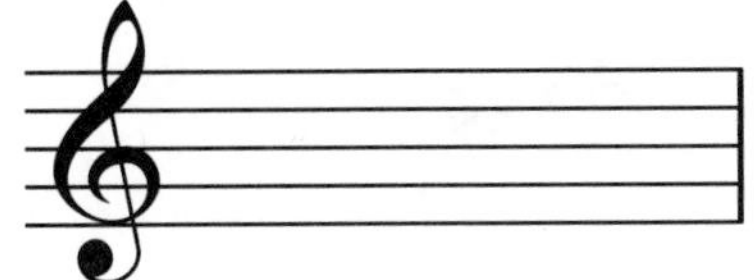

B♭ Major 9

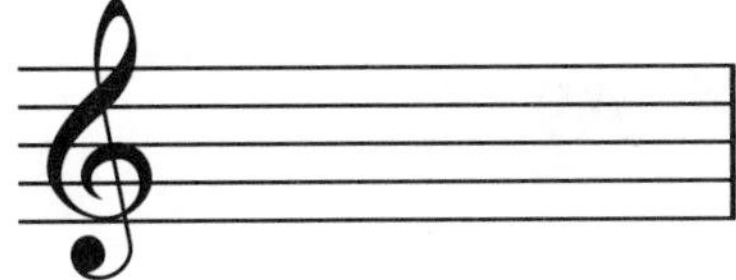

A♭ Minor 7♭5

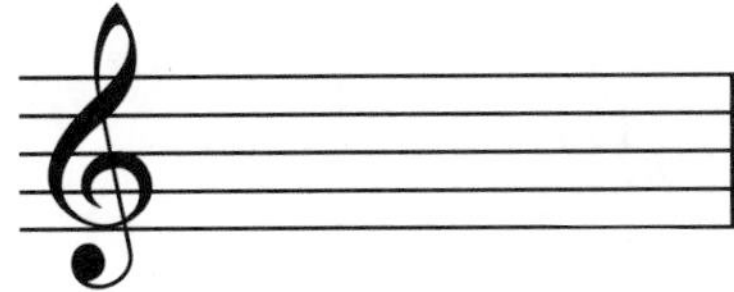

E♭9

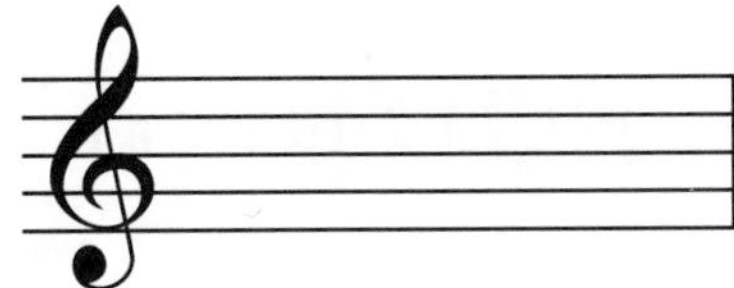

Spell the Following Altered Jazz Chords

F Major 7 #11

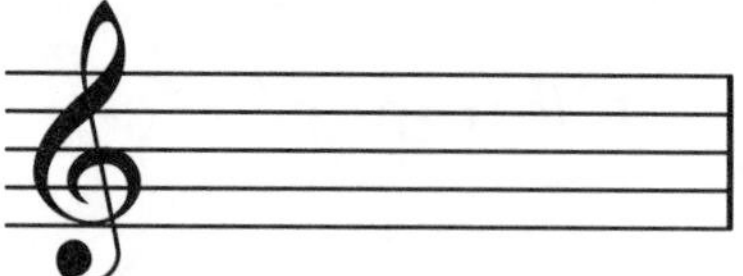

G7 ♯9

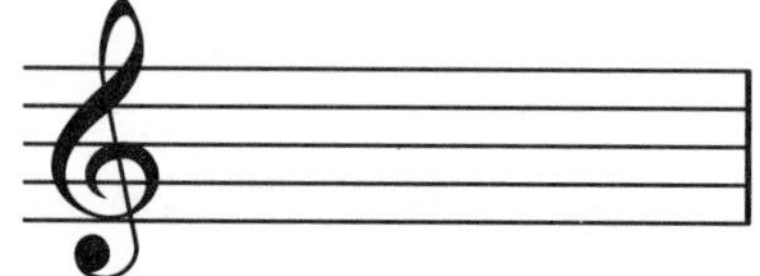

A9 ♭5

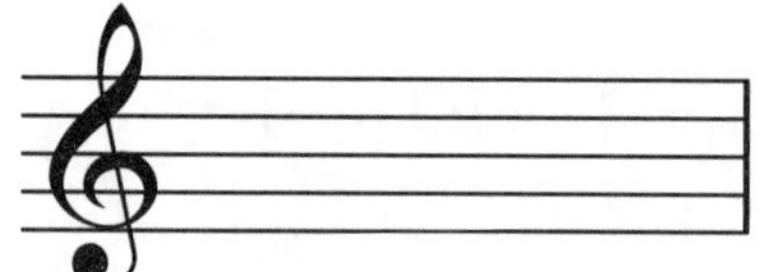

E7 ♯5

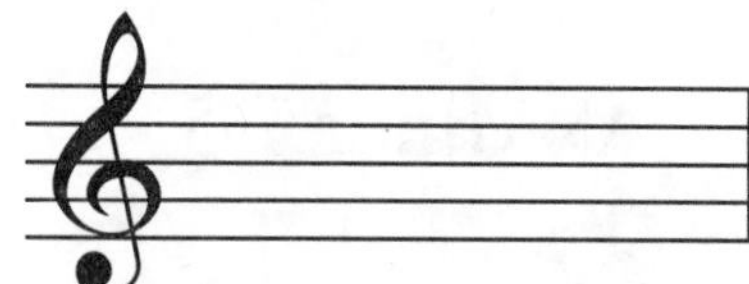

B7(♯9 ♯ 11 ♭ 13)

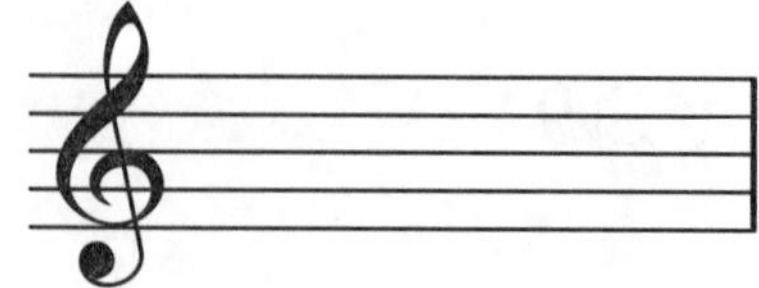

Name the Following Jazz Chords (Extended and Altered)

Transpose the Notes to Concert Key
B♭ Trumpet →
Concert Pitch
French Horn →
Concert Pitch
B♭ Clarinet →
Concert Pitch
E♭ Alto Saxophone →
Concert Pitch
B♭ Tenor Saxophone →
Concert Pitch

Transpose the Concert Notes to Transposing

Concert Pitch →

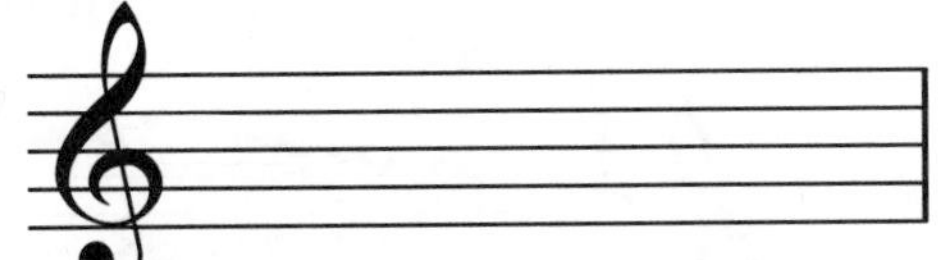

B♭ Trumpet

Concert Pitch →

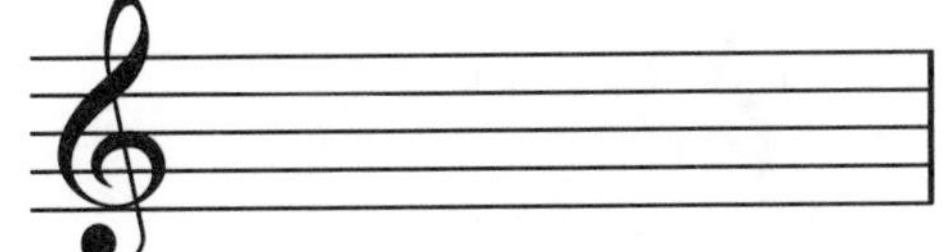

French Horn

Concert Pitch →

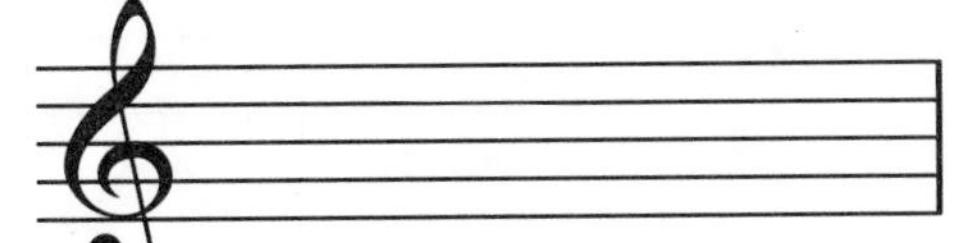

B♭ Clarinet

Concert Pitch →

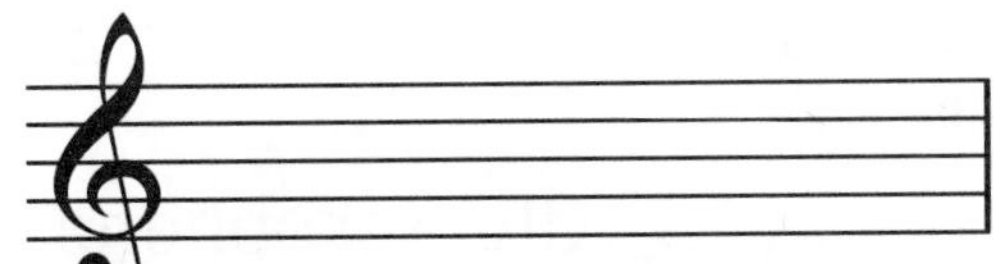

E♭ Alto Saxophone

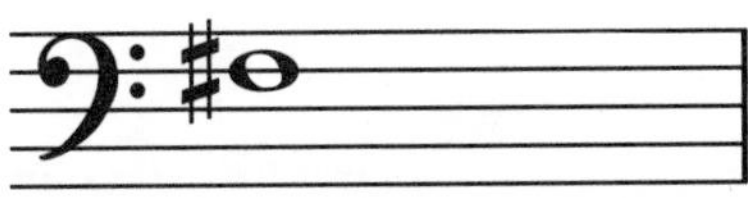

Concert Pitch →

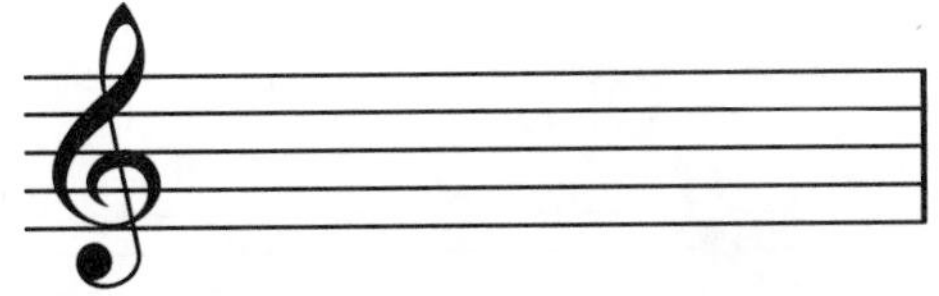

B♭ Tenor Saxophone

Transpose This Melody So Each
Instrument Plays in Unison
B♭ Clarinet
Flute
Trombone
E♭ Alto Saxophone
Oboe

Appendix A

Glossary

$\frac{4}{4}$ time

Also called "common time" and is abbreviated by this symbol **c**; denotes that four beats are found in each measure

12-Bar Major Blues

A set progression of chords that takes twelve bars or measures to complete and resolves to a major or dominant chord

12-Bar Minor Blues

A set progression of chords that takes twelve bars or measures to complete and resolves to a minor chord

Aeolian Mode

A major scale played from its sixth note (also the minor scale)

Arpeggio

The notes of a chord played one note at a time

Augmentation Dot

Also called a dot; increases the duration of the dotted note by one half

Augmented Interval

Any interval that is one half step larger than major or perfect

Bass Clef

A symbol used for instruments that have a lower pitch, commonly called the F clef

Borrow Chords

A chord that exists in the parallel major or minor key that you can "borrow" in your present key

C Clef

A clef that has two semicircles that curve into the middle of the staff and point toward middle C

Chord

Three or more notes sounded simultaneously

Chord Alterations

Chords that have fifths or ninths that have been altered

Chord Progression

The movement of chords from one point to another

Chord Substitution

When one chord can take the place of another chord

Chord Tones

Melodic notes that are contained within the supporting harmony

Circle of Keys

A visual organization of all the possible musical keys

Clef

A symbol that sits at the beginning of every staff of music that defines which note is where

Common Chords

Chords that are shared between two different keys

Compound Meter

Meter that breaks itself into groups of three notes

Concert Key

Instruments that adhere to the physical definitions of pitch (i.e., A = 440 Hz)

Concert Pitch

Instruments that play in concert key

Deceptive Resolution

A substitution when one chord resolves to an unexpected resolution, typically when the tonic is expected and not heard

Diatonic

Using the notes from only one scale/key to make chords or melodies

Diminished Interval

Any interval that is one half step smaller than a minor or perfect interval

Diminished Scale

A symmetrical scale built on repeating intervals, always half steps and whole steps. There are two varieties of diminished scales: one that starts with the pattern whole step, half step intervals, and one that uses half step, whole step interval patterns

Dominant

The fifth chord or tone of a scale

Dominant Seventh Chord

A major triad with a minor seventh interval added

Dorian Mode

A major scale played from its second note

Eighth Note

A rythmn that receives half of one count; its duration is one half of a beat

Enharmonic

Where two notes sound the same yet are different notes on paper

Extended Chords

Chords that contain 9th, 11th, or 13th intervals in them

First Inversion

Whenever the third of the chord is in the bass

Fully Diminished Seventh Chord

A diminished triad with a diminished seventh interval added

Grand Staff

When the bass clef and the treble clef are grouped together; often used for piano

Half Diminished Chord

A diminished triad with a minor seventh interval added

Half Note

A rhythm that receives two counts; its duration is two beats

Half Step

The smallest interval

Harmonic Minor

A minor scale with the 7th note raised up one half step

Harmonic Rhythm

The speed at which the harmony progresses from chord to chord

Harmonization

Using chords and melodies together; making harmony by stacking scale tones as triads

Instrument Ranges

The lowest and highest notes a particular instrument can physically play

Interval

The distance from one note to another

Inverted Chords

Any chord or triad where the root is not the lowest-sounding pitch

Ionian Mode

The major scale

Key

Defines the basic pitches for a piece of music

Key Signature

Used to indicate that a certain note or notes is going to be sharp or flat for the entire piece

Lead Sheet

Simplified shorthand for a musical piece found in jazz

Leading Tone

The seventh note of a major scale—a tone that pulls heavily to the tonic

Locrian Mode

A major scale played from its seventh note

Lydian Mode

A major scale played from its fourth note

Major Intervals

Intervallic distances of seconds, thirds, sixths, and sevenths

Major Scale

A seven-note scale based on the interval pattern of WWHWWWH

Major Seventh Chord

A major triad with a major seventh interval added

Mediant

The third chord or tone of a scale

Melodic Harmonization

Harmonizing a melody with chords or other melodic lines

Melodic Minor

A minor scale with the 6th and 7th note raised up one half step

Minor Intervals

Intervallic distances of seconds, thirds, sixths, and sevenths; exactly one half step smaller than a major interval

Minor Scale

A seven-note scale based on the interval pattern of WHWWHWW

Minor Seventh Chord

A minor triad with a minor seventh interval added

Mixolydian Mode

A major scale played from its fifth note

Mode

The notes of a major scale starting from any note but the expected tonic

Modulation

The art of shifting the tonal center to another key and staying there

Orchestration

The art of arranging music for multiple instruments

Passing Tones

Melodic notes that are not contained within the supporting harmony

Pentatonic Scales

A scale that contains only five notes; can be major or minor

Perfect Intervals

Intervallic distances of unison (no interval at all), fourth, fifth, and octave

Perfect Pitch

The natural ability to name a note just by listening to it (also called absolute pitch)

Phrygian Mode

A major scale played from its third note

Primary Chords

The I, IV, and V chords of any major key

Quarter Note

A rhythm that receives one count; its duration is one beat

Relative Minor

The minor key that is shared within a major key signature

Relative Pitch

The learned ability to name and recognize chords and intervals by ear comparatively, not absolutely

Resolution

The feeling of rest in a harmony

Roman Numerals

A standard way for music theorists to name and help analyze chords and chord progressions

Root Position

A chord that has its root as the lowest sounding pitch

Scale

A grouping of notes together that makes a key

Second Inversion

Whenever the fifth of the chord is in the bass

Secondary Chords

The ii, iii, and vi chords of any major key

Secondary Diminished Chords

Any diminished chord that is not functioning as a true leading tone chord

Secondary Dominant Chords

Any dominant chord that is not the fifth chord of a key; a dominant chord that resolves to any chord other than tonic

Seventh Chord

Any triad with an added seventh interval

Simple Meter

Meters that contain groupings of two or four notes

Solar Harmony

The system of harmony that revolves around the tonic chord being the most important harmony

Subdominant

The fourth chord or tone of a scale

Submediant or Super Dominant

The sixth chord or tone of a scale

Supertonic

The second chord or tone of a scale

Tablature

A graphical system that guitar players use for reading numbers instead of notes

Tertian Harmony

Harmony based on chords built from third intervals

Third Inversion

Whenever the seventh of the chord is in the bass

Tonic

The first chord or tone of a scale

Transposing

Changing the key of a melody while keeping its intervallic relationship intact

Transposing Instrument

Any instrument that plays in a key other than concert pitch

Treble Clef

A symbol that circles around the note G, commonly called the G clef

Triad

A three-note chord, built with third intervals

Tuplets

A grouping of odd groups of notes divided equally into one or more beats

Voice Leading

The art of connecting chord to chord in the smoothest manner possible

Whole Note

A rhythm that receives four counts; its duration is four beats

Whole Step

The distance of two half steps combined

Whole Tone Scale

A symmetrical scale built entirely with whole steps

Appendix B

Additional Resources

Here is a list of important books that you should know about. Some of these were referenced in this book, and all of them will deepen your knowledge of music in general.

Books

Black, Dave, and Gerou, Tom. *Essential Dictionary of Orchestration.* Los Angeles: Alfred Publishing Co.

Gerou, Tom, and Lusk, Linda. *Essential Dictionary of Music Notation.* Los Angeles: Alfred Publishing Co.

Harnsberger, Lindsey C. *Essential Dictionary of Music.* Los Angeles: Alfred Publishing Co.

Kennan, Kent. *Counterpoint.* Upper Saddle River, NJ: Prentice Hall.

Kennan, Kent, and Grantham, Donald. *The Technique of Orchestration.* Englewood Cliffs, NJ: Prentice Hall.

Piston, Walter. *Harmony.* New York: W.W. Norton & Company.

Roeder, Michael Thomas. *A History of the Concerto.* Portland, OR: Amadeus Press.

Stolba, K. Marie. *The Development of Western Music: A History.* Madison, WI: Brown and Benchmark.

White, John D. *Comprehensive Musical Analysis.* Metuchen, NJ: Scarecrow Press.

Web Sites

www.musictheory.net
One of the best online resources for music theory.

www.sibelius.com
Makers of the Sibelius brand of score writing and music theory software for Windows and Macintosh.

www.music.vt.edu/musicdictionary/
Excellent general music theory site.

INDEX

A

Accidentals
- harmonizing and, 177
- in relative minor keys, 75–76

Aeolian scale (mode), 85, 87, 88
Alto clef. *See* C clef
Augmented intervals, 31
Augmented triads
- alternative view of, 116–17
- described, 115–16
- etude, 181
- formula for, 116
- in jazz, 212
- with sevenths, 130–31

B

Bach Prelude in C, 137–40
Bars, 7
Bass clef
- compared to treble clef, 4
- defined, 4
- middle C and, 5
- notes of, 4

B-flat instrument transpositions, 228
Blues forms, 219–22
- 12-bar major, 220–21
- 12-bar minor, 221–22

Books, resources, 263
Borrowed chords
- etude, 245
- major keys borrowing from minor, 200–201
- minor keys borrowing from major, 198–200

C

C clef, 5–7
- as alto clef, 5–6
- as movable clef, 6
- notes of, 5–6

C major scale
- chords in, 118–19
- defined, 37–38
- deriving minor scale from, 52–53
- intervals, 21–23, 37
- piano keyboard showing, 19
- related key, 72
- scale definition and, 37
- tone numbers, 44

C minor scale
- definitive approach and, 48–49
- derivative approach and, 52–53
- intervals, 23–25

Chant, transposing, 227
Chord inversions, 123, 132–40
- Bach Prelude in C and, 137–40
- etudes, 184–86
- functions of, 123
- quick study on, 137–40
- reasons for, 137
- seventh chords, 135–37, 185

triads, 133–35, 184
Chord ladder, 149–52
Chord progressions, 141–52, 153–64
chord ladder and, 149–52
chord stacks and, 142
deceptive resolutions, 152
defined, 142
diatonic, 144–47, 213–15
dominant chords in minor keys, 158–61
etudes, 187–88
gravity and, 148–49
harmonic rhythm and, 161–62
historical perspective, 142–45
minor, 156–58, 188, 215–17
movements in fifths, 150–52
primary chords and, 145–46
Roman numerals and. *See* Roman numerals
secondary chords and, 146–47
solar harmony and, 145, 147, 148–49
tonic/dominant relationships, 154–58
V and I chord balance, 154–56
voice leading and, 137, 162–64, 174, 175
voices in motion, 154–56
Chord progressions (jazz), 212–19
chord alterations and, 218–19
diatonic, 213–15
minor, 215–18
overview, 212–13
substitutions/ enhancements, 218
Chord tones, 169–70
Chord(s), 108–22
alterations, 131, 212, 218–19
building, 110–13
defined, 109
diatonic. *See* Diatonic chords (triads)
etudes, 185, 186, 243–45, 247–49
extended, 210–12
jazz, 210–12, 247–49
lines of music and, historical perspective, 142–43
major. *See* Major triads (chords)
minor, 112–13
modulation of, 201–6
primary, 145–46
in scales, 118–19
secondary. *See* Secondary chords; Secondary dominant chords
stacks, 118, 119, 142
supportive, 166–67
See also Chord inversions; Chord progressions; Seventh chords; Triads
Chromatic harmony, 196–98
Chromatic intervals, 32–33
Circle of keys
major keys, 66–67, 73, 201–3
relative minor keys, 70–71, 73, 76–77, 201–3
Clefs
bass, 4
C, 5–7
defined, 3
grand staff and, 4–5
middle C and, 5
note naming practice for, 6–7
treble (G), 3–4
Color, of minor scales, 48
Compound meter, 13–14
Concert pitch (C), 224, 225

D

Diatonic chords (triads), 119–22
creating (in C major), 118–19
defined, 119
etudes, 182–83
order of, 119–20

Roman numerals
delineating, 120–22
Diatonic progressions, 144–47, 213–15
Diatonic seventh chords, 124–25
Diminished intervals, 32
Diminished scales, 93–94, 107
Diminished triads, 114–15
alternative view of, 115
described, 114
etude, 181
formula for, 116
half and whole, 129–30
in jazz, 212
with sevenths, 128–30
Dominant chords
altered, 218–19
defined, 121
extended, 211–12
in minor keys, 158–61
minor scale harmony and, 122
secondary, 190–94
tonic and, 154–58
Dominant notes, 45, 53, 54
Dorian scale (mode), 82–83, 87, 88, 90
Dotted notes, 10–11

E

E-flat instrument transpositions, 229
Eighth notes, defined, 9
Eighth rests, 12
Enharmonics, 18, 26, 41–42
Etude, purpose of, 95
Etude one, 96–107
naming intervals, 97
naming key signatures, 104
naming scales, 102–3
writing intervals, 98–99
writing modal scales, 105–6
writing scales, 100–102
writing special scales, 107
Etude three, 242–52
jazz chords, 247–49
spelling chords, 243–45, 247–49
transposing, 250–52
writing/harmonizing melody, 246
Etude two, 178–88
adding key signatures, 182–83
naming inversions, 186
naming seventh chords, 186
naming triads, 182–83, 186
spelling scales, 182–83
spelling triads, 179–81
writing inverted seventh chords, 185
writing inverted triads, 184
European music tradition, 2
Exercises. *See Etude references*
Extended chords, 210–12
dominant, 211–12
major, 210
minor, 211
Extended intervals, 209–10

F

F instrument transpositions, 230
Fifths, movements in, 150–52
Figured bass, 133, 134, 135, 137
Flats
learning key names, 69–70
remembering, 68

G

G clef. *See* Treble clef
Glossary, 253–62
Grand staff, 4–5
Gravity, 148–49

H

Half notes, defined, 8–9
Half rests, 12
Half step intervals, 18–19
Harmonic minor, 54–55, 57, 107, 122, 128
Harmonic rhythm, 161–62
Harmony, 189–206
  borrowed chords and, 198–201, 245
  chromatic, 196–98
  etudes, 245–49
  intervals for, 174–75
  in minor scales, 122
  modal mixture, 198–201
  modulation and, 201–6
  secondary chords and, 190
  single line, 175–77
  thirds and, 173
  See also Jazz; Melodic harmonization

I

Instruments
  analyzing scores and, 231–37
  B-flat, transpositions, 228
  concert pitch (C), 224
  E-flat, transpositions, 229
  F, transpositions, 230
  octave transposing for, 230–31
  ranges of, 237–41
  reasons for transposing, 226
  that transpose, 225
  transposing chant for, 227
  transposing etudes for, 250–52
Intervals, 16–35
  advanced, 30–33
  augmented, 31
  in C major scale, 21–23
  in C minor scale, 23–25
  chromatic, 32–33
  defined, 17
  diminished, 32
  distance of, 25–26
  distinguishing types of, 32
  enharmonics and, 18, 26, 41–42
  etudes, 97–99
  extended, 209–10
  formula, for major scales, 37–38
  formula, for minor scales, 49–50
  formula, for modal scales, 87
  half steps, 18–19
  for harmonizing melodies, 174–75
  inverted, 33–35
  major, 27
  minor, 28–29
  perfect, 29–30, 34–35
  piano keyboard showing, 17–18
  quality of, 25–26
  rule of nine, 34
  from scales, 21–26
  simple, 26–30
  types of, 17
  whole steps, 19–21
Inversions. *See* Chord inversions
Inverted intervals, 33–35
Ionian scale, 81–82, 87, 88

J

Jazz, 207–22
  augmented chords in, 212
  blues forms, 219–22
  chord alterations in, 218–19
  diatonic progressions in, 213–15
  diminished seventh chord in, 212
  etudes, 247–49
  extended chords in, 210–12
  extended intervals in, 209–10
  minor progressions in, 215–17
  overview, 208–9

progressions in, 212–19
substitutions/ enhancements in, 218
12-bar major blues, 220–21
uniqueness of, 208

K

Key signatures
defined, 65–66
etudes, 104, 182–83
remembering flats and sharps, 68
shared, 71–72
system of, 68–71
Keys
changing, 76–78, 201–6. *See also* Transposing
circle of major, 66–67, 73
circle of relative minor, 70–71, 73, 76–77
controlling, for melodic harmonization, 170–72
defined, 65
determining, 74
learning names of, 69–70
major. *See* Major keys
minor. *See* Minor keys; Relative minor keys
moving in fourths and fifths, 70–71
related, 201–3

L

Ladder. *See* Chord ladder
Leading tones, 45, 53, 54
defined, 75
knowing, value of, 76
in minor keys, 75–76
in scales, 55, 75
tonic/dominant chords and, 154–56, 158
Lines of music, importance of, 142–43
Locrian scale (mode), 86, 87, 88
Lydian scale (mode), 83–84, 87, 88

M

Major intervals, 27
Major keys
borrowing chords from minor keys, 200–201
circle of, 66–67, 73, 201–3
minor keys borrowing chords from, 198–200
Major pentatonic scale, 90–91
Major scales
all, illustrated, 41–43
defined, 37–38
deriving minor scales from, 52–53
enharmonic notes and, 41–42
etudes, 100, 102–3, 182
interval formula, 37–38
scale tones (by number/ degree), 44–45
spelling (building), 38–43
unifying, in music, 45–46
See also C major scale
Major sevenths, 126–27
Major triads (chords), 110–11
alternative view of, 111
described, 126
etude, 179
extended, 210
formula for, 110, 116
with sevenths, 126–27
Measures, 7
Mediant notes, 45, 53
Melodic harmonization, 165–77
accidentals and, 177
chord tones and, 169–70
etude, 246
intervals for, 174–75
inverse of thirds and, 174
key control and, 170–72
melody/harmony correlation, 166–67
passing tones and, 169–70
point-to-point harmonization, 167–69
single line harmony, 175–77
thirds and, 173

Melodic harmonization—*continued*
true melodic harmony, 172–75
Melodic minor, 56–57, 107
Melody
defined, 166
supportive chords and, 166–67
Meter(s)
compound, 13–14
odd, 14–15
simple, 12–13
Middle C, 5
Minor chord progressions, 156–58, 187, 215–17
Minor intervals, 28–29
Minor keys
borrowing chords from major keys, 198–200
dominant chords in, 158–61
major keys borrowing chords from, 200–201
naming, 72–73
secondary dominant chords and, 194
See also Relative minor keys
Minor pentatonic scale, 91
Minor scales, 47–63
all, illustrated, 58–63
anomalies, 57
defined, 48
definitive approach of forming, 48–51
degrees in, 53–54
derivative approach of forming, 52–53
etudes, 101–3, 107, 183
harmonic minor, 54–55, 57, 107, 122, 128
harmony in, 122
interval formula, 49–50
melodic minor, 56–57, 107
minor colors and, 48
varieties of, 54–57
See also C minor scale
Minor sevenths, 127–28
Minor triads, 112–13
alternative view of, 112–13
described, 112
etude, 180
extended, 211
formula for, 112, 116
Mixolydian scale (mode), 84–85, 87, 88, 89
Modal mixture, 198–201
Modal scales, 81–87
Aeolian, 85, 87, 88
Dorian, 82–83, 87, 88, 90
etudes, 105–6
interval formulas, 87
Ionian, 81–82, 87, 88
Locrian, 86, 87, 88
Lydian, 83–84, 87, 88
Mixolydian, 84–85, 87, 88, 89
Phrygian, 83, 87, 88
practice exercise, 89–90
relating/learning tips, 86–87
Mode(s), 79–90
defined, 80–81
history of, 81
learning, 86–87
Modulation, 201–6
common chords and, 204–6
defined, 201
related keys and, 201–3
secondary dominant chords and, 203–4
Movements. *See* Chord progressions; Chord progressions (jazz)

N

Notes
of alto clef, 5–6
of bass clef, 4
distance between. *See* Intervals
naming practice, 6–7
review, 2–3
of treble clef, 3–4

O

Octatonic scales, 93–94
Octave transposes, 230–31
Odd time/meter, 14–15
One hundred and twenty-eighth notes, 10
Organization, of music. *See* Key signatures; Keys

P

Passing tones, 169–70
Pentatonic scales, 90–91
Perfect intervals, 29–30, 34–35
Phrygian scale (mode), 83, 87, 88
Piano keyboard, showing intervals, 17–18
Point-to-point harmonization, 167–69
Prelude in C, 137–40
Primary chords, 145–46
Progressions. *See* Chord progressions; Chord progressions (jazz)

Q

Quarter notes, defined, 8
Quarter rests, 12

R

Ranges, of instruments, 237–41
Related keys, 201–3
Relative minor keys
  accidentals in, 75–76
  circle of, 70–71, 73, 76–77, 201–3
  determining, 74–76
  naming, 72–73
  shared signatures, 71–72
Resources, 263
Rests, defined, 12
Rhythm(s)
  augmentation dots (dotted notes), 10–11
  basic note values, 8–11
  defined, 8
  tuplets, 11
  See also Meter(s); Time signature(s)
Roman numerals
  assigning (etude), 187–88
  for chord progressions, 44, 187–88
  delineating triads, 120–22
  diatonic seventh chords and, 125
  etudes, 187–88
  inverted seventh chords and, 137
  inverted triads and, 133, 135
Rule of nine, 34

S

Scale(s)
  chords in, 118–19
  defined, 37
  diminished, 93–94, 107
  etudes, 100–103, 107, 182–83
  natural vs. man-made, 114
  octatonic, 93–94
  pentatonic, 90–91
  spelling, 38–43, 182–83
  tones (by number/degree), 44–45
  unifying, in music, 45–46
  whole tone, 92–93, 107
  See also C major scale; C minor scale; Major scales; Minor scales; Modal scales
Scores, analyzing, 231–37

Secondary chords
chord progression and, 146–47
chromatic, 192
diminished, 194–96
dominant, 190–94
harmony and, 190–96
minor keys and, 194
where to use, 193–94
Secondary dominant chords, 190–94, 203–4
Seventh chords, 123–32
augmented triads with, 130–31
construction of, 125–31
defined, 124
diatonic, 124–25
diminished triads with, 128–30
dominant, 127, 132, 154, 211
etudes, 185–86
formulas derived from major scale, 132
inverted, 135–37, 185
major triads with, 126–27
minor triads with, 127–28
recap of, 131–32, 136–37
triads compared to, 124
types of, 125
Shared key signatures, 71–72
Sharps
learning key names, 69
remembering, 68
Simple meter, 12–13
Single line harmony, 175–77
Sixteenth notes, defined, 9
Sixteenth rests, 12
Sixty-fourth notes, 10
Solar harmony, 145, 147, 148–49
Subdominant notes, 45, 53
Submediant, superdominant notes, 45, 53
Supertonic notes, 45, 53
Supportive chords, 166–67

T

Theory, explained, xi–xii
Thirds
inverse of, 174
true melodic harmony and, 173
Thirty-second notes, 10
Time signature(s), 7–8
common time, 7
interpreting, 7
odd, 14–15
See also Rhythm(s)
Tonic notes, 45, 53, 54
Transposing, 223–37
analyzing scores and, 231–37
B-flat instruments, 228
chant for, 227
concert pitch (C) and, 224, 225
defined, 224
E-flat instruments, 229
etudes, 250–52
F instruments, 230
how it works, 225–26
instruments, common, 225
octave transposes, 230–31
reasons for, 226
what it means, 225–26
Treble clef, 3–4
bass clef compared to, 4
as G clef, 4
notes of, 3–4
Triads
alternative views of, 111, 113, 115, 116–17
augmented, 115–17, 130–31, 181
components of, 111
corresponding to scales, 113
defined, 109
derivative approach of forming, 111, 112, 113, 115, 116–18
diatonic, 119–22, 182–83
diminished, 114–15, 116, 128–30, 181
etudes, 179–86

formulas for, summarized, 115–16
inverted. *See* Chord inversions
major, 110–11, 116, 126–27, 179, 210
major third interval, 111
minor, 112–13, 116, 127–28, 180, 211
minor chord progressions and, 156–58
minor thirds, 112
order of, 119–20
perfect fifth interval, 111, 113
remembering order of, 112
Roman numerals for, 120–22
in scales, 118–19
seventh chords compared to, 124
ways to form, 111
See also Chord(s)
Triplets, 11
Tritones, 32, 155
True melodic harmony, 172–75
Tuplets, 11
12-bar major blues, 220–21
12-bar minor blues, 221–22

V

Voice leading, 137, 162–64, 174, 175
Voices in motion, 154–56

W

Web sites, 263
Whole notes, defined, 9
Whole rests, 12
Whole step intervals, 19–21
Whole tone scale, 92–93, 107

Software License Agreement

YOU SHOULD CAREFULLY READ THE FOLLOWING TERMS AND CONDITIONS BEFORE USING THIS SOFTWARE PRODUCT. INSTALLING AND USING THIS PRODUCT INDICATES YOUR ACCEPTANCE OF THESE CONDITIONS. IF YOU DO NOT AGREE WITH THESE TERMS AND CONDITIONS, DO NOT INSTALL THE SOFTWARE AND RETURN THIS PACKAGE PROMPTLY FOR A FULL REFUND.

1. Grant of License
This software package is protected under United States copyright law and international treaty. You are hereby entitled to one copy of the enclosed software and are allowed by law to make one backup copy or to copy the contents of the disks onto a single hard disk and keep the originals as your backup or archival copy. United States copyright law prohibits you from making a copy of this software for use on any computer other than your own computer. United States copyright law also prohibits you from copying any written material included in this software package without first obtaining the permission of F+W Publications, Inc.

2. Restrictions
You, the end-user, are hereby prohibited from the following:
You may not rent or lease the Software or make copies to rent or lease for profit or for any other purpose.
You may not disassemble or reverse compile for the purposes of reverse engineering the Software.
You may not modify or adapt the Software or documentation in whole or in part, including, but not limited to, translating or creating derivative works.

3. Transfer
You may transfer the Software to another person, provided that (a) you transfer all of the Software and documentation to the same transferee; (b) you do not retain any copies; and (c) the transferee is informed of and agrees to the terms and conditions of this Agreement.

4. Termination
This Agreement and your license to use the Software can be terminated without notice if you fail to comply with any of the provisions set forth in this Agreement. Upon termination of this Agreement, you promise to destroy all copies of the software including backup or archival copies as well as any documentation associated with the Software. All disclaimers of warranties and limitation of liability set forth in this Agreement shall survive any termination of this Agreement.

5. Limited Warranty
F+W Publications, Inc. warrants that the Software will perform according to the manual and other written materials accompanying the Software for a period of 30 days from the date of receipt. F+W Publications, Inc. does not accept responsibility for any malfunctioning computer hardware or any incompatibilities with existing or new computer hardware technology.

6. Customer Remedies
F+W Publications, Inc.'s entire liability and your exclusive remedy shall be, at the option of F+W Publications, Inc., either refund of your purchase price or repair and/or replacement of Software that does not meet this Limited Warranty. Proof of purchase shall be required. This Limited Warranty will be voided if Software failure was caused by abuse, neglect, accident or misapplication. All replacement Software will be warranted based on the remainder of the warranty or the full 30 days, whichever is shorter and will be subject to the terms of the Agreement.

7. No Other Warranties
F+W PUBLICATIONS, INC., TO THE FULLEST EXTENT OF THE LAW, DISCLAIMS ALL OTHER WARRANTIES, OTHER THAN THE LIMITED WARRANTY IN PARAGRAPH 5, EITHER EXPRESS OR IMPLIED, ASSOCIATED WITH ITS SOFTWARE, INCLUDING BUT NOT LIMITED TO IMPLIED WARRANTIES OF MERCHANTABILITY AND FITNESS FOR A PARTICULAR PURPOSE, WITH REGARD TO THE SOFTWARE AND ITS ACCOMPANYING WRITTEN MATERIALS. THIS LIMITED WARRANTY GIVES YOU SPECIFIC LEGAL RIGHTS. DEPENDING UPON WHERE THIS SOFTWARE WAS PURCHASED, YOU MAY HAVE OTHER RIGHTS.

8. Limitations on Remedies
TO THE MAXIMUM EXTENT PERMITTED BY LAW, F+W PUBLICATIONS, INC. SHALL NOT BE HELD LIABLE FOR ANY DAMAGES WHATSOEVER, INCLUDING WITHOUT LIMITATION, ANY LOSS FROM PERSONAL INJURY, LOSS OF BUSINESS PROFITS, BUSINESS INTERRUPTION, BUSINESS INFORMATION OR ANY OTHER PECUNIARY LOSS ARISING OUT OF THE USE OF THIS SOFTWARE.
This applies even if F+W Publications, Inc. has been advised of the possibility of such damages. F+W Publications, Inc.'s entire liability under any provision of this agreement shall be limited to the amount actually paid by you for the Software. Because some states may not allow for this type of limitation of liability, the above limitation may not apply to you.
THE WARRANTY AND REMEDIES SET FORTH ABOVE ARE EXCLUSIVE AND IN LIEU OF ALL OTHERS, ORAL OR WRITTEN, EXPRESS OR IMPLIED. No F+W Publications, Inc. dealer, distributor, agent, or employee is authorized to make any modification or addition to the warranty.

9. General
This Agreement shall be governed by the laws of the United States of America and the Commonwealth of Massachusetts. If you have any questions concerning this Agreement, contact F+W Publications, Inc., via Adams Media at 508-427-7100. Or write to us at: Adams Media, an F+W Publications Company, 57 Littlefield Street, Avon, MA 02322.